CW00373519

Progressivism and the World of Reform

Progressivism and the World of Reform

NEW ZEALAND AND THE ORIGINS OF THE AMERICAN WELFARE STATE

Peter J. Coleman

UNIVERSITY PRESS OF KANSAS

Published by the University Press of Kansas (Lawrence, Kansas 66045), which was organized by the Kansas Board of Regents and is operated and funded by Emporia State University, Fort Hays State University, Kansas State University, Pittsburg State University, the University of Kansas, and Wichita State University

Library of Congress Cataloging-in-Publication Data
Coleman, Peter J.
Progressivism and the world of reform.
Bibliography: p.
Includes index.
1. United States—Social conditions—1865–1918.
2. Progressivism (United States politics) 3. New Zealand—Social conditions. 4. United States—Social policy. 5. Welfare state. I. Title.
HN57.C582 1987 306'.0973 87-6187
ISBN 0-7006-0321-2

British Library Cataloguing in Publication Data is available.

Printed in the United States of America
10 9 8 7 6 5 4 3 2 1

To the memory of
WALTER PRESCOTT WEBB
Scholar of the New World

CONTENTS

Preface ix

PART 1: DEMOCRATIC MISSIONS

1 The Mission of the American Democracy 3

2 The Mission of the New Zealand Democracy 16

PART 2: THE ANTIPODEAN CONNECTION

3 The Antipodes through American Eyes 45

4 New Zealandizing the United States 76

5 Maximum Hours, Minimum Wages 98

6 The Compulsory Arbitration of Labor Disputes 130

PART 3: THE INTERNATIONAL CONTEXT

7 American Progressivism and the World of Reform 155

Notes 191

A Note on Sources 239

Index 241

PREFACE

Readers may find it helpful to know something about the origins and history of this book. It has been a long time in the making. Its beginnings go back three decades, to 1950, when I came to the United States to study at the University of Texas with the late Walter Prescott Webb. With the presumptuous arrogance of the graduate student, I had written to him expressing reservations about his *Great Plains,*[1] the book that had established his reputation as an imaginative and pathbreaking scholar. I said, in effect, that he had ignored the truly important consequences of environment. If the vast, treeless, flat, semiarid interior reaches of the continent had indeed imposed fundamental adaptations on settlers, surely this influence should have manifested itself in social and political attitudes, behavior, and institutions. And yet his *Great Plains* was totally silent on so crucial a matter. What I proposed to him, therefore, was that I undertake a comparative study of the evolution of New World societies, looking at the behavior of some Great Plains states and at the British dominions south of the equator.

And so I arrived in Austin a few days after Labor Day, 1950, clothed in the heavy Harris tweed I had worn when I left New Zealand's winter behind me a month earlier and armed with a ship's trunk load of research notes on political experimentation in New Zealand between 1891 and 1911. What I was not to know was that Webb had long since outgrown the Great Plains and that he would soon bring to publication the *Great Frontier,* a concept he had been working on since the late 1930s.[2] He was a decade ahead of me.

Since he was a man of tunnel vision and was interested primarily in knowing what would confirm and enlarge his concept of the transforming role of the Great Frontier in the modern world, he persuaded me to abandon my original proposal and to concentrate instead on an intensive study of New Zealand as an example of the evolution of a Great Frontier society. Though he never said so, Webb was probably disappointed. For not only did I fail to enlarge our understanding of his Great

Frontier thesis, I reacted so vigorously against the Texas department's overwhelming preoccupation with Turner's frontier interpretation that I argued that New Zealand was more the product of what settlers brought with them from the British Isles as hopes and aspirations for a New World society than of frontier influences. For example, the refusal of the first boatload of settlers to go ashore at Wellington in 1839 until they were guaranteed an eight-hour working day said more about the reform milieu whence they came than it did about the impact of Turner's frontier environment.

Two articles eventually grew out of the dissertation, one, "The New Zealand Frontier and the Turner Thesis," the other, "The Spirit of New Zealand Liberalism in the Nineteenth Century."[3] The latter, which appeared in the *Journal of Modern History* and was directed primarily at American scholars, closed with the suggestion that the effect of Australian and New Zealand reform on American progressivism deserved more study. "A careful search of the pamphlet and newspaper literature . . . might show that much material from the South Seas reached American readers," I wrote in 1958, and I reported that such topics as the compulsory arbitration of labor disputes were widely debated by high school and collegiate clubs and that Louis D. Brandeis used the example of New Zealand to persuade the Supreme Court of the United States to hold minimum-wage legislation for women constitutional.[4]

Little did I realize at that time just how vast the literature would turn out to be, or that the antipodean connection would manifest itself in such an extraordinary variety of ways. From the perspective of 1986, of course, it seems naive and not a little absurd that Americans should really have supposed that the social, economic, and political experiments being carried out in Australasia at the turn of the century had created a Pacific paradise and that the United States could finally achieve its democratic destiny as the "world's last best hope" by emulating the antipodean reform example.

We have learned since the 1930s, and especially since the 1950s, that the modern welfare state, while it may solve certain kinds of problems, often does so at the cost of creating new sets of problems, that "reform" can gradually take on a self-perpetuating life of its own completely separate from whatever human problems it was originally intended to cure, and that the democratic humanism supposedly born out of what was called "state socialism" two generations ago may prove over the longer term to deny more individual freedom and dignity than it created.

But these are observations based on hindsight and the perspective of postindustrial America. We too easily forget the passionate urgency reformers brought to their cause eight decades ago, and we too easily forget their optimistic assumptions about the perfectibility of man and society. Girded in the new armor of the social sciences, they persuaded themselves, and tried to persuade the larger public, that knowledge was power, that the social and economic problems of their times were susceptible of scientific analysis, understanding, and solution. We may no longer share their faith and diamond-bright hopes, but our skepticism should not be allowed to cloud our understanding of the world of reform as the reformers themselves saw it.

That is to say, although this book is ultimately a study in propaganda and of the struggle, largely unsuccessful, to mold American thinking and behavior along antipodean lines, it does not assume that what Australians and New Zealanders did at the turn of the century was necessarily what the rest of the western world should have copied. Nor does it assume that those Pacific colonists even served their own best interests. Those are questions for others to answer. What the book does suggest is that for almost three decades American reformers of various stripes and occupations—Populists, Progressives, liberals, socialists, journalists, lawyers, clergymen, economists, sociologists, legislators, social workers, labor leaders—held up the Australasian colonies as examples of what the United States could become if it only had the wit and the will to work along similar legislative lines.

And in a curious, some might even think perverse, way, the book also reflects some of the anti-Turnerian bias I espoused three decades ago. More impressive to me than the unique and independent arrival at common solutions out of a common frontier heritage is the cross-fertilization between countries of ideas and movements. Chartism, not frontierism, was the midwife at the birth of the New Zealand democracy, and Edward

Bellamy, Henry George, Karl Marx, and John Stuart Mill were the pediatricians who nurtured the attitudes of later waves of colonists, the ones who ultimately became the foot soldiers in the Liberal army in the 1890s. Above all, it was the determination to prevent the emergence in New Zealand of the evils of the Old World—landlordism, poverty, unemployment, sweated labor, soup kitchens, crippling strikes and lockouts—that provided the Liberals with their legislative mandate. This was a vision of just society to which all classes could subscribe. Thus imported rather than home-grown ideas and attitudes counted most.

This is not to dismiss Turner's views entirely. What the frontier offered newcomers was an opportunity to put into effect mankind's deepest longings for human dignity. That is what the shipboard strike in Wellington harbor in 1839 was all about. And it was a replication, on a different stage and at a later time, of what the Pilgrims had agreed to in their Mayflower compact. That too was the theme the late Richard Hofstadter set out in his appraisal of Turner's thesis in *The Progressive Historians* in 1968.[5]

It follows from this line of reasoning that I was quite wrong thirty years ago in supposing that it would be possible to enlarge our understanding of the Great Frontier by the kind of comparative study I had in mind. Or perhaps I really mean that I lack the rich wisdom of the Australian scholar of the frontier, the late John B. Hancock, to carry off so enormous a comparative undertaking.[6] In any event, though we can all agree that the people of the Great Plains were and are a distinct breed (even if we have trouble defining their distinctiveness with any precision, let alone documenting our impressions), this book rests on the assumption that plainsmen at the turn of the century were more citizens of the larger world of transatlantic culture and ideas than they were isolated spirits, free to create a totally new society. On the contrary, they too drank deeply at the well of contemporary ideas—Edward Bellamy, Henry George, Karl Marx, John Stuart Mill, and their translators and popularizers—and they too drank deeply at the well of those other spokesmen for reform—Victor S. Clark, John R. Commons, Richard T. Ely, Benjamin Orange Flower, Henry Demarest Lloyd, Hugh H. Lusk,

Frank Parsons, James E. Le Rossignol, William E. Smythe, H. de R. Walker, and Julius A. Wayland—who thought, if only briefly, that they had discovered in the South Pacific mankind's ultimate direction and salvation.

Finally, it must also be said that antipodean ideas penetrated the plains states with approximately the same intensity and consequences as they penetrated the Northeast or the Pacific West. One would be hard pressed to demonstrate, one way or the other, that the distinct environment of the Great Plains produced, so far as New Zealand influences were concerned, political attitudes and institutions markedly at variance with those of, say, Massachusetts or California. Where there were differences—and there were some—they appear to reflect differences in social and economic development, mainly disparities in industrialization and urbanization, and what might be thought of as fortuitous differences in the presence or absence of reform leaders.

Without in any way subscribing to a great man or great woman theory of history, it can nevertheless be asked, Would the "New Zealandizing" of America have been very different had William E. Smythe chosen to remain in Nebraska rather than migrate to California? Would the political history of Minnesota have been significantly different had Harris Weinstock, the California dry goods merchant and labor reformer, set up shop in Minneapolis rather than Sacramento? What would have been the result had Jane Addams organized Hull House in St. Louis rather than Chicago? These are unanswerable questions, of course, but they serve to remind us that a study such as this can report and assess what happened only through the eyes and mouths of those who actively involved themselves in antipodean matters.

That Julius Wayland chose to build his socialist publishing empire in so improbable a place as Girard, Kansas, surely tells us little about the attitudes of Kansans toward socialism and New Zealand. On the other hand, Boston did provide Progressives with a congenial intellectual and reform milieu, but that would have been true had New Zealand never been colonized or had it never embarked on a program of legislative reform in the 1890s. The point is that a number of Boston Progressives—Conrad Reno, Frank Parsons, Louis Brandeis, Benjamin Flower, and Elizabeth Evans, among others—for very different reasons, drew from the antipodean record lessons that served their particular reform purposes. In so doing, they influenced not only the history of Massachusetts but also the shape and direction of Progressivism as a national phenomenon.

As usual, it is a pleasure to acknowledge the support and encouragement I have received over the years. Some of the data and ideas have been previously presented, though in very different form, to the staff seminar at the State Historical Society of Wisconsin (1964), Dartmouth College and Boston University (1965), the Universities of Auckland and Waikato and the Wellington History Association (1970), the University of Illinois at Chicago (1978), the Organization of American Historians (1980), the American Historical Association (1982), the University of Alabama (1982), four New Zealand universities (Auckland, Waikato, Victoria, and Canterbury, 1982), and the Australian and New Zealand American Studies Association (1982, 1984, 1986). I am grateful to the panelists and audiences at those presentations for their helpful suggestions and criticism, to the editors of the *Journal of Modern History, Pacific Historical Review, Journal of American History, Continuity, Wilson Quarterly,* and *Wisconsin Magazine of History* for their assistance in the articles that appeared between 1958 and 1986, and to my students, who over the years have helped me to clarify and deepen my thinking about the "World of Reform."

I must also acknowledge with gratitude the financial support provided by the Henry E. Huntington Library and Art Gallery, the State Historical Society of Wisconsin, the Graduate Research Board of the University of Illinois at Chicago, and the United States Educational Foundation in New Zealand.

Archivists and librarians have been unusually helpful to me over the years, most especially in Madison, Sacramento, Washington, D.C., and Wellington. For archival records and for both manuscript and printed materials, I would like to thank, in the United States, the Claremont College Library, Huntington Library, San Marino, the State Historical Society of Wisconsin Library, Madison, the University of California libraries at both Berkeley and Los Angeles, the University of Illinois at Chicago Library, the University of Wisconsin Library, Madison, and the

Wayne State University Library, Detroit; in New Zealand, the Alexander Turnbull Library, Wellington, the Canterbury Museum, Christchurch, the General Assembly Library, Wellington, the Hocken Library, Dunedin, and the libraries at the University of Auckland and Victoria University of Wellington. I am especially grateful to the interlibrary loan system, which has kept me supplied with a steady stream of material, some of it obscure and difficult to locate.

Thanks are also due to all those typists in the History Department at the University of Illinois at Chicago who have painstakingly typed successive versions of the manuscript and who have uncomplainingly worked their way through what at times must have seemed like an avalanche of footnotes.

Finally, I am particularly indebted to my best and oldest friend, sometime colleague, and shrewd critic, Forrest McDonald, whose sharp eye, extraordinary knowledge, deep wisdom, and organizational skill have made this book, along with my earlier ones, the better for his support and encouragement.

Peter J. Coleman
Glenview, Illinois
August 1986

Part 1
DEMOCRATIC MISSIONS

1 The Mission of the American Democracy

From the beginnings of settlement Americans have always been conscious of a special destiny. The colonists, especially in New England, took that responsibility seriously, seeing themselves as a chosen people singled out by Divine Providence to accomplish His earthly will. That sense of mission persisted long after society became increasingly secularized. "It is now your turn to figure on the face of the earth, and in the annals of the world," declared the South Carolina politician and doctor David Ramsay in 1793 in his *History of the American Revolution.* "Perfect the good work you have begun by . . . ensuring to . . . future generations the blessings for which you have successfully contended."[1] "The rest of the nations must soon be in our rear," announced Herman Melville in 1850. "We are . . . the advance-guard, sent on through the wilderness of untried things, to break a new path in the New World that is ours. In our youth is our strength; in our inexperience, our wisdom."[2] "Fortunate shall they be esteemed by future generations who are privileged to . . . battle for the rights, for the hopes, for the enduring good, of Humanity in all time to come," proclaimed the editor Horace Greeley in the 1840s. "It is a distinction to which the loftiest might well aspire, but which proffers opportunity alike to the humblest. Who would slumber through life ingloriously when such crowns are to be won?"[3]

These declarations of purpose, responsibility, and opportunity catch the flavor of American nationalism in the generations between the Revolution and the Civil War. Self-serving and reassuring, such optimistic professions of faith in the mission of American democracy shaped and defined how rich and poor alike perceived the meaning of their individual lives as well as the destiny of the Republic at large.

This public philosophy served the Republic well over the short term. It reassured an emerging nation by dispelling doubts about the viability of the Democracy; it encouraged westward expansion by providing a rationale transcending individual ambition; it buttressed reform effort in such disparate fields as penology, education, and women's rights; it justified improvements in the transportation network; it served as a beacon to migrants from the Old World and as a set of values by which they could be Americanized; and it made it easier to bear hardships or make sacrifices in the confident belief that better lives lay ahead.

Over the longer term, however, this public philosophy proved a mixed blessing. By encouraging expansionism, it contributed to sectional tensions and thus to the coming of the Civil War; by giving immigrants inflated expectations about the promise of American life, it led eventually to disillusionment and even to disaffection; by exaggerating the abundance of natural resources, it encouraged a profligacy of exploitation; by establishing growth as the principal measure of national progress, it emphasized material values and accelerated change at the expense of societal values and continuity; and by inculcating the belief that the United States was already the best of societies and shortly to achieve perfection, it eventually invited invidious comparisons between rhetorical myth and harsh reality.

While the antebellum United States had not lacked for homegrown or foreign critics, it was not until the closing decades of the century that the nation's achievements and future course came into serious question. The result was a diverse but broadly based reform movement combining proposals of both domestic and foreign origin. In the United States as elsewhere public policy then shifted fundamentally toward the new liberalism of state interventionism, thereby beginning the process that led toward what we have come to think of as the modern welfare state.

This emerging new liberalism—whether local, state or national, rural or urban—was the American version of a worldwide reform movement remarkably similar in its description of problems, diagnosis of underlying causes, and formulation of solutions. Although ordinary citizens probably knew little of what was happening in Europe and elsewhere, many reform leaders were well informed about foreign trends and could be thought of as links in an international information network. Members corresponded and visited with each other, attended international conferences, read the same books, periodicals, and reports, and studied the same issues.

But the Progressive movement was not merely similar to the new liberalism elsewhere. It also borrowed from foreign experience in three crucial ways. First, Europeans supplied many of the ideas about modern society and the modern state that formed the intellectual foundation for American reform. The new social sciences—education, economics, political science, sociology, and psychology—all drew heavily on European scholarship, as did the helping professions—medicine and social work—the basic sciences—especially biology and botany—and architecture and city planning. This infusion of ideas, knowledge, and analytical methodologies reinforced emerging American assumptions that human beings and their social and economic arrangements were not locked into some immutable web of natural laws but that human problems were susceptible to rational analysis, understanding, and correction. Similarly, political ideas, whether drawn from Britain's Christian and Fabian socialism, France's syndicalism, Germany's statism, or Russia's anarchism, gave Americans both a critique of the world of capitalism and an agenda for the reconstruction of the Republic.

Second, the worldwide reform movement provided Progressives with a broad range of legislative and regulatory suggestions from which to draw in formulating their own solutions to America's problems. They canvassed the world in search of models adaptable to domestic needs, institutions, and traditions. They looked to Ireland for ideas on land reform, to Britain for guidance on town planning, to Denmark and the Low Countries for rural credit models, to Germany for social insurance programs, and to Switzerland for ways to democratize political life. Whether acting as public officials, academics, journalists, clergymen, or concerned private citizens, Progressives wanted to know what the Old World had to teach the New; they especially wanted to establish from foreign experience the standards by which Americans could judge the quality of their own lives and accomplishments.

Third, the new liberalism abroad provided Americans with

more than just ideas and models. It gave them as well both a touchstone of what could be accomplished and an invigorating lift to their own reforming efforts. They could point to the results achieved by specific measures to prove that reforms proposed for Americans would produce similar benefits, and in what were often long, arduous, and frustrating campaigns they could take heart that others elsewhere had successfully marched the same road to reform.

Although Americans continued to look primarily eastward to Europe for ideas, models, and inspiration, by the opening of the twentieth century some of them began looking westward to the Antipodes. What they discovered in the Australasian colonies was a critique of modern trends confirming their own perceptions that Old World problems were about to engulf the New. Phrased in colonial metaphors redolent of American thinking, voiced by settlers with roots even younger than the founding of the Republic, and touched off by concerns much like their own over the mission and destiny of communities far from the centers of civilization, these criticisms reinforced the American sense of impending crisis.

The Australasian colonies, particularly New Zealand, also came to be seen, in the United States as in Europe, as experimental laboratories where new economic, political, and social arrangements were being tested in small-scale but practical settings. For Americans, the validity of these reform models gained additional power from the fact that they were being tried in new societies, countries coming to nationhood with New World aspirations and values, communities peopled by immigrants who, like themselves, had fled Europe to take up new lives and new ways, settlers who, in Frederick Jackson Turner's words, had dared to break the cake of custom by building outposts free from the restraints of tradition and established ways of doing things.

Important to Progressives as well was the comprehensiveness of South Pacific reform and the rapidity with which the new liberalism came into operation. No significant aspect of life seemed to have escaped legislative attention—not rural needs, not the aged, babies, or the unemployed. And the transformation seemed to have been accomplished within only a few years. That record impressed American reformers. It invigorated their own commitments by providing working examples of what they too could achieve.

Although the Antipodes supplied the United States with ideas, models, and hope, and although reformers in both hemispheres broadly shared the same goals, the differences between the two movements should not be overlooked. In America, much was made of the need to reform the political system through such devices as the direct election of senators, the secret ballot, municipal home rule, women's suffrage, and the initiative, referendum, and recall. Direct democracy was expected to produce two short-term effects: it would make the people's representatives more responsive to the democratic will, and it would liberate the legislative process from the baneful influence of special interests. Over the longer term, changing the electoral and law-making systems would open the way to social and economic reform. Like the Chartists before them, Populists and Progressives saw the democratization of political institutions as an essential first step toward the achievement of their larger purpose.

Though New Zealand Liberals readily appreciated that the enactment of their program also hinged on electoral and more especially on legislative reforms (making each voter's ballot count equally and forcing the appointive upper house to be more responsive to electoral mandates), there were no American equivalents to these antipodean political and constitutional arrangements. Nor was there in the New Zealand parliamentary system any perceived need for the American concepts of initiative and recall. Most issues and points of view were fully aired in the General Assembly, and any failure to enact important measures reflected the absence of a political consensus rather than a conspiracy by the "interests" to frustrate the popular will. Nor did the recall idea attract support. Triennial elections satisfied voters. The referendum already existed in two areas: local property taxation and liquor licensing. To be sure, the Liberals did abolish the principle of lifetime appointments to the Legislative Council, but there was no significant sentiment for an elective upper chamber.[4]

Votes for women was an entirely different matter. There constitutional and political differences between the two countries mattered little. In both, the suffrage movement was strikingly similar in origin, meaning, relationship to other reform efforts, and larger purpose. There was one important difference: serious consideration had been given to extending the vote to New Zealand women in national elections as early as 1879 and when the suffrage did come, in 1893, it was a generation sooner than in the United States.

Another noteworthy difference between the two reform movements can be seen in their divergence on the question of political and business morality. Although New Zealand had not been immune from public scandal, especially in land acquisition and development, voters saw the overall tone of political life as honest and principled if not always edifying and admirable. They often grumbled, as voters are wont to do, about the quality of representation and debate. They also accepted, even if they did not always approve, the class structure of nineteenth-century politics (some members of parliament were clearly understood to represent large landholding or commercial interests as distinct from small farming or workingmen's interests). But few charged and still fewer believed that politicians were for sale. Voters were probably entirely too sanguine about the purity of public life. Considering the limited information available, they are hardly to be blamed. In any event, cleaning out the legislative cesspool was not part of the New Zealand reform agenda.[5]

In the United States, by contrast, both politicians and their handling of the public's affairs came under attack. With good reason. Every level of government—local, state, federal—critics charged, was poisoned and corrupt. Those politicians not owned outright by the railroads, coal companies, bankers, lumber barons, cattle kings, merchants, or industrialists simply practiced their own brand of legislative entrepreneurship by selling their votes to the highest bidder. Politics had become a business and professional politicians peddled their services for whatever the traffic would bear. And judges and public servants, taking their cue from elected officials and commonly acting in collusion with them, engaged in a wondrous variety of larceny and malfeasance ranging from the sale of favors and the falsification of records to selectively enforcing the law and diverting public revenues into their own pockets. These charges grossly exaggerated the extent and depth of corruption, but there was sufficient truth in them to make the purification of public life an important reform issue.

Nor did New Zealand liberalism draw much strength from attacking either business morality or the concentration of economic power, which were important American concerns. If there were sharp business practices in some colonial firms, which there were, they brought few demands for public regulation, and the antitrust movement won few adherents. Many fields, especially overseas trade, shipping, and farm services, certainly lacked vigorous competition, and banks, insurance companies, commission houses, meat packers, shipping lines, and brewers were suspect, especially if they were owned abroad.[6] Farmers themselves defused some of the issues by forming cooperatives and processing companies and the Liberals dealt with other problems (insurance underwriting, mortgage lending, and coal mining) by setting up state agencies to compete with private firms. The government did take control of the Bank of New Zealand in 1894, but that was to avoid a financial crisis and not a response to demands that the banking business be nationalized, a view held by only a tiny minority of voters. From the outset, municipalities supplied most of the electrical service, and although most urban transit systems and gas companies were privately owned neither public ownership nor public regulation became political issues.

Colonial conditions also explain the absence of a municipal component to the reform movement. City services had yet to be strained by the rate or scale of development. Corruption and "bossism" were absent. By European or American standards, slums did not exist, though the housing stock was often dilapidated and inadequate. There were no serious health problems associated with overcrowding, contaminated water supplies, or inadequate sanitation. There were problems of poverty, alcoholism, drug abuse, and child neglect; and medical services needed improvement. Some ethnic, racial, and religious bigotry and discrimination could also be found in the cities, directed particularly against the Chinese, southern Europeans, Maoris, Irish Catholics, and Jews. There was class feeling as well, especially among the unemployed, and urban elites had little in common with the working poor. Substantial merchants, large property owners, and professional people still controlled most city councils so that municipal government could hardly be described as democratic. Nevertheless, the tensions characteristic of American cities were muted and urban problems so modest that the national reform movement had no parallel in local affairs.

Absent as well from the New Zealand reform agenda were many other issues central to American Progressivism. Since most colonial railways were state owned and operated, antipodean liberalism paid little attention to either nationalization or regulation. Instead, politicians concentrated on expanding the rail network to link the main commercial centers and to open undeveloped country to commercial farming. Similarly, government agencies provided telegraph and telephone services and the post office, a savings bank. Consequently, those American reform concerns had no antipodean parallels. Even civil service reform, though needed, never became a serious matter in New Zealand until after the Liberal era, partly because voters had yet to become concerned about the cost and quality of administration, and partly because Liberal politicians still found the benefits of patronage to outweigh the disadvantages of having to choose between qualified applicants. Both the United States and New Zealand were pioneers in the setting aside of public land for national parks, but the colonial conservation movement had the preservation of natural beauty as its primary goal rather than the management of scarce natural resources. There were no lumber barons or mining magnates in the Antipodes to serve as lightning rods for a conservation ethic.[7]

To be sure, colonial experts played some part in formulating and executing the Liberal program, especially in the fields of agriculture, child and maternal care, education, labor, and public health, but there was no New Zealand equivalent of the American effort to rationalize either government or business.[8] Robert Wiebe's "Search for Order" had no significant parallel in colonial liberalism.

In short, even in microcosm, many of the issues central to American Progressivism had no New Zealand equivalents. The colony was too young, too small, too uncomplicated, and too unlike the United States in its political habits and constitutional arrangements.

These differences notwithstanding, some of which went unnoticed at the time by acts of either omission or commission, many Progressives became fascinated by antipodean liberalism. What they saw, or sometimes thought they saw, seemed to provide compelling answers to perplexing questions about modern life, ranging from the proper functions of government, relations between capital and labor, and exploitation in the workplace to security in old age, infant mortality, and rural impoverishment. The ways in which they perceived and acted on those assessments of Australasian reform says something important about Progressivism in the United States.

The assessment of American reform advanced here reflects an effort to broaden the framework of analysis by putting more emphasis than before on the external forces shaping Progressivism. Doing so in no way minimizes the importance of recent scholarship. The achievements are impressive, particularly in sharpening the focus, though at the cost of narrowing the perspective so as somewhat to lose sight of the American experience in the larger, worldwide trend toward the interventionist welfare state.

It is a cliché to say that we grow up with built in assumptions about the uniqueness of our New World experience. But it is also true. Try as we may to see things otherwise, we are drawn understandably to an interest in what sets us apart from the rest of the world. It would be uncharitable to suggest that Americans suppose that they invented democracy or discovered reform. Yet there is enough truth in the comment to explain why Progressivism has been studied so exclusively in American terms. As historians and especially in our role as teachers, it is as if we have been programmed to emphasize the unique at the expense of the universal.

This tendency to highlight what was distinctive about the American experience gathered strength over time and became unusually powerful for students of the Progressive period. The United States by the turn of the century looked quite unlike any other country. It seemed more complex and diverse than ever before, and its constitutional and political arrangements had a character all their own. To understand Progressivism, therefore, scholars found it necessary to study each facet of it in depth. Thus their research turned sharply inward. One result has been that the effort to draw all the data together to reach an overarching synthesis of Progressivism, even as a purely American phenomenon, has become increasingly difficult—so much so, in fact, that some historians have simply written off the task in frustration.[9] A second result of this inward view was that a larger sense of the content, process, and meaning of reform reaching beyond American shores still lies pretty much below the historical horizon.

We are only too aware that Progressivism seemed to be one thing in national affairs, something often quite different in state politics, and yet a third thing in the local arena. And at each of these levels of jurisdiction, there were broad as well as specific regional variations to further complicate the task of defining Progressive goals, constituencies, and outcomes. Issues of conservation and irrigation mattered more in the West than elsewhere, problems of rural poverty and race had a special intensity in the South, absentee ownership of natural resources deeply affected Appalachia but hardly concerned New England, and the quality of urban life was irrelevant to most voters on the High Plains.[10]

Substantial as they may seem, these variations may not be as unique as we suppose. Reform everywhere—whether in Canada, Australia, Italy, or Germany—involved comparable complexities, often of a remarkably similar character; regional differences from east to west or north to south, cultural and religious variations in Old World countries as well as in New, urban and rural distinctions everywhere.

These regional and other differences remind us that the reform movements everywhere had more in common than we have recognized and that the particularity of American historiography over recent decades has tended to obscure, not clarify, the worldwide thrust of change. The reform pathways in the United

States—the actors, issues, and processes—varied from region to region, state to state, and city to city, as numerous studies have shown. What these studies have not revealed are the linkages and similarities between domestic and foreign experience.

Two other related factors help to explain why historians have been drawn inward rather than outward. The first is our recognition that, more than anything else, what sets the Progressive period apart from what came before was the increase in legislative activity. Such was the case at every level of government from the village board to the Congress. To understand what happened, therefore, we have had to concentrate on the politics of the period. We have wanted to know, for example, who supported or opposed zoning ordinances, how constituencies were mobilized for or against, who shaped the administration of the law, and what the consequences were. Looked at in this way, the study of politics puts a premium on the particular, the special, the distinct and thus gives to American progressivism characteristics that set it apart from reform elsewhere.[11]

In the second place, our capacity to separate out what was particular and distinctive about American political life has been greatly strengthened in recent years by our methodological borrowings from other disciplines. Anthropology has enriched our understanding of the underlying and persistent strength of ethnic and cultural forces; sociology has given us the tools to analyze organizations and group relationships; and mathematics has enabled us to quantify, measure, and compare. As a consequence, we know more about Progressivism than an earlier generation of historians would have though possible.

What we know, of course, is what we should have known all along but have apparently forgotten—that all societies, including very small ones, are pluralistic, and that while individuals and groups may seem to march to the same drum cadence, they may in fact hear different beats. Initially, students identified only two beats, though they could not agree on what they were. David P. Thelen, for example, generalized from the Wisconsin experience and identified the dominant Progressive tune as one of outrage over universal problems, including inequitable taxation and hazards to public health. Melvin G. Holli, by contrast, argued from Mayor Pingree's Detroit in favor of institutional reform at the expense of Thelen's social concerns.[12]

Others drew contrasts between East and West or new immigrants versus old stock. More recently, scholars have identified a multiplicity of competing tunes with results sounding more like a piece by Charles Ives than like a Bach chorale.

Though each of these contributions has in its own way enriched our understanding of Progressivism, particularity of understanding rather than universality has been the consequence. Every American tree has been painstakingly identified, numbered, and described, but we know less than we should about the forest in general or its ecosystem in particular. And we know still less about the relationship between the American trend toward the welfare state and similar trends elsewhere.

To these considerations must be added several others: the possible constitutional limits on state interventionism; self-imposed limits arising from relationships between the states; and limits thought to have their origins in flaws in the political process itself. In the first, it is easy to see that constitutional impediments complicated the reform task and thus gave American Progressivism distinctive features. Could the state intervene between employer and worker to specify who might work, for how many hours, when, in any twenty-four hour period, and at what minimum rates of pay? Some other countries had comparable constitutional problems. But even if such interventions could survive constitutional scrutiny, would a higher standard imposed on employers in Massachusetts put them at a competitive disadvantage with firms in Connecticut or South Carolina? These were substantial concerns and have served to strengthen our impression of Progressivism as a movement overwhelmingly reflective of problems anchored in what is special to the United States. Add to these factors the perception that reform in America would make little headway until various institutional impediments were removed. What was required was the popular election of senators, direct democracy (the initiative, referendum, and recall), the Australian ballot, votes for women, city-wide elections in place of parochial ward politics. With the exception of bringing women into political life, most of these reform concerns have been treated as if they were distinctively American problems. In fact, the removal of institutional impediments to change was crucial in other countries as well, and Benjamin O. Flower's *Twentieth Century Magazine* had regular monthly columns on worldwide trends in municipal government and proportional representation, as well as other areas. On these, as on so many other issues, American reform was linked to an international information network. By treating these questions in isolation as if they were distinctive American concerns, historians have minimized the broad similarity of both the reform objectives and the processes of reform throughout the developed world.

This study is a modest attempt to broaden our understanding of Progressivism by examining the links to antipodean liberalism and in the concluding chapter by suggesting some of the ways in which the American reform effort can be placed in a worldwide context.

Accordingly, the book is laid out in three parts. The first examines the parallels between the New Zealand and American reform movements; the second investigates the antipodean impact on Progressivism; and the third both evaluates that impact and sets out a tentative analysis of foreign influences on American reform.

2 The Mission of the New Zealand Democracy

New Zealanders no less than Americans invested their colonial lives with a sense of destiny. It was not many years after the arrival of the first emigrant ships in 1840 that they began to speak self-consciously about their special mission in the world. "New Zealand . . . enjoys . . . the distinction of being the political laboratory of the world," declared O. T. J. Alpers, a teacher at the Christchurch Boys' High School, in 1894. "Every possible experiment in legislation and government—from labour laws to advertising on postage stamps—is being tested. . . ." "The fierce search light of the civilized world is turned full upon you," announced the United States consul at a political rally in Auckland in 1893, "and your every action . . . watched with fear and trembling." The mission of the New Zealand democracy, wrote a pamphleteer in 1892, should be to "hasten . . . that 'new era' of human life now in its birththroes throughout the world, an era in which the spirit of brotherhood . . . will supplant . . . the spirit of individualism."[1]

These self-congratulatory assessments of the inner spirit and larger purpose of antipodean colonization reflected the common tendency of European settlers at other places and times to invest their efforts with a significance transcending the workaday struggle of farm making or community building. The Puritan vision of "a city on a hill" in New England, the "manifest destiny" of America to carry democracy, republicanism, and civilization to the shores of the Pacific and beyond, or the Afrikaner's determination to preserve an Old Testament society on the high veldt are familiar examples of similar needs and aspirations.

The New Zealand version of national destiny was doubtless a necessary form of reassurance to colonists who were separated by more than 13,000 miles of ocean from their kinsfolk in the mother country. They needed to justify their sacrifices to themselves and to distant relatives by linking their efforts to a higher purpose. After all, the colony had barely celebrated its fiftieth anniversary when Alpers and others began talking about New Zealand's special place in the world, and growth had been painfully slow, especially over the first two decades of colonization (1840–1860). It had taken the Otago gold rush in the sixties to push the number of settlers beyond 100,000 and massive recruiting efforts in the seventies to carry the total over 400,000. Even so, by 1890 the number of white colonists had barely reached 600,000; natural increase was only beginning to outrank immigration as the vehicle of growth; the leading communities of Auckland, Wellington, Christchurch, and Dunedin compared unfavorably with the smaller English provincial towns; and thousands of settlers in the country districts enjoyed neither comfort nor prosperity.

The origins of what was to become the "mission of the New Zealand democracy" are to be found in the optimistic theories of the perfectability of man and society that so dominated Western thought in the age of rationalism and utilitarianism. It is especially significant that the arrival of the first New Zealand Company settlers in January 1840, and the proclamation of British sovereignty the following month placed colonization within the context of profound political and social change underway in the mother country. The reform of Parliament, Roman Catholic emancipation, changes in the system of public welfare, the reorganization of local government, improvements in municipal service, the abolition of slavery in the colonies, prison reform, and the enactment of factory legislation—each in its own way reflected the conviction that man's condition could be improved by the application of rational principles. Also noteworthy were the rise of Chartism among the middling and working classes and the demands for political reform as a necessary first step in bringing about social and economic improvement. Reflecting the spirit of the age, the colonists arrived in New Zealand confident of their ability to shape their destiny.

To some extent their thinking was influenced by the colonization concepts formulated by Edward Gibbon Wakefield in the 1830s. Though associated with the Whig radicals of the day,

Wakefield's view of colonization was essentially backward-looking and conservative. Deeply troubled by the agricultural and industrial revolutions, he proposed to recreate in the South Seas an older and more admirable England, an England free of the social and economic distress he saw on all sides.

Wakefield's formula consisted vaguely of transferring a vertical cross section of English rural society to the Antipodes and freezing the social structure by fixing the price of land at a level so high that only the gentry could afford to buy. This would guarantee an adequate supply of labor to the squirearchy, provide steady employment for properly deferential laborers and artisans, and preserve rural harmony and tranquillity in the foreseeable future.

It should come as no surprise that a concept of colonization formulated in a cell in Newgate Gaol and based on nothing more substantial than a few secondhand accounts of conditions overseas should have proved totally impractical. In the event, theories of colonization proved no match for the stern realities of time, place, climate, topography, or markets. They swept the Wakefieldian vision aside. Settlers concentrated on surviving in a strange, alien environment. At best, they paid no more than lip service to the notion of planned colonization. But what Wakefield left behind was an influential legacy—the idea that colonial life could be ordered in such a way that the grinding poverty of industrial England or the chronic anarchy of rural affairs could be forever ended.[2]

The humanitarian liberalism of the thirties and forties reinforced this view that colonists could somehow look forward to a better life in the New World than in the Old. Powerfully but not exclusively motivated by an evangelical wish to christianize, civilize, and protect the heathen from the ungodly exploitation of rapacious settlers, colonial reformers and philanthropists gradually came to believe that colonization could not be halted and that the Maori could be protected only by the imposition of British law and order. What emerged from this debate over policy goals was the assumption that the interests of Maori and settler could be harmonized for the benefit of both. Ultimately, the assumption proved no more valuable than the Wakefieldian concept of planned colonization and within two decades Maori and *pakeha* were locked in battle. Control of the land was the ostensible cause and from the settler's point of view it was the fundamental issue. For the Maori, however, their very survival as a people was at stake. Despite the failure of the colonial reformers to reconcile these conflicting interests, they too left a legacy—an uncritical acceptance by settlers of the idea that New Zealand was a "progressive" society and that a better world was in the making.

This is not to suggest that many colonists thought very deeply about national destiny. On the contrary, few had either the time or the inclination to reflect on such matters. Most were fully occupied carving farms out of the bush, opening the back country to settlement, sluicing for gold, or in countless other ways eking out livelihoods. Their interests were practical rather than philosophical.

Out of such concerns emerged an early tendency to expect government to play an active role in economic development and in some instances to provide services more commonly supplied in other societies by private business. Thus successive governments actively campaigned for emigrants, offering optimistic accounts of colonial life and free passages and land as inducements. These activities massively expanded in the seventies when the government borrowed millions of pounds on the London money market and embarked on vast public works schemes. Roads, bridges, railways, telegraph lines, a cable to Australia, and steamship service to San Francisco were the result. By the end of the decade, population had doubled and more than 130,000 new settlers had arrived. During the same period the government also created the Post Office Savings Bank (1865), entered the life insurance business (1869), and with the establishment of the Public Trust Office (1872), began competing with private firms in the field of estate management.

While these development programs derived overwhelmingly from pragmatic necessity and political expediency, they were accompanied nevertheless by the first stirrings of a national sense of destiny. Mary Ann Muller, for example, in *An Appeal to the Men of New Zealand* (Nelson, 1869), urged the suffrage for women with what were to become classic reform arguments. "Why ever pursue the hard beaten track of ages?" she asked.

"Have we not enough cobwebs and mists to cloud our mental gaze, enough fetters to impede our onward progress . . . that we must voluntarily shackle ourselves with old world prejudices. . . ?" If women were to be enfranchised eventually, she asserted, there was no virtue in New Zealand's merely following the rest of the world. "Why not take the initiative?" The colony "has but to inaugurate this new position [and] all will applaud."[3]

Similar arguments were made in the seventies and eighties by reformers pressing other causes. Colonists were repeatedly reminded of both their unique opportunities and their obligations. Thus an editor defended the establishment of the Government Life Insurance Office by asserting that settlers looked forward to the creation of a society that would be a model to the rest of the world. He was confident that foreign governments would interest themselves in what New Zealand was doing. "We have a country founded under circumstances . . . of the best kind," declared Sir George Grey, first a governor and then premier, in 1878. In urging the General Assembly to reform the electoral system, Grey asked whether "such an opportunity [had] presented [itself] before of moulding a nation which would be an example to all times?" Electoral reform, commented another liberal spokesman, W. L. Rees of Auckland, would be a credit to New Zealand by keeping the colony abreast of the policies of the foremost communities of the world. On a somewhat more philosophical note, James E. Fitzgerald, a politician and journalist, observed that because New Zealand was free from "tradition . . . precedent . . . and old-world prejudices," it could legislate an equitable distribution of national income. It might be "the imperishable glory of statesmen in these new born nations," he declared, so to improve social and economic conditions that poverty would not be the consequence of artificial law, nor crime prompted by "the cravings of want, and matured by the sense of wrong." Even civil servants found such rationalizations attractive. "If state-aided emigration is to be one of the earliest solutions to some modern social problems," one of them observed, "New Zealand possesses the extraordinary capacity in a field where the experiment can be tested with an almost certainty of success, because population is its greatest want."[4]

By the last decade of the nineteenth century, therefore, New Zealanders were becoming accustomed to hearing a flattering view of their place and destiny in the world order. The colony should guide the spirit of the age. Other countries were watching New Zealand's deviation from the "beaten track of Conservatism" by establishing state railways, telegraphs, life insurance, and savings banks. Colonists were told that their political life was more vital than in older countries, that they did not have to wait for others to establish precedents, and that New Zealand's leadership would be followed because they "know we are putting into a concrete form the great theories of civilization that are moving the world today." Indeed, Sir Robert Stout once made this remarkable request of his fellow politicians: "I ask the House to make these experiments," he declared. "I ask the House to believe that these experiments may be made. I ask the House to think that even if these experiments fail it is our duty to make them."[5] In short, New Zealand had both the opportunity and the obligation to lead mankind into the promised land.

Powerful social and economic trends in the seventies and eighties reinforced this sense of mission. Interacting with and complementing each other, these developments radicalized popular attitudes and brought the Liberal party of John Ballance into office, and it so reformed the statute book as to give the colony its reputation as a legislative laboratory.

The most fundamental force leading to political change was demographic. The gold rush of the sixties and the Vogel program of the seventies brought very different settlers to the colony. For the most part urban and working class in origin and attitude, these newcomers were less deferential toward the established social and political order than their predecessors had been. When the gold diggings played out, many miners roamed the country seeking work, eventually drifting to the towns where they formed the beginnings of an urban proletariat. Their numbers were swelled in the eighties when depression forced a drastic curtailment of public works schemes and threw thousands of newcomers out of work.

The inability of the rural economy to absorb large numbers of farm workers intensified the urban trend and exacerbated discontent. The underlying cause was simple. The Wakefieldian idea of rural harmony and stability had been based on a hopelessly impractical concept of labor-intensive agriculture. Each farm unit was to be a more or less self-contained, self-sufficient squirearchy. But the realities of colonial life were very different. From the inception of organized settlement, there had been a desperate search for exportable cash products. Only in that way could citizens and governments alike finance the flow of essential developmental credit and pay for the vast assortment of imported necessities. Masts, spars, sawn lumber, flax, and gold figured prominently on early bills of lading, but it was the development of the pastoral economy and the export of wool that finally gave New Zealand its capacity to survive and prosper.

Wool growing was capital- rather than labor-intensive, however, and it required the dispersion of settlers over wide areas. After mid-century, as a consequence, the large runholders and their mercantile and financial allies in the commercial centers became the dominant force in colonial life and they came to equate their own self-interest with the interest of New Zealand at large.

Pastoral preeminence might have gone unchallenged had the demand for wool stayed high. But the Panic of 1873 broke the market and threw the colony into a depression that persisted throughout the eighties and beyond. Foreclosures and bankruptcies piled one upon the other, the cost of money soared, unemployment lines grew longer, and soup kitchens appeared in some towns. Accompanying these frightening trends was the rise of the sweatshop in the garment industry and a bitterly fought strike in the shipping industry.

Many colonists concluded that the Old World was about to overtake the New. Whether influenced by the Wakefieldian vision of a model society, by an optimistic belief in the capacity of man and society to progress, or by a simpler faith in their own chances for self-improvement, settlers began comparing promise with reality. Alarmists drew the obvious conclusion: that the increase in poverty, slums, disease, unemployment, sweated labor, and violent industrial disputes in the towns, and the growth of land monopoly, rack renting, and absentee landlordism in the countryside were leading to serfdom and provided clear proof that the colony was slipping back toward Old World conditions.

A few colonists had taken up this cry as early as the seventies. It grew louder in the eighties as the depression deepened. Lengthening the working day produced "great evil to the mind, body and soul" and had brought "wretchedness" to English women, complained one settler in 1872. No "sophistry" could conceal the increase in misery and poverty or the social distress that foreshadowed crisis. Even the colony's simple industrial system came under attack: factories would only make "a few men gods of wealth, and the rest mean drudges toiling for the smallest pittance." Just as it had done in England, the "ghastly being," Progress, would soon turn the people into serfs. Before long, predicted one critic, the colony would reveal "the hideous face of the old civilization." The emigration agent in England, complained a new settler in 1880, had failed to tell him that he "would find a soup kitchen here, [and] that he would . . . be dependent on the earnings of his little children." "There were cases of need almost as deplorable as any in the crowded purlieus of the cities of older lands," reported the Rev. W. J. Williams in a sermon he called "The Bitter Cry of Christchurch." There were "homes from which furniture had gone bit by bit to purchase bread; homes where was to be found the bitter cry of children . . . for food; homes where they had no fuel to keep them warm, nothing to cover them but mere rags." Has "it come to this," fumed the Rev. Rutherford Waddell in a sermon entitled "The Sin of Cheapness" and charging that Dunedin was riddled with sweated labor, "that we are willing to permit in our midst a system that in this young fair land threatens to reproduce . . . those very evils that are eating the heart and soul out of the older countries?" He and others warned: unless prompt action were taken, "we shall find, as population increases and the struggle for existence becomes keener, that these very evils will have struck deep their roots in our midst."[6]

Concern for New Zealand's future was especially strong among land reformers. Unless prevented, the "desolating monster" of land monopoly would soon force settlers into the towns where, left to rot in pauperism, they would "swell the ranks of poverty and crime." They "will sink deeper . . . in degradation" and men will sit down "every evening with poverty, a grim and terrible companion." Such a system "not only robs the living but robs generations unborn." Our "children . . . will experience the bitter grinding poverty now so prevalent in Britain. . . . Like causes produce like results." Monopoly and landlordism seemed to have fled "the old world to find refuge in the new." In Europe these evils had "shoved . . . millions into sweltering misery, and driven them into . . . crime . . . or death." Thousands of acres would support only sheep, "humanity being represented by a shepherd and his dog" until such time "as serfs . . . can be imported, . . . receiving a wage barely enough to keep body and soul together." New Zealand would then replicate the United Kingdom's "hideous contrast of wealth and poverty," a few "governing families"—a bloated aristocracy of unsurpassed cruelty—would then monopolize all positions of influence. "Should not priest and pulpit, people and Parliament [unite] to save our grand and great-grandchildren from . . . such a curse?" No "progress could be expected unless every relic of [European] feudalism . . . was swept away."[7]

The depth of these misgivings explains why Henry George's *Progress and Poverty* had such an impact on antipodean thinking. From it most Australasians had learned all they knew about classical economics, John Stuart Mill's idea for recapturing the unearned increment on land values for the public benefit, or Alfred Russel Wallace's proposals for land nationalization. For many colonials George became a modern prophet, a revered authority who expressed their own longings for a just order. More than any other single individual he laid the attitudinal basis for the modern New Zealand state.

Throughout the hard times of the eighties, the colonial debate over land and tax policy drew its fire and much of its rhetoric from George's analysis. From one end of New Zealand to the other, the call for reform went out. Landlords, declared one speaker, "have been enriched at the expense of the people, for their lands so easily acquired have been increased in value a hundred fold by the natural progress of the country, and by the expenditure of money which the people have to pay for." "Allow absolute individual ownership of the land to continue, and the moneyed class will gradually absorb the smaller holdings. Thus not only the rent, but the 'unearned increment' due solely to increase of population and the people's labour, will pass into private hands instead of going toward the abolition of customs duties, taxation, etc." "We believe that the surface of the earth was created for the mutual sustenance . . . of all mankind," argued R. D. L. Duffus, a leading Auckland single-taxer, "and not solely for the benefit . . . of those who . . . monopolize it, and who . . . live in idleness, luxury, and dissipation, feasting upon . . . the industry of others, while the people . . . are living . . . on the very verge of starvation."[8]

Progress and Poverty appealed particularly to the New Zealand Knights of Labour, a group organized by the Christchurch unemployed in 1887. The movement spread rapidly in the early nineties, when an American organizer toured the colony "explaining, exhorting, arranging and founding" affiliates of the parent order in the United States. Before long the Knights had some fifty assemblies, perhaps five thousand members, and the support of fourteen members of Parliament. Though the organization lost strength in the second half of the decade, it continued to support land and tax reforms.[9]

Edward Bellamy's utopian novel *Looking Backward* reached New Zealand's readers at the depths of the depression. Bellamy's indictment of the existing order reinforced Henry George's criticisms from a socialist perspective, while his vision of the future raised the hopes of thousands of colonists. Bellamy's ideas shaped the thinking of labor leaders, politicians, and reformers; crept into parliamentary debates and the editorial pages of liberal newspapers; and brought an entire generation of settlers to new ways of viewing the role of the state in the modern world.

It was against this background of widespread distress, disillusionment, and dissatisfaction that the Liberals, led by John Ballance, came to power in January 1891. Although the party's election manifesto made only traditionally modest promises, such as frugality in government, tariff protection for colonial industries, and the settlement of more families on the land, some candidates, especially in the cities, ran on platforms appealing to both workers and middle-class radicals. Their ideas came to dominate the new government's legislative agenda.

Under a succession of leaders—Richard John Seddon from 1893 to 1906 and Sir Joseph G. Ward until 1912—the Liberals pushed their reform program through the legislature, adding new proposals as they went along, partly to sustain their political momentum so as to retain power. But over the two decades the party became increasingly conservative and cautious as ideology gave way to pragmatism. This trend reflected public attitudes, especially in rural areas, which became increasingly conservative with the growth of farm incomes, but it ran counter to a rising militancy in some sections of the labor movement, most notably in coal and gold mining and in transportation.

Seddon had some success in counteracting these centripetal forces of the Right and the Left. By far the most charismatic figure in the history of New Zealand politics, he built a modern political organization by demanding pledges of support from candidates in return for the party's official endorsement. He also reinforced loyalty through patronage appointments, pork barrel expenditures in the constituencies of faithful party members, and at election time by campaigning vigorously on their behalf. And throughout their two decades in office, the Liberals shrewdly cultivated for their own political advantage the image of New Zealand as the world's legislative laboratory.

Initially, the Liberals put forward a program to deal with the colony's economic and social crisis, but they quickly learned, as the Chartists had done before them, that they had first to remove the political obstacles to their proposals. In the process, they rediscovered several political truths—that conservative obstructionism could be turned to the ministry's advantage, that electoral reform could itself be made an effective issue, and that control of the Treasury benches gave them the power to spend public funds where they would do Liberals the most political good.

When the Ballance ministry took office it could hardly be said that the political system was democratic in the modern sense. Only males could vote, property owning still conferred special privileges at election time, the apportionment of seats in the House of Representatives discriminated against urban voters, and the Legislative Council behaved like a conservative gentlemen's club in its devotion to class, property, and interest. The outgoing prime minister, Sir Harry A. Atkinson, had even persuaded the governor to appoint six additional conservatives to the council as a further precaution against radicalism.

Atkinson's strategy proved so effective that it quickly led first to a political impasse and then to a constitutional crisis. In 1891 and to a lesser extent in 1892 the Legislative Council either threw out or drastically amended virtually every significant Liberal proposal. Though this gave Ballance and his colleagues time in which to rally popular support as well as to improve various details of their program, a confrontation between the two houses could not be avoided. It came early in 1892 when Ballance requested the appointment of several new councillors. Successive governors refused his request. Only the intervention of the Colonial Office, which ruled that a governor must accept the advice of his chief minister, settled the question. The appointment in 1893 of twelve additional members did not give the Liberals control of the council, but it conveyed a clear message: further obstructionism would lead to further appointments. That threat sufficed to break the legislative impasse without turning the council into a meek rubber stamp of the majority will in the House.[10]

Ballance was undoubtedly shrewd in stopping short of packing the council with pliant Liberals. He conveyed a reassuring sense of political restraint and responsibility, especially to middle class voters who held the balance of power in many electorates, he emphasized by comparison the outrageousness of Atkinson's earlier use of the appointing power, and perhaps most significantly by leaving some doubt as to how the Council would treat the reform program in the next session of the General Assembly, he provided party workers with an essential spur in the forthcoming election campaign. Nothing would persuade councillors to let the Liberal legislation go through so much as a resounding victory at the polls.

But if the Liberals were not above turning the struggle with the Legislative Council to their political advantage, nor were they above trying to consolidate their power by changing the electoral system. Two measures, one minor, the other major, came in 1893. The first modified the voting advantage of property owners by extending the principle of "one man one vote" to the rule that a voter could register in only one electorate. By prohibiting multiple registrations, this prevented the affluent from waiting for campaign trends to appear and then casting their ballots in marginal districts where a shift of a few votes from one candidate to another often meant the difference between victory or defeat. Since multiple registration had most affected urban and suburban districts, areas in which the Liberals held a number of marginal seats, this reform weakened the Conservatives.[11]

The major change made New Zealand the first country to give women the right to vote in national elections. The reform was a testament to the power of organization. To be sure, by the nineties a national consensus for the expansion of voting rights had probably emerged. After all, women had been voting in various local elections since 1867. Most men saw the logic of enlarging their participation and expected the change to come sooner rather than later. But the Women's Christian Temperance Union and the Franchise League accelerated the timetable. That their campaign avoided confrontational, militant tactics masked its intensity and determination. Leaders began unobtrusively with petitions, anonymous newspaper articles and pamphlets, letter writing, and private meetings with editors and politicians. Then the campaign came out into the open with public rallies and lobbying in the corridors and galleries of the General Assembly itself.

The movement faced three obstacles. First, diehard opponents saw only disaster in granting women the vote. Second, the brewing and liquor industries worked vigorously against the reform, understandably fearing that prohibition would surely follow. And third, many politicians, even those who believed that women should be brought into national political life, simply preferred to sit on their hands. Whether Conservative or Liberal, they thought the electoral consequences unpredictable but generally supposed that most women would vote for the other party.

This was especially troublesome to the Liberals. Seddon had only just replaced Ballance as prime minister, his leadership remained untested in both the House and the colony, and the party's hold on power was in doubt. In these circumstances Seddon hesitated to offend the suffrage movement by blocking reform, but feared that if women won the vote they would support Conservatives in the next election. He chose to straddle the issue by openly supporting the measure in the House while covertly working for its defeat in the council. The strategy backfired. Instead of letting the diehard majority in the Council work its will, his surreptitious intervention tipped the scale the other way and women got the vote.[12]

In the event, Seddon had no cause to regret his tactics. The Liberals won a stunning victory in the next election. Where there were clear choices between candidates, women tended to vote for temperance Liberals and against antifeminist Conservatives. Their votes were probably decisive in some constituencies and in the colony as a whole women accentuated the pronounced Liberal swing.[13]

Several other factors contributed to the Liberal victory. Despite the hard times, Seddon persuaded voters that the party's reform program offered effective solutions to the colony's economic problems. The Conservatives, by contrast, rejected interventionism and offered voters little more than government retrenchment. The Liberals also attacked the council's obstructionism, arguing that only a strong electoral mandate would persuade the upper house to abandon its opposition to reform.

Both Ballance and Seddon made the land question their first priority. Monopoly was the central issue. Fewer than a tenth of the holders controlled almost half the land. They included fifty absentees who between them held more than a million acres. And with much of the best land in large estates, barely one colonist in ten earned a livelihood from farming. Critics complained that monopoly retarded development, locked out thousands of potential farmers, and threatened to fasten a plutocracy on the colony.

If reformers could agree on the causes of the problem, they disagreed on the cure. The most doctrinaire would settle for nothing less than land nationalization. Single-taxers disagreed. They thought it would be sufficient to force large estate holders to improve their properties and to siphon the speculative profits of the land into the public treasury for the benefit of all. Practical reformers, by far the majority, cared little for ideology, only for results.

Their leader was the minister of lands and agriculture, John McKenzie, a Scottish settler who brought to the monopoly issue a passion so intense that he could not always keep it under control. Single-minded in purpose, he pursued the goal of opening the land to ordinary colonists, but compromised wherever necessary to get as much of his program through as possible. The program had four elements. First, a graduated land tax in 1891 encouraged higher productivity to offset the higher tax burden. Owners unable or unwilling to make capital improvements were expected to sell off some or all of their holdings. Second, McKenzie obtained authority to repurchase estates, by forced sale if necessary, for subdivision and resettlement by small farmers. Here McKenzie sided with the land nationalizers without committing the government to wholesale repurchase. Third, he also reformed the land-tenure system, though there were limits to what he could do; two acres out of three were already in freehold. For the remaining land, McKenzie gave farmers three choices: outright purchase for those who had the capital; a 25-year leasehold with the right to purchase the freehold title but with the periodic revaluation of the rent; or a 999-year leasehold at a fixed rental, which was a freehold title in all but name. Both leaseholds encouraged investment in improvements rather than in land acquisition. Finally, the Liberals put the government into the money-lending business. The work of the colonial treasurer, Ward, rather than McKenzie, the Government Advances to Settlers Act of 1894 supplied small farmers with developmental capital at interest rates well below what private lenders charged. Without cheap money, most farmers would have had to struggle for years to make their holdings profitable.

Buttressing their claims with impressive statistics about the redistribution of land ownership and the sharp rise in farm output, the Liberals, throughout the nineties and beyond, trumpeted their land reforms as a brilliant solution to grave social and economic problems. They made much of the repurchase in 1893 of the Cheviot estate in North Canterbury and the subdivision of this 84,000-acre tract into 320 separate farms. So successful was this venture that over the next fifteen years the government broke up another million acres, invested heavily in access roads and bridges, and settled several thousand more families. There seemed every reason to believe that the Liberals had destroyed monopoly, appeased land hunger, and blocked, in McKenzie's words, "a recurrence of those causes which led to poverty and misery in the older countries."[14]

The Liberals claimed more than their due. Market forces had a greater impact on the rise in farm prosperity than did legislation. They gave holders of large estates, including banks and insurance companies—which had acquired many properties through foreclosure—their first opportunity in more than a decade to sell out on a rising land market. The development of the export trade in cheese, butter, and mutton reinforced the trend. Smaller farms then became economical as meat and dairy products began to challenge the primacy of wool as the colony's leading export. The reform program certainly encouraged closer settlement, but the legislation would have had little impact if economic conditions had not encouraged changes in the structure of farming. Moreover, the land tax proved worthless as a weapon against monopoly. The rates were too low to break up the large estates, and with the rise in wool prices, the tax burden steadily declined.[15]

If the Liberals claimed too much, they more than fulfilled the election contract. In doing so, they revolutionized political life. Thereafter, no party could win office without being responsive to electoral needs. Whether conservative or liberal, governments would be expected to legislate for the benefit of the typical voter. No longer would it be possible to oppose change as a matter of principle or to equate the national welfare with the interest of the few.

McKenzie's tireless struggle for rural improvement was matched by William Pember Reeves's parallel attack on urban distress. Sweated labor and the maritime strike replaced land monopoly and absentee ownership as the symbols of discontent, but unlike McKenzie, the son of an evicted Scottish crofter, Reeves came from comfortable, educated circumstances. He had no firsthand experience of poverty or hunger, unemployment or exploitation. Reeves was an authentic colonial intellectual. Widely read in Bellamy, George, Mill, Spencer, Wallace, and especially the Fabians, he brought bookish learning to social and economic problems. Nevertheless, his legislative program was more practical than theoretical. "If industries cannot prosper without the sweating of women, children, and men, and without bringing in their train the evils of the Old World, well, we should do better to get on without them. I would rather that New Zealand had a million inhabitants, happy, prosperous and satisfied, than two million living many of them in dirty streets of black hovels, in the midst of dreary poverty."[16]

Reeves believed that the fastest and most effective way to deal with urban distress was by improving working conditions. He went about it in two ways: by establishing minimum standards of employment and by redressing the bargaining inequality between employers and employees. State intervention in the work contract roused great opposition in conservative circles, but the Reeves program no longer seems radical. Like Franklin Delano Roosevelt in the United States in the thirties, Reeves was considered an enemy to his class, and like the Democrats, the Liberals were thought to be bent on the destruction of business. The reality was very different: Reeves merely altered the terms of competition; support for trade unions protected workers from those who would exploit the inequality in bargaining power. Thus were urban conditions to be ameliorated.

There was nothing especially new or radical in this Liberal program to regulate working conditions. European and American reformers had shared similar goals since the early years of the century. Though scattered labor laws had been enacted piecemeal over the preceding generation, New Zealand workers enjoyed little protection when the Liberals took office in 1891. Shipowners had to provide seamen with adequate accommodations, food, and medical care, and apprentices had to be supplied with food, clothing, bedding, and a moral education. Aside from a safety law for factory machinery and boilers, another making it easier for injured workers to recover damages, and a third protecting wages when contractors failed, only the working conditions of women and children were controlled. But as the growth of sweated labor had revealed, the legislation was a sham.

What distinguished the Liberal reform program from efforts elsewhere was its comprehensiveness and administration.

Reeves and his successor achieved comprehensiveness in two ways: by defining the unit of regulation as an industrial establishment employing two or more workers and by extending the basic principles of the labor code to new categories of employees. Thus even the smallest workshop had to provide minimum working conditions. There had to be adequate safety devices, good ventilation, proper sanitation and cleanliness, decent eating space, and regular mealtimes. The length of the working day and week was strictly controlled, especially for women and youths. Men could not work more than 48 hours a week, women and children were limited to 45 hours, children under fourteen could not be employed in factories at all, overtime was carefully regulated, and paid holidays had to be given. By 1911 comparable protection had been given to clerks in shops and offices, household servants, miners, seamen, sheep shearers, farm laborers, and kauri gum diggers, and the labor code had been brought together in a series of consolidating statutes. Included were measures requiring the inspection of machinery and scaffolding, regulating employment agencies, protecting workers' wages, and making employers liable for death or injury caused by negligence or default.[17]

What was both noteworthy and unusual was that the Liberals, unlike most previous reformers in New Zealand or elsewhere, paid scrupulous attention to the administration of the labor code. Here Reeves proved himself both practical and sensible. Like McKenzie in the field of land reform, he knew that only systematic enforcement of the regulations would achieve the results he sought. The establishment of the Department of Labor in 1892 with the energetic and devoted Edward Tregear as its chief officer was followed by the appointment of an effective staff of inspectors and a steady stream of reports on working conditions and recommendations for amending legislation.

The Liberal program brought significant improvements in the lives of working people. Vigorously opposed at the outset by most employers, the labor code barked loudly but bit infrequently. In practice, the regulations proved less burdensome than anticipated, though businessmen continued to grumble about government harassment and the growing complexity of the regulations. Rising prosperity made it easier to pay for such improvements as safety, sanitation, and ventilation. The regulation of shopping hours had no significant impact on the volume of retail sales, and the protective tariff along with New Zealand's remoteness combined to insulate local producers from foreign competition. Few, if any, owners had to make a choice between coming up to the national standard for working conditions or closing down their businesses.

While Reeves put great emphasis on the labor code and its administration, he was sufficiently a man of the nineteenth century to prefer private agreements between employers and employees to state regulation. As he saw it, in the past, labor contracts had provided workers with little protection because bargaining power had been almost always monopolized by employers. The only way to prevent exploitation, he reasoned, was by equalizing the strength of the negotiating parties. Since the threat of withholding their labor was the workers' only real weapon, Reeves concluded that balanced power was best accomplished by encouraging trade unionism. As the Maritime Strike had plainly shown, the Union Steamship Company could be absolutely ruthless and totally without compassion in defending its interests. Unless power was matched with power, the labor contract would always be one-sided.

Ever the intellectual who conceived of the antagonists more in idealized than real terms, Reeves struggled for a rational solution to industrial strife. It consisted of a system of state conciliation and arbitration in which associations of employers and employees were to settle their differences across the bargaining table instead of the picket line. From his study of similar schemes in other countries, Reeves concluded that conciliation by a neutral negotiator would never work unless the opposing parties knew that the state could force an equitable agreement on them. The threat of compulsory arbitration had to be a tangible presence at the bargaining table.[18]

The concept of compulsion as the ultimate answer to strikes and lockouts was both innovative and revolutionary. Since there was no labor trouble for more than a decade after 1894, it was mistakenly assumed that Reeves had provided the world with the definitive solution to industrial conflict. Though not widely copied by other countries, the reform nevertheless attracted widespread foreign attention. Time would show that strikes could not be legislated away even in New Zealand and that the threat of compulsion did not encourage negotiated settlements, as Reeves had assumed it would. On the contrary, it had just the opposite effect. Owners and workers alike merely went through the motions of conciliation, preferring to carry their disputes to the Arbitration Court, where a judge made the final determination. But within this framework, court-imposed awards gradually superseded many aspects of the labor code, especially on matters affecting wage rates, hours of employment, and working conditions, and the compulsory arbitration system did more to shape twentieth-century New Zealand life than did any other Liberal measure.

Reeves left the government in 1896 to become agent general for the colony in London and later the director of the London School of Economics. His portfolio as minister of labor was then assumed by the premier, "King Dick" Seddon, who, while he allowed Tregear's work of enforcement and codification to continue, showed more interest in winning elections than in supporting abstract principles. What drove Reeves out of the ministry was his weak stomach for the crude give-and-take of colonial politics. Though he had demonstrated skill, patience, and determination in pushing his program through the General Assembly, he was too fastidious, scrupulous, and aloof to be comfortable with his cabinet colleagues or with Seddon's rough leadership and populism.[19]

Perhaps because he saw labor problems in practical and human rather than abstract and intellectual terms, Seddon put a somewhat higher priority on dealing with unemployment than did Reeves. Though he too came from a well-educated, middle-class family, Seddon never aspired to a profession. Instead, he served an engineering apprenticeship and worked in foundries and railway workshops in Liverpool and Melbourne as well as on the Australian and New Zealand gold fields before eventually becoming the keeper of a general store. Thus Seddon's empathy for the plight of workers and their families, especially the unemployed, came naturally. It is also significant that Seddon, unlike Reeves, served a long apprenticeship in local and regional politics before entering the General Assembly. Indeed, he gave up county affairs only when he became a cabinet minister in 1891 and could no longer carry the double burden. This experience with local needs and concerns doubtless strengthened Seddon's pragmatic pork-barrel approach to politics.[20]

Seddon, Reeves, and McKenzie brought the combined resources of the Departments of Public Works, Labour, and Agriculture to bear on unemployment. The problem had three aspects. First, the Liberals had to find ways to expand job opportunities. That was Seddon's responsibility. Despite pressure to keep spending down, he followed the long-standing New Zealand strategy of expanding railway, road, and bridge construction. In the short run, this created jobs for almost 40,000 men; over the longer term it opened more country to economic development and provided a more permanent employment base. Especially significant were the replacement of subcontracting on government projects by worker cooperatives and the greatly enlarged role of the Department of Public Works in the design, execution, and supervision of engineering projects. In effect, Seddon took the government into the construction business. Worker cooperatives, an unusual feature of Seddon's program, were a large-scale extension of the system that he had used so effectively during his gold-mining days. Gangs of navvies contracted directly with the project engineer, set their own work rules, and shared the proceeds when they completed the job. The government supplied materials, professional supervision, and accommodations; the workers, foremen, tools, and muscles; and the cooperative, organization, food, and recreation.

Reeves concentrated on the second aspect of the problem—bringing workers and jobs together. As the depression of the eighties steadily worsened, the jobless and landless had drifted to the towns where long periods of idleness and hunger had crushed hope and initiative. Many abandoned the search for work or became less proficient through inactivity. Jobs had to be found for such men, if necessary by moving them to country districts and construction projects. This took the government into the employment agency business. Agents around the country gathered information about the local demand for labor and the department undertook to supply the needed number of workers. If, as was often the case, an applicant did not have the fare to get to his new job, he received a free pass on the government-owned railway. In addition to the 40,000 jobs created by Seddon's public works projects, another 20,000 workers were placed in private employment. With their dependents, this meant that the state assisted more than one person in six.

McKenzie tackled the third aspect of the labor problem—preventing the drift of workers back to the towns as soon as construction projects or seasonal farm jobs ended. He devised two solutions. Workers hired on cooperative public works projects were offered small farms of ten to fifteen acres as an inducement to stay in the country, and many unemployed were taught the rudiments of agriculture on state farms before being placed on properties of their own.[21]

The cumulative importance of these Liberal reforms lay not so much in what they accomplished in putting the landless on to farms or the unemployed back to work as in their rejection of laissez faire as an acceptable principle of public policy. In its place came the concept that government had an obligation to deal with social and economic distress. To some extent, the assumption of such responsibilities reflected the steady democratization of political life. No party could be elected to or sustained in office unless it responded to the demands of the electorate. More fundamentally, voters expected their governments to intervene in what had formerly been private affairs and to use the power of the state in positive ways for what was broadly perceived to be the public social and economic good.

These attitudes and expectations made it possible for the Liberals to carry the government into a series of economic activities that seemed to foreshadow a full-scale program of what at the time was called state socialism. Actually there was no such program. The Liberals, particularly under Seddon, accepted or rejected proposals for new state-owned enterprises as public need rather than abstract principle dictated. In 1904 they included the opening of state coal mines, which sold their output to private consumers and government agencies, especially the railways, the largest single consumer in the country. This was justified on the pragmatic grounds that private supplies were inadequate and prices, particularly for householders, were too high. Similar considerations applied in the insurance, home-rental, and money-lending fields. In 1901 the Government Life Insurance Office opened an accident branch to insure employers against the liabilities imposed on them under the Workers' Compensation Act, and in 1905, over the vehement protests of private underwriters, a State Fire Insurance Office was established to force down premiums, especially for home owners. Soaring rents, notably when prosperity returned to the towns, took the government into the housing business in 1905 with a program of building and renting cottages at rates substantially below what private landlords charged. This was followed a year later by the establishment of a government department to lend money on first mortgages to poorer workers so that they could buy their own homes. Interest rates were set below market rates. In this way the Liberals did for urban workers what they had done a decade earlier for farmers through the Advances to Settlers Act. The Liberals even took the government into the business of redeeming trading stamps as a way of protecting consumers against the possibility of the issuer defaulting on its obligations.[22]

Quite different motives underlay the government's takeover of the Bank of New Zealand in 1894, at that time the largest financial institution in the colony. Faced with a liquidity crisis brought on by a combination of mismanagement and excessive credit extension, the bank saved itself from immediate bankruptcy by asking the government to guarantee a substantial new issue of preferential stock. In return for its support, the government took control of the bank. This arrangement saved many thousands of depositors from certain ruin and protected very substantial sums of public money as well. Had the government not intervened, the crisis would have overwhelmed the colony and brought untold damage. Though a tiny minority of colonists had been advocating state banking for decades, the ministry's intervention carried with it no ideological implications. In giving the measure their support, even conservatives recognized that the colony had no other choice.[23]

Though the Liberals had no coherent social program comparable to their land and labor platform, the Ballance-Seddon-Ward era brought a good deal of incidental legislation in areas as diverse as education, health, and women's rights. Most measures were sponsored either by professional civil servants or by pressure groups outside the ministry.

The only measure to attract significant foreign attention was the creation in 1898 of a system of old-age pensions. It allowed Seddon to declare himself a "humanist" and to create a larger-than-life impression of a political leader devoted to the welfare of his subjects and filled with compassion for the unfortunate: the old, widowed, orphaned, sick, crippled, poor, unemployed. "If we deal with [the problems of age and poverty] now," Seddon declared, "the curse of the older countries will never come to New Zealand. There are those here who have seen what has happened in the older world: and I say what a blot it is on our civilization." The illusion of the compassionate father figure succeeded because Seddon genuinely believed himself to be such a leader, though his decision to push the measure through the General Assembly owed more to election strategy than to his conversion to abstract principles of social justice. As he was later to advise a cabinet colleague on the proper way to handle voters: "You should always keep something up your sleeve for next year. Keep the bastards on a string and then they'll keep you in Office."[24]

This contemptuous attitude helps to explain the backwardness of social services and the difficulty in bringing about improvements. The Department of Health, which was established in 1900, for example, made only slow progress in controlling disease or improving sanitation. Though authorized to begin the medical inspection of school children, the department waited in vain for the Liberals to vote the necessary funds. Two measures aside—state examination and registration of nurses, and the establishment of state maternity hospitals to improve the care of mothers and the training of midwives—the Liberals did little to raise the level of public health or to expand medical services.

Nor did the Liberals make a strong record in the field of women's rights. While the extension of the suffrage and the improvement of working conditions were noteworthy advances, successive ministries dealt with various forms of sex discrimination either reluctantly or not at all. The result was some progress, but it was generally tardy and always piecemeal. The Divorce Act of 1898 expanded the grounds on which a marriage could be dissolved; measures passed in 1895 and 1900 protected the family home against the husband's creditors and prevented him from bequeathing the property without providing for his wife and children. Reformers made especially slow progress in securing the repeal of two measures that indirectly sanctioned prostitution. It took years of agitation to get the age of consent raised from twelve to sixteen, and it was not until 1910 that the Contagious Diseases Act was finally abolished.

The Liberals had a somewhat better record in education, though there too the party had no clearly defined program, contenting itself with "do-nothingism" until such time as reformers or voters persuaded it otherwise. Civil servants and education reformers, mainly labor activists, put their principal emphasis on expanding opportunities. By 1911 they had created a system of technical education over the opposition of the traditionalists and had established the principle of free secondary and university education for qualified students.[25]

Looking back over the years from 1891 to 1911, it is clear that the radical, experimental reform phase had run its course by 1894. By that time McKenzie and Reeves had achieved most of their goals in land and labor. For the most part, what followed was consolidation and codification. Party leaders then turned down the flame of reform. To be sure, they kept the "mission of the New Zealand democracy" alive with such measures as old-age pensions, but their hearts were in officeholding rather than in remaking the world.

And so it should have come as no surprise to New Zealanders that many of the English and European observers who came to look at the new utopia went away unimpressed. With Anthony Trollope, who had visited the colony in the seventies, they praised the rough openness and equality of colonial democracy but shuddered at the absence of cultivated manners or commitment to political principle. They considered New Zealand's claims to have found the blueprint for utopia as puffed up as Seddon himself ("a frog who wished to swell to the size of an ox," as André Siegfried called him).[26] It was both laughable and preposterous for the premier to talk of the colony as "God's Own Country."

Not all foreigners shared this assessment. Perhaps because they too were acolytes for the New World optimism (but perhaps more because they had a vested interest in capitalizing on the supposed success of the New Zealand experiments), many American visitors and writers lionized the colony and made its social and economic experiments the model for what should be done at home. As the Boston reformer Frank Parsons put it in 1904, "The Island Commonwealth has shown the way to the solution of the great problems of wealth diffusion and equalization of opportunity. A new civilization has come. A new age has dawned. New Zealand is the birth place of the 20th Century."[27]

Part 2
THE ANTIPODEAN CONNECTION

3 *The Antipodes through American Eyes*

For most of the nineteenth century the Australasian colonies lay well beyond the frontiers of American interest. At one time New England whalers and sealers cruised the South Pacific and in the fifties and sixties the Australian and New Zealand goldfields attracted Americans, especially Californians. But neither colonial products nor colonial markets attracted much attention, though a regular mail service via San Francisco brought some contact as Antipodeans crossed North America on their way to and from Europe. Inevitably, colonists knew a great deal more about the United States than Americans knew about the Antipodes, and the flow of information and ideas was mostly one-sided, as the impact of Bellamy, George, or the Knights of Labor demonstrates.

This relationship began changing in the early nineties, when news of progressive reforms in Australasia began filtering into the United States. Initially, newspaper coverage consisted of little more than occasional factual reports, usually brief, of elections and important legislation. English and American periodicals, by contrast, became the prime sources of both fact and commentary, but as interest in the Antipodes increased, newspapers paid more attention to South Pacific developments in their news and editorial pages. Gradually a crude propaganda network emerged devoted to extolling or condemning the merits of antipodean reform in general or specific laws in particular. Colonists on both sides of the ideological fence fed this rising interest by writing for American newspapers, periodicals, and publishers, by supplying Americans with information, including official reports, and by even coming to the United States to lecture to American audiences. In these ways many Americans came to believe that the ideals of Bellamy, George, and Populism had proved themselves in the South Pacific and were now ready to be reimplanted in their native soil.

Three themes dominated American perceptions of Australasian reform. First, many commentators conveyed an impression that the Pacific colonies had achieved a quality of democracy such as Americans had only dreamed of. They had triumphed over the "interests" by making government the servant of the "wealth producers" rather than the "wealth consumers." In America, by contrast, government had been captured by predatory wealth, and democracy was a cruel hoax.

Second, the expansion of the functions of the colonial state was beneficial. Settlers obtained both opportunity and security. This true democracy released energies for the fulfillment of man's highest aspirations. America, ran the liturgy, would reap the same benefits by throwing off the shackles of plutocracy and letting the people's will prevail.

Third, these romantic perceptions of antipodean progress had little appeal for Americans of a more pragmatic cast of mind. Theirs was a more limited agenda. They focused on specific policy issues and accepted or rejected Australasian models on a case-by-case basis. Less interested in the overall meaning of the new liberalism in the South Pacific, they were more concerned with what the United States could learn and borrow from foreign experience, and they paid more attention to scholars than to journalists.

The American irrigation engineer and chairman of the State Rivers and Water Supply Commission of Victoria, Elwood Mead, reflected these themes in an article entitled "What Australia Can Teach America." He argued that "Australia began earlier and has done far more toward solving the problems of . . . public utilities, and the . . . conservation of natural resources than America. Much of the American . . . legislation . . . has been sordid, short-sighted, selfish; that of Australia has been . . . enlightened and . . . sound."

These differences, Mead believed, reflected differences in government. Australians "have learned that they can act together wisely and efficiently in carrying out great works for the common good," he declared; "it is the welfare of the many, rather than the enrichment of the few, which is the governing principle."

Unless the United States enlisted this same "efficiency . . . in the service of the public . . . the aggregation of our resources in a few hands must continue . . . while the crown of democracy and . . . opportunity for the common man will pass" to Australia.[1]

Mead's observations, made in 1911, differed very little from those made when outsiders first began noticing antipodean reform. A. G. Fradenburgh, then a graduate student at the University of Wisconsin and later dean of Brooklyn College, said much the same thing in 1894. Quoting a speech by Arthur Clyden at the National Liberal Club in London, he characterized state socialism as a "supreme attempt by old-world victims of bad government to prevent a recurrence of the evils in their new homes by boldly radical legislation. . . ."

Fradenburgh argued that New Zealand's experiments supported private enterprise. The state had entered the underwriting, trusteeship, and railroad businesses because its access to credit gave it advantages. Similarly, only the government could maintain a network of employment agencies or break up the large estates and settle working farmers on the land. He especially liked the village settlement program. The benefits "can hardly be exaggerated. The movement is, above all, a democratic one," and he expected it to continue with demonstration farms, cheaper credit for farmers, and pensions for civil servants and the aged.[2]

Scattered news reports aside, most Americans learned little about Australasian reform until the end of the nineties. That was not the case with a small but influential circle of reformers—clergymen, editors, educators, journalists, labor leaders, and lawyers. They made it their business to know and to share with each other news of advances taking place in even the most remote corners of the globe. A diverse group, they included the journalist Henry Demarest Lloyd, who began corresponding with colonial leaders as early as 1893; Richard T. Ely of the University of Wisconsin, who drew on Australian experience in the debate over state ownership of railroads; William D. P. Bliss, the Episcopal founder of the Society of Christian Socialists, who published data on the antipodean experiments in *A Handbook of Socialism* (1895) and his *Encyclopedia of Social Reform* (1897); the Boston reformer Frank Parsons, who became an early advocate of the Australasian method of settling labor disputes by compulsory arbitration; Dr. J. M. Peebles, the Michigan publicist of causes ranging from vegetarianism and temperance to abolitionism and universal suffrage, who linked New Zealand's prosperity to the success of its reform program; and Julius A. Wayland, the Kansas socialist, who held up the New Zealand example to readers of his *Appeal to Reason.*[3]

These reformers acquired their knowledge where they could—from reports published by the American and Australasian governments, essays in English periodicals, summaries in the *Review of Reviews,* scholarly articles and books, newspaper accounts drawn from correspondents in the colonies or the English press, travel to the South Pacific, and contacts with visitors from the colonies.

They shared their information and assessments in a variety of forums, such as meetings of the Nineteenth Century Club and the Brotherhood of the Kingdom (Walter Rauschenbusch's intimate fellowship of Christian Socialists), private conversations and correspondence, study clubs, essays, classrooms, pulpits, and lecture platforms. The Cornell economist Jeremiah W. Jenks, for example, encouraged his students to study New Zealand reforms. He thought the subject so important that he acquired a complete set of the colony's statutes for his seminar library, "the only set of statutes . . . besides those of . . . New York, that are in that room." Hugh H. Lusk, a former member of the New Zealand General Assembly, joined the reform network in 1897. He became friendly with Lloyd and began lecturing on Australasian reform at the Cooper Union. In articles for *Arena, Forum, Harper's Weekly,* and *Outlook,* and especially in *Our Foes at Home* (1899), Lusk urged Americans to adapt antipodean principles to their own needs.[4]

For the most part, this initial interest in the Antipodes merely reflected gratification in colonial reform accomplishments. Typically, observers found in them confirmation for their own preferences for policies ranging from the public ownership of the railroads to the breaking up of large estates into working farms. They applauded "the real christianity of those new peoples," the "remarkable revelations of what man can and will do for himself when all barriers are torn away from . . . 'Labor' applied to 'Land,' " and some affirmed that the "New Zealand people are practically and successfully testing the elementary principles of socialism." Only occasionally, as in the Illinois struggle for the eight-hour day for women or in Lusk's writings, did they press for antipodean solutions to American problems.[5]

What had been a passive interest in colonial reform changed dramatically to an active campaign to "New Zealandize" America, following Lloyd's return from an extended tour of Australasia in 1899. Discouraged by the demise of the Populist crusade, frightened by the growing inequality of wealth and power in the United States, and troubled by the *Ritchie* decision striking down the eight-hour day for Illinois women, Lloyd turned to the Antipodes, hoping to revitalize the reform cause by shaming Americans to action. "I am going to study this democratic efflorescence," he told an English friend, "to rouse [our people] from their pessimism about the possibility of progress in self-government."[6]

Perhaps it was already too late, for Lloyd saw the colonies as the world's last best hope, the one remaining area where mankind could make a fresh start. Nevertheless, he believed it important "to be able to say that I have seen at first hand . . . the things which our leaders here tell us cannot be done." If he could prove to the American people "that they are still economic barbarians," perhaps he could inspire them "to the point of naturalizing all the reforms that have been successfully instituted in different parts of the world." If that could be done, Lloyd declared, "we should have a very nearly ideal Utopia right here and now."[7]

Lloyd recognized the difficulty of the task. He knew, of course, just how closely the public identified him with the reform cause and that he would have to overcome the presumption that he was a prejudiced observer. This problem was compounded by the fact that he already knew, long before he left for the South Pacific, what he was going to report. What he did not know was that once in the field, the more he studied antipodean achievements, the more impressed he would become. "I think it is the most truly Christian country of the earth," he wrote from the colony in April 1899. "Here they seem to think the Golden Rule is worthy of practical application." He confessed to a New Zealand politician that "My greatest trouble is going to be to avoid getting a reputation of being a Munchhausen by simply telling the truth about you."[8]

Lloyd dealt with the credibility problem in two ways. First, so far as possible he affected the role of objective reporter rather than advocate. In books, articles, interviews, letters to editors, and speeches, and as an expert witness on labor affairs, he provided Americans with vivid and very human descriptions of colonial laws and the way they worked. He took his readers into a quiet provincial courtroom to witness the peaceful resolution of a labor dispute, and they stood beside him as he chose by lottery the working farmers who were to lease properties acquired by the state through compulsory repurchase from large estate holders. From Lloyd they learned that New Zealand had neither millionaires nor tramps, that economic growth and prosperity marched hand in hand with the world's most comprehensive labor code, that country children rode to and from school free of charge on the state-owned railways, that government employment bureaus found jobs for workers and even provided train tickets to get them there, that the elderly received pensions financed from general revenues, that farmers could borrow from the government at below-market rates, and that lockouts and strikes were a thing of the past.[9]

Second, Lloyd reinforced his posture of objectivity by stopping far short of endorsing all he had seen. He criticized worker cooperatives in public projects, unemployment programs in rural areas, and the weaknesses of the Australasian labor movement. "This Newest England is no Utopia, no paradise," he declared; it had reached "no final 'social solutions.' " In Lloyd's view, Americans would be ill-advised to borrow wholesale from the colonial statute books. As an older and more complex country with its own institutions and traditions, the United States should devise its own, and preferably more advanced, solutions. The Antipodes merely offered proof that ordinary people, "with no theoretical socialism impelling them," could reach for and achieve a social, economic, and political order more humane, just, and democratic than the world had yet seen. Such a goal,

Lloyd argued, was as much within the American as the colonial grasp.[10]

This public display of objectivity was camouflage. Lloyd's intention was to lay out an invidious comparative model. He encouraged his readers, usually by implication but sometimes explicitly, to equate New Zealand with civilization, the United States with barbarism. The idea of a country with neither tramps nor millionaires, neither lockouts nor strikes, neither an industrial plutocracy nor a landed aristocracy, neither exploitation in the working years nor insecurity in old age, came to symbolize all that was wrong with America.

If Lloyd's two books on Australasian reforms, *A Country without Strikes* and *Newest England,* had only a modest circulation, between his return to the United States in June 1899, and his death in September 1903, his ideas nevertheless reached millions of readers through newspapers and periodicals. Hundreds of reviews of his books appeared, as did countless editorials, he granted many interviews, some of which were syndicated, and he went on a lecture tour of the western states, which was widely covered by the press. Audiences may have been smaller than he had hoped, but they were always well informed, often enthusiastic, and commonly engaged in spirited discussion after Lloyd's formal remarks. He also wrote for *Ainslee's, Atlantic Monthly, Boyce's Weekly, Good Housekeeping, Independent, National Geographic, Outlook,* and the *Sunday School Times.*[11]

For a time these forums shaped the tone of the American debate on important issues as well as some aspects of the reform agenda itself. One reader vowed to visit New Zealand himself so that he could "taunt our people . . . with their . . . political and social shortcomings." George H. Gates, president of what is now Grinnell College, supposed that "we fool Americans will go on for fifty or seventy-five years before we . . . undertake . . . what they have already achieved in New Zealand," and Henry Latchford, a friend of Lloyd's, declared that democracy was "having a fairer chance in the Australasian colonies" than in the United States. Tom Watson, the Georgia Populist, predicted that the "struggles and triumphs of true democracy in New Zealand will become a source of inspiration to those who would achieve the same results in our own land," and a midwestern clergyman thought that if "America had New Zealandized herself before she entered upon the Cuban problem, it would have been settled in a [more equitable] way."[12]

Lloyd's ideas also gained a friendly reception on many college campuses and in some sections of the press. Classes and debating teams drew on his works at such schools as Chicago, Columbia, Cornell, Earlham, Harvard, Nebraska, and Wisconsin. They "bring gladness and courage to every reader," declared the *Social Gospel,* while the *Chicago Tribune* predicted that they would exert a "valuable influence in guiding Americans in the solution of these same problems, though under radically different conditions." *Outlook* found them to be "full of practical suggestion respecting the problems pressing in upon our own country" and thought that New Zealand provided "the necessary means for the best development both of individual character and of the highest social order." The colony had created the "democracy of the future" by destroying the "plutocracy at the top" and the "proletariat at the bottom." Similarly, the *New York Journal* had the New Zealand middle class absorbing "all the other classes."[13]

As these reactions show, Lloyd made considerable headway in "New Zealandising the rest of the world," as one Bostonian put it. "It was a brilliant bit of controversial tactics," noted the *Boston Transcript,* "while all the world is discussing the great social questions, to make the trip to New Zealand and study the reforms . . . in actual operation."[14]

Lloyd's campaign attracted many followers, including the editor of *Arena,* Benjamin Orange Flower. Over fifteen years Flower lavished praise on colonial reform in editorials, reviews, essays, and a book on Progressive leaders, and he opened his columns to articles and letters about Australasian accomplishments written by both Americans and Antipodeans.

Arena reported that *Newest England* was filled with "data and practical illustrations . . . wherever the people would preserve free government from the encroachment of tyranny, oppression, and injustice. . . ." Lloyd's writings on social democracy were "solid, practical, and vital"; *Newest England* should be "in the library of every reading American. It is a sane, thoughtful work that will make for democracy." More "than in any other land in the world the people are the government" in New Zealand. There "we find the democratic ideal of a government of the people, by the people, and for the people prevailing." In the United States, by contrast, there was "government of the corporations, by the corporations, for the exploitation of the producing and consuming masses. . . ." An "enormously-rich privileged class" had honeycombed all levels of government with graft, corruption, and bossism and had made itself "masters of the state as well as masters of the bread. . . ."[15]

Flower announced his "Program of Progress" in an editorial in 1901. "New Zealand is to-day leading the nations in the successful inauguration of many of the most wise and practical legislative measures demanded . . . to meet changed conditions. . . ." The "wealth-creators" in New Zealand had "banded together and won the battle for democracy. . . ." He judged Seddon to have been the "greatest constructive liberal statesman of the last fifty years" and "a master-builder." Seddon's "ideals and deeds shine as a beacon throughout the world of reactionary thought, pointing to the justice-kissed heights of pure democracy, where man counts more than money, . . . and where the principles of the Golden Rule become the practical ideal of the State."[16]

Lloyd also drew Flower's friend, Frank Parsons, to an active role in the antipodean cause. Legal textbook writer for Little, Brown and lecturer at the Boston University Law School, Parsons wrote prodigiously on a range of reform issues—municipal government, direct democracy, public ownership of railroads and utilities, industrial arbitration, slum clearance, unemployment relief. He also lectured widely in the Boston area, taught briefly (1897–1899) at Kansas State Agricultural College alongside other reform activists, and served as the first dean of extension education for the Ruskin College of Social Science, which he helped to found.[17]

Like Lloyd, Parsons saw New Zealand as a model society, a foreshadowing of the "mutualism" mankind could achieve in the future, confirmation that reform was no idle, utopian dream. Though he had shown some interest in the Antipodes in the nineties, it was not until the fall of 1901 that Parsons singled out New Zealand more broadly as an example of what lay ahead for democratic societies. "Progressive taxation of monopoly values, incomes, and inheritance, division of large estates, labor legislation, compulsory arbitration, public recognition of the right to employment, and old-age pensions," he told *Arena* readers, "indicate the strength of . . . equalization in the most advanced communities."[18]

Three years later the Philadelphia editor and reformer, C. F. Taylor, published *The Story of New Zealand,* Parsons's massive volume based on an evolutionary concept of historical progress. Unlike Lloyd's *Newest England,* which purported to be an objective report on antipodean conditions, Parsons's *Story of New Zealand* made no pretense to objectivity. It was written "to prepare the way for a democratic renaissance" in the United States by demonstrating the success of a "government dominated by the ideal of the welfare, development, and prosperity of all the people, just as our Republic illustrated the results of a government of privilege, operating through a money-controlled machine, for the selfish enrichment and aggrandizement of the few."[19]

Taylor also published an abridged paper edition that dealt only with the reform movement. He hoped to reach "the masses, . . . particularly . . . the mind and thought of our voters" and to inspire them "to emulate the example of New Zealand" by bringing government "close to the people" and making it serve their interests. For that reason, Taylor waived the copyright. "All are freely invited to spread the facts contained in this book as widely as possible."[20]

Wherever feasible, Parsons contrasted New Zealand with the United States. "New Zealand's distinction," he wrote, "lies in her practical application of the principles of civic and economic justice. . . . She leads the world in the discovery . . . of effective measures for the equalization of opportunity, wealth and power, and the uplift of the common people. . . . America aims at the dollar; New Zealand at the man."[21]

Parsons elaborated with some seventy comparisons, such as "In America the people have the *right* to govern; in New Zealand they *do* govern," "Here political corruption is a byword, there political corruption is unknown," "Here the railways are managed for private profit, there the railways are run for public service," and "The United States is a land of industrial conflict; New Zealand is the land of industrial peace." He then summarized his thesis in column form, setting out the eighteen most important differences between the two countries. The United States list included such items as "Dollar the king," "Government loans to banks," "Taxation for revenue." The New Zealand opposites were "Manhood the king," "Government loans to farmers," "Taxation for the public good."[22]

There was no reason, Parsons believed, why the United States—"the grandest nation on earth"—should not "move forward toward industrial justice with a momentum that will carry humanity with her. . . . It is only necessary to put the proper men in control and change the course of the ship for the true port. . . ."[23]

The Story of New Zealand charted the course Americans should follow. "The new light that has been growing for years in the Southern sky, till now it illumines the world, is . . . but the rising glory of a new civilization," Parsons declared. "The Aurora Socialis of New Zealand is . . . whiter, clearer, steadier than its predecessors, tho it . . . draws its political electricity from the same great dynamos of liberty, equality and fraternity" as did the Declaration of Independence and the French Revolution.[24]

Though in Arthur Mann's words, "poorly organized, dull, rambling, and over long,"[25] *The Story of New Zealand* attracted considerable attention in reform circles. Flower's *Arena*, of course, was lavish in its praise, declaring "that no book has appeared in the last decade whose circulation would do more to further the principles of free institutions, the cause of justice and the peaceable evolution of our republic from its present condition of social and political chaos." The volume "offers the remedy for the crying evils that are so fraught with peril to republican institutions, in a peaceful and orderly manner and in line with the evolutionary sweep of government."[26] The *Independent* was briefer and less fulsome than Flower, but the reviewer reported that the book came "as a revelation. We are moved with wonder and almost envy when we see how easily this favored land has dealt with the evils that threaten the very existence of democracy in our own country. The list of progressive and radical measures successfully carried out is amazing." Indeed, the *Independent* was so impressed that it included *The Story of New Zealand* in its "Books of the Year."[27]

The testimonials Taylor received and published on the cover of the abridged edition were, as might be expected, laudatory, but they, too, convey some sense of the way that reformers responded to Parsons's message. E. B. Andrews, the economist and former president of Brown University, hoped that the book would "be read by millions, for it will usefully clear away superstitions which clog the progress of economic legislation in the United States," and former Senator R. F. Pettigrew of South Dakota described it as "the story of a wonderful revolution, where the rights of man have triumphed and equality of opportunity is established. . . ." The influential Rev. Josiah Strong also endorsed the book, telling Taylor that "New Zealand is a social laboratory from which the world should learn much," and the Rev. Russell H. Conwell, the pastor of the Philadelphia Baptist Temple, the largest Protestant church in the country, predicted that New Zealand's "advanced theories of government . . . must soon conquer the world." *City and State* agreed, declaring that the message "ought to go out into all the earth," while the publisher Dr. I. S. E. Funk was convinced that the colony's aggressive reform spirit "has fastened upon that country the eyes of all progressive people throughout the world."[28]

Parsons's study is indeed monumentally tedious for the modern reader, but at the time it was a crucial contribution to the cause of reform in America. A deeply religious, virtually ascetic man, Parsons demonstrated that the progressive, social science theories of modern liberalism were not the vague, utopian pipe dreams of armchair critics and scholars, but practical solutions to contemporary problems. With the New Zealand experience of fourteen years as a working guide, reform proposals could no longer be dismissed as visionary. That was the crusade to which Parsons devoted himself. He worked at it with such single purpose and devotion that in the end it killed him. Never in robust health, he died in 1908 before reaching his fifty-fourth birthday.[29]

If Parsons can be seen as the scholar turned reformer, then William E. Smythe of San Diego was more like Lloyd, the journalist turned reformer. He was a contributing editor to *Out West,* a magazine published by Charles F. Lumis and formerly called *Land of Sunshine: An Illustrated Monthly of Southern California.* A curiously eclectic periodical, *Out West* devoted much space to such subjects as the history of California, Indian and Mexican art, the Wild West, and Los Angeles. By contrast, the editorial pages were outspoken on political issues and for a time led a vigorous campaign for the adoption of the New Zealand reform program in California.

Lloyd's *Newest England* inspired the campaign, and Smythe organized and managed it. The founder and president of the California Constructive League, one of the many progressive organizations that mushroomed at the turn of the century, Smythe was something of a Horace Greeley type, much given to enthusiasms and passing fads. Born in Massachusetts in 1861, he turned to journalism and publishing, moving successively westward in the Populist years through Nebraska, Colorado, and Utah before finally settling in southern California. Beginning in 1891 he helped organize and promote the national irrigation movement and eventually succeeded in getting Congress to dedicate the proceeds from the sale of western lands to reclamation projects.[30]

While still active in the irrigation cause, in 1901 Smythe was impressed by Lloyd's articles and books about New Zealand. "I consider her as having an especial right to be considered the political brain of the modern world," Lloyd told Smythe.[31]

"We are going to . . . fight to build up California on New Zealand lines," Smythe replied, and opened his campaign to "make another New Zealand of the empire state of the West" in his "Twentieth Century West" column in *The Land of Sunshine.* His "Program for California" had five components, two drawn from New Zealand and one from European models: constructive legislation; irrigation of public and private lands at national and state expense; *"the New Zealand method of purchasing, improving, and leasing the great estates as a means of giving the masses of men easy access to the soil"*; *"the New*

Zealand system of compulsory arbitration for the settlement of all disputes between capital and labor"; and co-operatives similar to the ones in Belgium and Holland.[32]

"The first great advantage of the New Zealand plan is that it kills land monopoly," he told his readers. "The second, that it kills land speculation. The third, that it throws wide open the door of opportunity to millions of people possessing very moderate means. The fourth, that by encouraging rapid settlement it benefits railroads, banks, merchants,—every element in the community."[33]

Smythe also condemned the failure of California to develop a system for dealing with industrial disputes. That was "an indictment of our intelligence, of our patriotism, of our Christianity." California, Smythe argued, should adopt the "sensible and statesmanlike" New Zealand system of compulsory arbitration.[34]

Smythe devised elaborate campaign strategies to New Zealandize California. They included organizing a statewide network of debating societies and political clubs to elect legislators sympathetic to his program, a lecture tour through the Sacramento and San Joaquin valleys and the southern coastal region, setting up a literary bureau to arrange lectures and distribute works to be published in a new series, the Constructive Library, and publishing a series of articles on New Zealand labor and land reforms in *Out West*.[35]

Over the next few months a stream of articles followed—on compulsory arbitration, Richard John Seddon, the land settlement program, state farm loans, and public works projects—with such titles as "The Government as a Colonizing Agency," "How the People Smashed the Money Ring," and "How Tramps Are Turned into Taxpayers." Throughout, Smythe hammered away at his New Zealand themes, reporting that many prominent Californians agreed with him that "New Zealand ideas are certainly . . . worthy of consideration in a state where industrial conditions and elements of population approximate so nearly to those of Australasia." Scientific "colonization and compelling peace between labor and capital" safeguarded the public interest so that "the people come out on top."[36]

Along the way, Smythe developed political ambitions and began campaigning for the Democratic congressional nomination in San Diego County. His first audience was "enthusiastically responsive" he told Lloyd in February 1902, and in May he reported that people who had formerly been uninterested in or opposed to public ownership of water resources, the New Zealand land system, and the cooperative movement had become enthusiastic converts to the cause.[37]

Smythe secured the nomination in August, loosely describing his platform as "the New Zealand ticket," but neither the crusade to New Zealandize the state through the California Constructive League nor the political campaign caught fire. Opponents argued that the water and land proposals could sap individualism, paralyze private enterprise, and transform civilization. Some critics described the New Zealand land policy as degrading. Compulsory arbitration encountered ever more vehement opposition, both capital and labor being too distrustful of the courts to brook judicial interference. Smythe got the message and as the election approached he had less and less to say on the subject. He had also hoped to build a following by distributing a cheap paper edition of Lloyd's *Newest England*, but he could not raise the $1,500 needed to underwrite a new printing. And curiously, he declined Lloyd's offer to campaign for him, believing him too radical for southern Californians. Instead, thinking that eastern newspaper coverage of the campaign would be worth a thousand votes, he asked Lloyd to arrange it.[38]

There is no evidence that Lloyd obliged, though even if he had, it seems unlikely that eastern press notices could have turned defeat into victory. Smythe consoled himself with his success in reducing Republican majorities in the district and by looking ahead somewhat wistfully to the gubernatorial race in 1906.

"I am very hopeful," he told Lloyd, "that we can prepare the public mind . . . for the making of another New Zealand, not only here, but in other western states."[39] Elsewhere, Smythe described his congressional campaign as an academic exercise intended merely to test and educate public opinion. In *Out West* over the next year, he continued to take occasional notice of

New Zealand reforms, but his crusade was clearly in decline and in January 1904, he gave up his political column, probably concluding that neither his California Constructive League nor "the New Zealand ticket" was the path to political office.[40]

But he was still a young man—barely forty-three—and within two years he had published two substantial books, a history of San Diego and *Constructive Democracy: The Economics of a Square Deal*, a complex tract for the times, setting out Smythe's political and economic views and proposing remedies for all that ailed the nation. Problems of capital and labor, particularly monopolies and what he called the "surplus man," were the central themes, while his solutions drew heavily on his earlier proposals for irrigation schemes, land reform, and industrial cooperatives.[41]

This meant that he drew heavily on New Zealand models. For example, the solution to the "surplus man" problem—Robert Hunter's vast army of impoverished Americans—was New Zealand's colonization program of destroying monopoly and settling the masses on the land. Any failure to create "new opportunities" for the poor would be "a pitiful travesty on social justice" and an admission "that our civilization is a failure. New Zealand refuses to humiliate herself by such an acknowledgment, and there is no reason why the United States should not rise to the level of New Zealand statesmanship. . . ." A program of low-interest loans, such as the Pacific colony had developed, would enlist plain American citizens "in the war against the wilderness" as a means of improving their "prospects in life." Such loans, Smythe argued, were not so much a favor to "the man as to the Nation, the hope of whose perpetuity lies in the prosperity and happiness of its citizens."[42]

Smythe enlarged on this theme in his chapter "An Army of Peace," in which he urged the adoption in the United States of the Australasian programs of putting the unemployed to work on public works programs for national development—farm making, railroad building, highway and bridge construction, land drainage programs, water conservation schemes, and similar projects. "We need an Army of Peace to develop the material resources of the United States. . . . Why not open recruiting stations in all cities, from sea to sea? . . . Does anyone doubt that the Army of Peace would return as many dividends—moral, social, and pecuniary—as the Army of War? . . . If there be such doubters, let them turn their eyes again to New Zealand, where the policy has proved to be sound. . . . *The value of improvements created far exceeds the cost.* Let American commercialism digest that interesting Fact!"[43]

By 1905, however, Smythe had abandoned his advocacy of the New Zealand system of compulsory arbitration of labor disputes, saying that although the idea "has had a large following among reformers" it "has never proven acceptable to either side of the labor controversy." Instead, Smythe proposed to regulate profits, contending that this would deprive corporations of any incentive to exploit workers and force them to concentrate on improving their products and working conditions. "The adoption of this plan would . . . even lead New Zealand," he declared, but there was probably even less chance of this solution being adopted than the compulsory arbitration one.[44]

Thus Smythe's campaign to "make another New Zealand . . . of the West" was short-lived, lasting less than five years, and apparently unpersuasive, for California adopted not a single element of his antipodean program. However, Smythe was simply ahead of his time. Within a few years voters accepted three labor reforms pioneered in New Zealand and within a decade rural reforms came as well. But so long as Smythe's campaign lasted, it was intense, reached thousands of westerners, and at the very least introduced them to strikingly different solutions to American problems.[45]

The fifth of these reformers to espouse New Zealand solutions to American problems, Julius A. Wayland, also took up the effort as a result of reading Lloyd's writings. And like Smythe, his involvement was both brief and intense, but because his socialist weekly, *Appeal to Reason,* had a large national circulation his message reached hundreds of thousands of Americans while Smythe's reached comparatively few, mainly in California and the West.

Drawn from that generation of American radicals born in the decade before the Civil War, Wayland grew up in small-town Indiana and roamed the Midwest as a printer before settling briefly in the late seventies in Harrisonville, Missouri, as a newspaper editor. Within four years he had moved to Pueblo, Colorado, where he was converted to socialism by an English shoemaker. As a job printer and real estate operator, Wayland was also a highly successful capitalist, shrewdly anticipating the Panic of 1893 by converting his holdings to gold.[46]

With a substantial capital at his disposal and by then determined to invest in an enterprise preaching socialism, Wayland returned to Indiana to found the *Coming Nation*, a propaganda weekly that quickly built up a circulation of at least fifty thousand, mainly in the rural West. The venture was so successful that Wayland's capital grew rapidly and embarrassingly. He solved the problem by founding a cooperative commonwealth in Tennessee, named after the English Christian socialist, John Ruskin. With 2,000 acres and 125 settlers, the community quickly prospered, but within a year it also fleeced Wayland of his investment, $100,000, and had even expropriated the *Coming Nation*, presses as well as title, expelling the editor and leaving him to fend for himself.

Wayland's resiliency was extraordinary. Within two years he had moved to Girard, Kansas, a small county seat in the southeastern corner of the state near the Ozarks, and had founded a new weekly, *Appeal to Reason*. Though circulation soon rose to 45,000, many readers canceled their subscriptions when Wayland attacked American imperialism during the Spanish-American War, and the newspaper did not begin to attract a large following until Fred Warren, a typesetter and editor, took over management of the enterprise in 1901.

Warren changed the paper's format and style, giving it a sensational, hard-hitting tone, mixing exposés of the Boy Scouts, White Slavery, and rape on the Santa Fe Railroad with socialistic propaganda. This muckraking style quickly drove circulation to 150,000 and to as high as 550,000 at the time of Wayland's death in 1912. The *Appeal to Reason* expanded so rapidly also because of the techniques it pioneered in selling subscriptions and in the enthusiastic loyalty it aroused in evangelistic supporters throughout the United States and Canada. Thousands of copies were given away, group subscriptions were organized through local socialist clubs, and there were 80,000 loyal readers who served as subscription agents, including the legendary Louis Klamrouth—Wayland's "mightiest war horse"—who cycled all over North America, taking more than 100,000 subscriptions and selling some 20,000 pamphlets.[47]

Southeastern Kansas was surely an improbable site for a publishing venture of this magnitude, not to say for the capital of socialist propaganda in the United States. Special issues of the *Appeal* required press runs of one to three million copies and twenty presses, including a huge Gosse press that could print and fold 25,000 newspapers an hour. Indeed, the volume of mail elicited by the *Appeal* and other publications was so large that Girard was the smallest community in the country to have a first-class post office. Mail trains had to be specially routed through the town to handle the huge volume of business, and once a single issue of the *Appeal* required four trains and forty cars to haul it away. Though the people of Girard were initially hostile to the enterprise, in time they came to tolerate it simply because it brought so much business and so many jobs to the community.[48]

Though the American socialist movement was badly splintered into several hostile factions, there was general agreement that Wayland and his *Appeal* did more than anyone else to win converts. The terse paragraphs, sensational muckraking, and down-to-earth editorials proved ideal ways of reaching the masses of ordinary people. But Wayland was also a practical socialist and he sought to demonstrate to his readers that it was not necessary to wait for the coming of a utopian society at some distant point in the future. Rather, the socialist's task was to deal immediately and step-by-step with whatever problems and with whatever means were at hand. And always the first step was to use the ballot box to elect genuine representatives of the people. Thus Wayland was perfectly willing to support Populism, even though the People's party platform fell far short of his socialist goals. If he could spread the socialist message by working with Populists, and if he could increase the *Appeal's* circulation, then he was ready to subordinate ideology to practical good sense.

It was for precisely these reasons that Wayland embraced New Zealand. Unlike Flower, Lloyd, Parsons, or Smythe, who generally believed that the solutions to the nation's ills were to be found in adapting colonial reforms to American needs, Wayland was too much the realist to believe that this was either the best strategy or much less that antipodean programs were really adaptable to the United States. It was not just that Wayland understood much better than the others that New Zealand was not a socialist country and therefore did not provide Americans with working socialistic examples to emulate. It was that he wanted to radicalize his readers by exposing every form of inhumanity, injustice, exploitation, and oppression and then fire their enthusiasm for the immediate reconstruction of society by demonstrating that ordinary people in other countries had quickly and successfully dealt with their problems. Unlike Smythe, Wayland did not want to New Zealandize America; he simply used the New Zealand example to inspire the American people to take up the cause of reform. But it was to be an American program, not a foreign one. In Wayland's view, this was not only sound politics but profitable journalism as well.

Wayland had first called attention to New Zealand reforms as early as January 1896, when Elmweed Pomeroy's column on direct legislation described the struggle for the eight-hour day and predicted early enactment. Scattered paragraphs of additional commentary, often drawn from the foreign press, continued over the next two years. Readers learned, for example, that the colony had "the most perfect land and labor laws in the world" and that it would be a paradise if it could only gain control of its money laws. Retail stores in the colony were closed on Wednesday afternoons because the clerks used the ballot box and unlike American workers did not allow "a Gompers, a McBride, an Arthur . . . to deliver them to their employers at every election."[49]

"IF A LITTLE SOCIALISM is a Good Thing for Labor in New Zealand," asked the caption to an extended interview with Dr. J. M. Peebles, "why not for American Labor?" In New Zealand, he reported, there "are not great soul-less syndicates, nor great heartless trust companies." Legislation provided equality of opportunity and checked "the overreaching of those possessed of miserly and wolfish propensities." If the United States took control of the railroads, telegraphs, and coal mines, there would be "no strikes, no beggars, and fewer syndicates and overbearing millionaires to oppress the honest hardworking toiler and tiller of the soil."[50]

Elsewhere, an Australian visitor was quoted from the *Washington Post* in support of the Australian system of taxing income and land, public ownership of railroads and telegraphs, and state development of the interior through the boring of artesian wells. "Does the fact that the government paid for the wells make them one whit less beneficial?" he asked.[51] A similar endorsement of "successful socialism," this time by an Auckland businessman, appeared in September 1897, attributing New Zealand's prosperity to the land tax, and praising public ownership of the telegraph, telephone, and railroad services, the post office savings bank, women's suffrage, the state life insurance office, and worker cooperatives. Wayland interpreted this to mean that the "New Zealand people are practically and successfully testing the elementary principles of socialism."[52] He also compared "our vicious system of private ownership" with the New Zealand system of public ownership and operation of the railroads, reporting that country children were carried to and from school free of charge and that the lines were beginning to earn money for the government. "The awful horribleness of socialism is enough to give anyone the creeps, isn't it?" he asked.[53]

"New Zealand socialists are organizing," Wayland declared in 1898, by providing "homes and pleasures" for the colony's aged citizens. "What a howl would go up from the tax-payers if Kansas were to do such a thing! That far away country is ahead of us."[54]

These notices of New Zealand "socialism" appearing randomly in the *Appeal to Reason* gave way late in 1898 to a concerted propaganda campaign that lasted for four years. It began in October with an extensive summary of colonial working conditions taken from an issue of the Labour Department's monthly journal that a New Zealand reader had sent to Wayland. Throughout, he held up the colony's achievements as models for the United States to follow, arguing that the success of antipodean reforms demonstrated the feasibility of socialism in America.[55]

To these ends he seized on whatever came to hand. The *Appeal* published excerpts from public lectures about New Zealand, letters from travelers and colonists, and news reports and articles culled from other newspapers and magazines. Interspersed were terse, polemical exhortations to political action. For example, he praised the state life insurance office with its low premiums and large investments in colonial development by commenting: "How different that is from the report of millions piled up in private vaults to make millionaires in the United States." The *Appeal* drew especially heavily on the Labour Department's journal for statistical information to prove the superiority of New Zealand's policies over those of the United States and for articles on the industrial code and its enforcement. Wayland urged his readers to send to the colony for copies and for a time he even imported copies to sell. The *Journal*, he told his readers, "is a bright oasis in the desert of wage-slavery." "Say, you socialist labor union member, send ten cents for a copy . . . and read . . . it to your fellow members. You will . . . arouse a new spirit in them. . . ."[56]

Virtually every facet of the New Zealand reform program, but particularly the labor and land laws, attracted Wayland's attention, and he especially emphasized the crucial importance of trade unionists' electing the "wisest, most radical leaders to office. . . ." They had secured the eight-hour day and were even considering reducing it to six. "So if a British colony dares to lead . . . surely it is not visionary to expect our Republic to fall in line." Wayland argued that "a peaceful revolution" could be achieved in two years if workers would "break away from the old parties. . . ." There "is not trampism or enforced idleness [in New Zealand]. Is it not worth while to throw all your political prejudices to the dogs and to vote [to bring] about the same conditions in the United States."[57]

Henry Demarest Lloyd reinforced Wayland's enthusiasm. "Your magazine articles on New Zealand," he told Lloyd in 1900, "have had an immense effect . . . this has been very noticeable at my desk. . . . I am constantly in receipt of requests for fresh information about New Zealand and the progress that has been made there." Ernest Hoeneck and his wife even emigrated to the colony because of what he had read in the *Appeal to Reason.* He thanked Wayland for the information, saying "we have been here only five months, but would not return to the States if our passage were paid and a bonus of $1,000 given."[58]

So great was the interest that in February 1900, Wayland devoted an entire issue of the *Appeal to Reason* to New Zealand. There were two long articles, one by the editor himself summarizing the main features of the colony's reforms, the other by a recent British immigrant, William Ranstead, reprinted from the London *Clarion.* Ranstead's message was simple. Having traveled all over the world, he had finally found the ideal place to settle. "Why should I ever leave such a country?" he asked. "Here there is no aristocracy, no snobbery. There are no very rich people and no poor. . . . There are no slums here, no miserable starving women, and no suffering children. . . . So you can tell my mutual friends I'm here for good. . . ."[59]

Wayland reiterated his message in later issues with banner headlines urging every union man to read the special issue. "NEW ZEALAND IS AHEAD OF US," he trumpeted. "FIND OUT ALL ABOUT IT!" "IF PEOPLE of the U.S. knew of conditions in New Zealand they would revolutionize the nation." He also congratulated himself for having first called American attention to the "wonderful change" that union labor had brought about in New Zealand and reported that American unions were "attracted to the same course of action. This may or may not be scientific socialism. I do not care a fig whether it is or not. . . ."[60]

Wayland was ahead of Lloyd in devising invidious comparisons, and he gave them a sharper edge with his biting sarcasm. "The capitalistic buccaneer don't seem to have much of an opportunity to ply his calling in New Zealand," he wrote, because the government was in the lending business. "The United States can't do what New Zealand does. Vegetables wouldn't grow if such a thing as government loans direct to farmers were suggested." "Yes, beware of New Zealand—it has not the contrasts of poverty and riches, oppressed and oppressors, corrupting corporations and bribery that this country has." "The heathen colony of New Zealand . . . appropriates $1,000,000 a year in old age pensions! Kansas people prefer to go to the poor house." In New Zealand workingmen were elected to high political office. "Here it is different. Only the rich can hold important places. . . . Is it because the laboring people there are more intelligent than here?" New Zealand had even solved the crime problem by providing the jobless with work. "If the same were done here we would not only save [a] billion dollars a year, but would have the products which their labor . . . would produce. But that would possibly be called paternalism. . . !" Similarly, New Zealand brought down the price of fuel by going into the coal business. "In America we don't do things that way. When the working people are overcharged . . . we have the police out in force to see that they submit peaceably to the skinning."[61]

In May 1900, the Kansas socialist launched a new journal, *Wayland's Monthly*, and devoted the entire first issue to "New Zealand in a Nutshell," a forty-five-page compilation on the colony's geography, history, political system, economy, and reforms culled from official and other sources, including testimonials "from those who have left America forever, never to return, and who have found their new home all and more than it was represented. . . ."[62] Wayland made his propaganda purpose clear. He wanted to supply persuasive facts to "the thousands whose only excuse for not openly embracing the cause of Socialism is their fear that it is not practical. . . . Shame be it to that American, while viewing the beauties of a little island in a far away sea, who will supinely bow his neck to the yoke and continue his part in the procession that leads only to degradation and an enslaved race!"[63] "There IS a way out," Wayland declared. "American workmen can lead in the new civilization, the brotherhood of man. It is no idle dream or Utopian vision. It is a practical fact, and our brothers across the Pacific have solved the first problems for us."[64]

"New Zealand in a Nutshell" carried the subtitle "A Country Without Strikes Where Labor Is Supreme" and devoted considerable space to the compulsory arbitration of labor disputes. Included were long extracts from the letters of an American emigrant to New Zealand, Frank G. Carpenter, articles by Lloyd and Lusk reprinted from the *New York Herald* and *World's Work*, and a copy of the labor code. With the exception of Lusks' contribution, most of the extracts were factual rather than polemical.[65]

Some measure of the influence of "New Zealand in a Nutshell" can be judged from the distribution figures. The initial printing, 10,000 copies, of *Wayland's Monthly* sold out within a month. It was then reissued as a pamphlet, republished in a revised edition as number 14 of *Wayland's Monthly* in June 1901, and again reissued in pamphlet form, selling for as little as three cents for bulk orders. By March 1902, 65,000 had been sold and by the end of the year the number reached 100,000. That was almost one copy for every hundred American voters.[66]

Wayland pushed sales vigorously, especially during the great anthracite strike in Pennsylvania. "NOW IS THE TIME to point out the only remedy—SOCIALISM," he advertised. "Naturally the unread man is skeptical, and like the Missourian, has to be 'shown.' This you can do by placing in his hands a copy of 'New Zealand In A Nutshell.' This little pamphlet will show how it is done in a country where . . . there have been no strikes. . . . This result . . . can be brought about in this country, if YOU will help in the great educational movement now in progress. . . . Circulate 'New Zealand in a Nutshell' NOW while the public mind is asking for something."[67]

It was not always easy to tell where Wayland's evangelism stopped and his hucksterism started. In June 1900, when circulation already exceeded 99,000, he complained that the *Appeal* was losing money and that the paper could survive only if the numbers could be lifted to 150,000. In addition to offering cash bonuses ranging from $25 to $1,000 to the most successful salesmen, Wayland promised to send an *Appeal* commissioner to New Zealand to observe and report on the colony's reform program. By implication, the editor conveyed two impressions: that the real truth about the success of New Zealand's socialism could be obtained only by sending an independent American observer who would have no ties to the capitalist press; and that the very survival of the *Appeal* depended upon increasing circulation by at least a half. Larger numbers would not only put the newspaper in the black, they would enable the *Appeal* to keep readers fully informed about New Zealand's progress and achievements. Wayland received dozens of applications for the post of commissioner, but he announced that no selection would be made until the circulation target had been reached and that the candidate would be chosen from among the *Appeal*'s most successful salesman. "Toward Utopia," he proclaimed, "Now for New Zealand," KEEP ON POUNDING! ON TO NEW ZEALAND!" "New Zealand in 60 Days," "Have You Will Force?"[68]

The campaign added some new subscribers within seven weeks, but fell far short of Wayland's goal. By July 1900, there was no more talk of sending a representative to New Zealand. Nevertheless, circulation continued to rise, reaching 141,000 subscribers by the end of the year and 400,000 by the end of 1902. And so the hundreds of New Zealand items Wayland published reached more and more readers. Wayland emphasized the success of compulsory arbitration of labor disputes, the cheapness of parcel postage rates, the dignity given to old-age pensioners, the profitability of the state-owned railroads and the favorable rates charged farmers, the prosperity of workers, the low cost of state loans and insurance, and the effectiveness of the attack on land monopoly. His propaganda brought hundreds of inquiries about the cost of emigrating to New Zealand; a Kansas socialist proposed to halt this loss of population by creating a county modeled on New Zealand lines; and Wayland claimed that hundreds of American newspapers had supported the cause by reprinting items from the *Appeal to Reason.*[69]

But although Wayland denounced what he saw as a concerted effort by the capitalist press to discredit New Zealand reform and tried to counter it by exposing what he believed to be the falsity of the accounts, Wayland's own position on New Zealand began to undergo a subtle change. In response to the question, "Is Socialism a failure in New Zealand?" he replied, "Socialism has never been established in New Zealand, hence can not be a failure."[70] Wayland continued to praise many aspects of colonial life, but he no longer held up New Zealand as a model for the United States to follow.

There were two underlying reasons for this shift. First, the emergence of a militant socialist movement in New Zealand, and particularly its denunciation of the Seddon government, made it difficult for the editor to maintain his former pragmatism. "Seddon is a capitalist fake," the *Appeal* charged in April 1903, "and has never had any intention of standing for the interests of the working class. The light is dawning, even in New Zealand."[71] Second, the formation of the American Socialist Party in 1901 brought many formerly fragmented radicals into a single organization with a common ideology. It was no longer possible for Wayland to preach his own brand of pragmatic socialism; he was obliged to follow more strictly the prevailing party line. And American socialists, like their antipodean brothers, saw Seddon's program, especially compulsory arbitration, as antithetical to trade unionism. Reformism only strengthened capitalism and made its overthrow more difficult.[72]

Beginning in the fall of 1902 the *Appeal* paid less and less attention to New Zealand, though scattered notices continued to appear from time to time under Warren's editorship and even after Wayland's death in 1912.[73]

In the meantime, Wayland had revived his old weekly, *Coming Nation*, which espoused socialist orthodoxy and denounced antipodean reformism. That view received powerful expression in four articles on New Zealand by Charles Edward Russell, the muckraker best known for his exposé of the "Beef Trust." Russell visited Australasia twice. On his first visit in 1906, though more critical than some other foreign journalists, he had a good deal of praise for antipodean accomplishments.[74]

And he, too, used the Lloyd-Parsons-Wayland technique of invidious comparisons. "In New Zealand," he wrote, "is no threat of accumulating millions, no trusts, no money mania, no corrupted legislatures, no extremes of condition, no surfeit, no poverty, . . . no destitution, no palaces, no slums, no unemployed, no epidemics, no overcrowding, no pest-holes, no noisome back streets, no heaps of unsanitary dwellings, no spots where people live without light, fresh air, and sunshine, no physical degeneration, no Hooligans, no tramps, no idlers, . . . no life-insurance scandals, no tax-dodging corporations, no boodling, no free-pass bribery, no watered stock, no fraudulent bonds, no rebates, no discriminations, no railroad combinations, no private graft for railroad presidents and managers, no refrigerator-car swindles, . . . and no government afraid to enforce the law upon the rich and the powerful."[75]

Russell concluded the series by asking if the New Zealand achievements were the result of "Fatuous Dreaming," and answered by saying that the colony "has shown that life is not necessarily a hideous battle-field on which each man lives by the slaughter of his fellow, that the slum is superfluous, poverty is not inevitable, and there are better uses for human life than to spend it in piling one dollar on top of another."[76]

But Russell formally joined the Socialist party in 1908, and when he revisited the Antipodes three years later he had more criticism than praise. It was a "hallucination" for Americans to think of Australasia as socialistic, he reported, and, as Wayland put it, Russell exposed the "weakness and hopeless insufficiency" of the reforms "as they have never been exposed before."[77]

This ideological change in no way minimizes Wayland's significance as a propagandist during that four-year period in which the *Appeal to Reason* and "New Zealand in a Nutshell" reached so many thousands of readers. By no means were all of them socialists, so that his shifting assessment probably had little impact. More important was the fact that Wayland, like Flower, Lloyd, Parsons, and Smythe, helped to expose an entire generation of Americans to a very different vision of what society could be, how it could be organized and governed, and what could be accomplished for humanity.

Hugh H. Lusk, the sixth of these propagandists, brought to the campaign quite different perspectives and commitments. Born in Scotland in 1837, he was taken to New Zealand in 1849, and he eventually entered the legal profession. Active in provincial and national politics in the seventies, he came to the

United States in the nineties, hoping to support himself from his writing and lecturing on social and economic problems.[78] Although he had left the colony too early to have had a hand in New Zealand's liberal experiments, he gave them his enthusiastic endorsement and vigorously campaigned for the American adoption of antipodean reform principles. Lusk's arguments gained credence from the frequently repeated description of him as a former member of parliament.

Lusk seems to have quickly acquired a circle of American reform contacts, especially Flower, Lloyd, and Parsons on the East Coast, Wayland in the Midwest, and Smythe on the Pacific Coast. Through them and others, he received speaking engagements and invitations to write for the leading American journals of opinion. For example, in April 1898, he told a joint conference of Catholic and Protestant Workingmen's Clubs in New York City that New Zealand had been trying to introduce Christian politics so that men could "live in peace and amity," a goal reflected in such measures as the attack on land monopoly, giving women the franchise, and the compulsory arbitration of industrial disputes.[79]

Lusk reiterated this theme a year later in an article for *Outlook*, "Industrial Emancipation in New Zealand," in which he asserted that in "nearly every line of political thought she has attempted new departures from the beaten track, and . . . put into practical operation the ideas that have elsewhere been scoffed at as the insubstantial dreams of visionary philosophers." But Lusk did not claim that the colony had deliberately set out to make itself "the guide and teacher of the rest of civilized humanity." Rather, reform had proceeded in an evolutionary way, dealing as they arose with such problems as working conditions, disputes between labor and capital, and the needs of the elderly. Nevertheless, because these reforms had not impaired the colony's growth and prosperity as their opponents had predicted, Lusk argued that it was proper to question "the truth of the doctrines so arrogantly declared to be the unalterable laws of economic science."[80]

In *Our Foes at Home* (1899), Lusk challenged conventional economic wisdom in much greater detail. Rejecting the tenets of the Manchester school of economics in favor of enlarging the role of the state according to the new liberalism of John Stuart Mill, Lusk branded the wealthy and powerful as the enemies of the United States and urged the breakup of trusts and large landed estates, public ownership of the banking system, tax reform, and measures to bring about fundamental improvements in the lives of working people.[81]

Throughout, Lusk took Australian and particularly New Zealand reform as his model, arguing that Americans should examine antipodean principles to see whether they "should guide future legislation." "The Australian system," he concluded, "is in no sense alien to the genius of the institutions of America. If it were adopted tomorrow it would be but a return to the principles of the purer days of the republic."[82] Lusk contended that it was still not too late to deal with the "evils that threaten . . . America." The "tyranny of capital" was not so old or entrenched as to be "beyond the reach of the people. . . ." The United States "must either, as now, lend itself to the purposes of the monopolist, the trust promoter and the millionaire . . . or it must give itself unreservedly to the interests of the people, to their social well-being and elevation. . . ."[83]

Over the next decade, Lusk remained an active if minor figure in the American Progressive movement, lecturing in such forums as the Cooper Union in New York City and writing for a broad spectrum of periodicals. And during the Great Anthracite Strike in 1902 he urged the Industrial Commission to recommend the compulsory arbitration of labor disputes. Throughout these years Lusk vigorously reiterated the themes laid out in *Our Foes at Home*, arguing that plutocracy had created a crisis in the United States that could be dealt with only if the American people acted quickly to reconstruct society according to the higher morality developed in the Antipodes.[84]

In 1913 his New York publisher also brought out *Social Welfare in New Zealand*, a thoughtful and readable summary of two decades of reform activity. Significantly, the subtitle was *The Result of Twenty Years of Progressive Social Legislation and Its Significance for the United States and Other Countries.* Arranged in four sections, "State Socialism: What It Means," "An Object-Lesson from New Zealand," "What It Has Meant to New

Zealand," and "What It May Mean for the World," the concluding four chapters argued that the colony's "steady discouragement . . . of grasping selfishness" had produced "economic success far greater . . . than that of any other national community in the world." It followed that Americans should give serious consideration to reforming the Republic along New Zealand lines.[85]

As activists and propagandists, Flower, Lloyd, Lusk, Parsons, Smythe, and Wayland drew highly subjective, self-serving portraits of antipodean liberalism. They saw in the colonial experiments what they wanted to see. Believing that social and economic justice could be won, they trumpeted the success of Australasian experiments and argued that they provided Americans with important lessons. But they were not disinterested observers. Wanting to reconstruct America along reformist or socialist lines, they chose to believe that antipodean successes proved that it could be done. Colonial liberalism also reinforced their determination to continue the struggle. Pessimism about the American future gave way to optimism. The Republic could indeed be "New Zealandized."

4 New Zealandizing the United States

The campaign to "New Zealandize" the United States drew its force and inspiration from the impression that the South Pacific colony had discovered a way to rescue the beleaguered American democracy from destruction. To hear the Flowers, Lloyds, Lusks, Parsonses, and Waylands tell it, antipodean reformers had abolished fear and want, given the aged security, opened land to the landless, provided shippers with low-cost rail services, reduced interest rates for farmers, banished strikes and lockouts, protected workers from exploitation, and brought women into the political process. Taken together, these and similar measures gave New Zealand its reputation as the world's most advanced democracy. This view gained wider currency and credibility when, one by one, the Australian colonies across the Tasman Sea followed in New Zealand's footsteps.

That is what Parsons meant when he proclaimed New Zealand "the birth place of the 20th Century." He was describing what we now think of as the origins of the modern welfare state and the mixed economy. Though often labeled "state socialism" or "state capitalism" by contemporaries, ideology played little part in the colonial experiments. Rather, most politicians, if they thought about the matter at all, would have described themselves as "humanists"—practical men in search of practical ways to improve the lot of their fellow human beings. As Seddon put it, "I desire to improve the condition of the people, to inspire them with hope, to provide for their comfort, and to improve them socially, morally and politically." According to Charles Edward Russell, New Zealand's leaders believed "it is better to have less wealth and more health."[1]

Nor was there much originality in the antipodean program. Most of the legislative ideas had been talked about in the English-speaking world for at least a generation. All that the colony could really claim was that it had acted while the rest of the world had talked. To many at home as well as abroad, that seemed justification enough, but the absence of a fully worked out theory of the state and the lack of inventiveness inclined European observers to dismiss the colonial accomplishments as hardly deserving serious attention.[2]

Americans, by contrast, were attracted by what repelled Europeans. When colonists talked of the "mission of the New Zealand democracy," Americans readily appreciated what that meant, just as they understood the colony's determination to prevent the spread of Old World problems to the New. More specifically, many reformers on both sides of the Pacific shared common attitudes and ideas. They had read the same works: John Stuart Mill and Alfred Russel Wallace, Christian and Fabian socialist writers, and above all Bellamy and George. The goal of reform was "to help the toilers to some degree of security and comfort. There is no brotherhood," declared an official, "except in love for the poor and helpless."[3] They were New Zealand words, but they could have easily have been written by Flower or Lloyd or Parsons. No wonder many Americans, rooted as they were in much the same reform tradition, found the antipodean experiments so exciting.

Other reasons reinforced the intensity of American interest in the antipodean experiments. Foremost, perhaps, was the rapidity and comprehensiveness of the colonial reconstruction. In just five years, 1893 to 1898, Lloyd and others believed, New Zealand had solved the great social and economic problems of the age. As the world's legislative laboratory, it had proved man's capacity to create a just and humane society for all. Given the same will and opportunity, Americans could as quickly and completely reconstruct their own democracy.

These optimistic assumptions meshed with the prevailing British orientation underlying the American outlook. Those most fascinated by the antipodean experiments were commonly Americans whose family origins were in the British Isles. They were attracted by the idea of grass-roots reform, especially when it drew its power from parliamentary institutions and universal adult suffrage. The English-speaking colonies provided reassuring confirmation that the United States, with its Anglo-American system of government and law, could achieve comparable results. Moreover, the striking absence of ideology in the colonies deepened the attraction, and antipodean achievements also meshed with the tradition of looking westward to the Pacific slope and beyond for the American future. Thus the success of the colonial experiments confirmed and validated the destiny of New World societies.

Paradoxically, American interest in the Antipodes may also have been heightened by the process by which they acquired their knowledge and understanding of colonial progress. Traditionally, Americans had looked eastward across the Atlantic for ideas, models, and inspiration. Throughout the nineteenth century, activists followed the trends of European reform, ranging from British Liberalism to Bismarckian statism, from Russian anarchism to French communism. This was especially true of those Americans who traveled in Europe or attended universities there. Particularly noteworthy was the influx of social science concepts and methodologies. European immigrants and their American-born children reinforced these Atlantic linkages, primarily as transmitters and interpreters of foreign reforms and as constituencies for such approaches in various parts of the United States.

There were no comparable linkages to the antipodean democracies. There were almost no Australasian immigrants in the United States in the nineties to transmit, interpret, or advocate antipodean solutions to American problems; few Americans visited the colonies, and so there was no steady flow of intelligence on reform matters across the Pacific; and there were no centers of culture and learning to attract American students. These obstacles obliged reformers to organize their own networks for gathering and disseminating information and evaluations. That process gave them a sense of discovery and achievement. It also gave them an inflated view of colonial progress and committed them to defend their interpretation.

So successful were they that many Americans caught what an Iowa man called "the New Zealand fever." This antipodean virus quickly entered the American bloodstream. When William Dean Howells heard a lecture about New Zealand in the spring of 1898 he told Sylvester Baxter that "it was like a dream of heaven." Eugene V. Brewster likened the colony to utopia. "It approaches Bellamy's ideal dream of 'Looking Backward'," he declared. "Reformers . . . rave over it. Socialists . . . point it out as a goal. . . . A model nation has been born." Others saw New Zealand as "the most progressive" government in the world. "Your economic advance," they proclaimed, "is the marvel of the years." They had "long admired the progressive and democratic spirit of your nation," and they saw its laws as a "true," "superb," and "rightful adjustment of conditions for the good of all." Emma Alice Wilkinson, an Oregon teacher, looked to New Zealand for a "Golden Rule Way" to deal with the "growing discontent and unrest among the laboring classes" of America.[4]

So powerful was "New Zealand fever" that some Americans talked of emigrating to the South Seas. They deluged British consulates and New Zealand officials with requests for information, often revealing their perceptions of the American crisis and their hopes for new lives in the Antipodes. A California group, for example, declared themselves "heartily in sympathy" with the colony's progressive "New Liberalism." They wanted to become citizens of a country "where human happiness and welfare are enlarged by the rightful restraint of avarice and greed." The American people, they reported, were "on the verge of ruin and bankruptcy, because of the swallowing up of all our industries by Trusts & Syndicates, and the monopoly by the few of the natural means of production."[5]

Others expressed similar concerns. "The common people," reported an Iowa group, "are becoming greatly oppressed by the 'Trusts' & Capitalism and if New Zealand offers us a better home we wish to take advantage of it." Some southern Californians also wanted a refuge from the " 'Cut-Throat' commercial spirit which so largely prevails in this country." Swedish-Americans from Denver looked to a better life under New Zealand's "faultless form of Government," as did a Minnesota man, who was troubled by high taxes and "the growth of trusts and great corporations."[6]

Still others chose to work for change at home. They saw New Zealand not as a haven but as a model and they discouraged emigration. "Agitate the idea of remaining in America," urged one radical in 1900. The best way to create "a New Zealand of our own" was to vote socialists into county offices, but George

B. Harrison disagreed, urging instead that radicals migrate to Oklahoma Territory and bring it into the Union as a socialist state. That same year Mrs. Annie L. Diggs ran for the Kansas legislature on a New Zealand platform, and in 1902, as we have seen, Smythe began talking about "New Zealandizing" California and the West.[7]

These manifestations of "New Zealand fever" showed how receptive some Americans were to the reconstruction of the United States along antipodean lines. Out of the colony's legislative laboratory had come a hopeful, even inspiring, vision of their own country's future, one where Emma Wilkinson's "discontent and fear" would be gone forever. But if the New Zealand road to reform clearly called for massive doses of state interventionism, less clear was the way to move the Republic in that direction. Overwhelmingly, that was a political problem. Voters first had to be persuaded that legislatures could indeed cure the nation's ills. Then specific remedies had to be proposed, support organized, competing interests reconciled, constitutional objections overcome. Just how far the campaign to "New Zealandize" America could go depended crucially on such practical considerations.

The American effort to enact old age pensions provides an instructive example of the reform process. Although Germany had created its system in the eighties, Americans paid little attention until the early nineties and another decade elapsed before the question attracted a substantial constituency. By that time the New Zealand program had been in operation for several years. The two systems were quite dissimilar. Both created pension rights, but Germany used the insurance principle by levying compulsory taxes on wages. It was thus a universal system based on weekly contributions to the fund. By contrast, New Zealand funded its pensions through general revenues, but eligibility hinged on residency, good character, and a means test.

Americans quickly learned about the colonial system and its underlying principles. As early as October 1898, while the measure was still being debated, the English magazine *Spectator* told its readers that New Zealand had become a laboratory of political and social experiment, "and though the rulers . . . are not exactly Edisons, they have a freedom of mind which one day may lead to considerable success." The *Spectator* predicted that state philanthropy, such as old-age pensions, would grow. The New Zealand program, therefore, should be watched "with keen interest, . . . though . . . its true . . . effects will only begin to be perceptible in the next generation."[8]

The New Zealand correspondent of the *New York Times,* J. Grattan Grey, reported in similar vein, declaring that "there is no colony in all Australasia which has made so much progress as New Zealand has done in the reform of old-land institutions and in its efforts to obliterate class distinctions and privileges. . . ." Grey believed that the experiment in old-age pensions was of importance to more than just the British Empire. "New Zealand has set an example to all the civilized nations of the world [by abolishing] the workhouse system as it exists in England."[9]

Articles by Lusk, Reeves, and Tregear in 1899 reinforced Grey's interpretation. They argued that society owed its poorer members honor, dignity, and a decent living in their retirement. The obligation was simple justice as well as a modest recognition and repayment of the contributions working people had made to the colony's progress in their productive years. As Lusk put it, New Zealand's greatest legislative advantage lay "mainly in seeing more clearly than many other communities evils that require to be met and the principles really applicable to dealing with them." The colony had recognized "a new code of social ethics"—"gratitude . . . to those who have served it well." Workers were as deserving as military veterans. Until there was a fairer distribution of the products of industry, it was "self-seeking hypocrisy . . . to discuss the moral benefits of thrift." Individual liberty, he argued, was impossible without economic security, which only decent working conditions, living wages, and old age pensions could provide. The colony had pointed "the way to a principle of justice and liberty which all other civilized nations will follow ere long." The world "owes something to New Zealand for making the experiment."[10]

These early commentaries on the pension law were intended to raise American consciousness and to evoke sympathetic responses. In Lloyd's *Newest England* (1900), the first substantial account of the colonial experiment, and in other writings, he saw "Our fellow democrats of Australasia . . . pioneering the way for us," and in *The Story of New Zealand* (1904) Parsons declared that *"What is now history"* in the colony *"is prophesy for the rest of the world."* Both declared the pension system popular, practical, and successful. Although not explicitly polemical, Reeves's *State Experiments in Australia & New Zealand* (1902) conveyed a similar message to his American readers. Further reinforcement of the arguments favoring an American pension plan came from an investigation of the New Zealand system by an Australian royal commission and on its recommendation the adoption of the program by the governments of New South Wales, Victoria, and the Commonwealth.[11]

Despite their enthusiastic advocacy, Lloyd and his emulators made little headway. Americans were not yet ready to give serious consideration to a pension system. In 1901 the Industrial Commission described the New Zealand law as "extraordinary," but thought legislation unlikely "for the present in the United States," and the *Independent* reported that the idea had not yet "seriously taken hold of the American public." Compulsion flawed the German system; paternalism, the New Zealand one. The New York businessman and philanthropist Lucien C. Warner only mildly disagreed. He had observed "an urgent demand" throughout the world for the "support of those who have passed the age of efficient work," but predicted after visiting New Zealand that the means test would destroy "the incentive for thrift . . . among the poor" and have a "demoralizing effect upon the people."[12]

And so the pension idea lay dormant until 1908, when the British government established a program based on the antipodean rather than the German model. It involved the redistribution of income rather than a tax on workers. American interest immediately revived. Prominent reformers, including Louis D. Brandeis, Richard Washburn Child, Rev. Edward Everett Hale, Anne Hard, Frank W. Lewis, and John A. Ryan began campaigning for old-age pensions; the John Stuart Kennedy Foundation sponsored a series of six lectures in New York by Columbia's Henry Rogers Seager; Massachusetts and New York appointed commissions to investigate; and the U.S. Bureau of Labor produced a massive report on foreign pension systems.[13]

Although these efforts produced no legislation until the New Deal, one consequence came almost immediately. Informed opinion firmly rejected the antipodean concept of paying pensions out of general revenue. The Massachusetts commission described the New Zealand law as "a counsel of despair. If such a scheme is defensible or excusable in this country," it declared, "then the whole economic and social system is a failure. The adoption of such a system would be a confession of its breakdown." Seager observed wryly that the colonists would have reacted to such a statement with "amused surprise," but what was nevertheless clear was that American thinking had shifted decisively in favor of the social insurance principle. Its protagonist was an immigrant from Russian Poland, Isaac Max Rubinow. As principal investigator for the Bureau of Labor on European pension systems and as teacher, writer, and actuarial consultant, he found moral as well as practical grounds for strongly favoring the German system of compulsory thrift, the central principle of the Social Security Act of 1936.[14]

The most that can be said for the antipodean influence, therefore, is that the New Zealand experiment helped to educate Americans to a larger awareness of the problems of age and poverty and to the possibilities of providing security through state intervention. But the New Zealand model, though influential in Australia and Great Britain, failed to attract a large or organized American following. The costs seemed prohibitive, even when a means test restricted eligibility. And informed observers noted the pressures throughout Australasia to expand the pension rolls and increase the weekly amounts. More troublesome still was the fear that a noncontributory system of state guaranteed security would discourage independence and thrift. Universal pensions seemed far beyond the reach of state revenues, but anything less would only encourage workers to waste their assets so as to make themselves eligible for state support.

If New Zealand failed to provide Americans with an acceptable pension model, the colony did provide California with a crucial element of its workmen's compensation system. By the close of the nineteenth century the traditional rules of employer liability had come under serious attack on the Continent as well as throughout the English-speaking world. Under challenge were three principles: that an injured worker could be compensated only if it could be shown that the employer was directly and personally responsible; that in accepting employment, workers also accepted the risks inherent in the job; and that the employer was not responsible for injuries caused by one's coworkers. Taken together, these principles made it virtually impossible for workers to be compensated for injuries. The rise of large firms and corporate ownership tipped the scales even further against employees.[15]

Nevertheless, the number of damage suits multiplied and, in especially heartrending cases, some courts began awarding compensation. The result was legal chaos. Employers no longer knew what their liability was, what the outcome of a particular suit might be, or how to protect themselves against claims. And even when workers did receive damages, lawyers and other middlemen commonly took most of the award in fees. Clearly there had to be a predictable, efficient, and inexpensive way of dealing with industrial injuries.[16]

In 1906 Congress followed the lead of Germany and Great Britain by establishing entirely new principles and beginning with New York in 1910 the states began to fall into line. The new statutes simply abandoned the old concept of liability. Except in exceptional circumstances, such as gross misconduct, an injured worker now had an absolute right to compensation, but benefits were fixed and an administrative agency replaced judges and juries. The new system had obvious merits. Deserving workers received limited but certain recompense for their injuries and, except for administrative costs, retained all of the money awarded; employers now knew that they were absolutely liable for all work-related injuries, whatever the cause, but they also knew that their liability was limited to the scale of benefits prescribed and that they had no need to hire expensive lawyers to defend themselves from claims.[17]

These principles left unresolved the question of how to guarantee compensation. Most states required employers to either establish a fund to cover potential claims or to buy liability insurance. Some states simply let employers choose between private underwriters; others created a state insurance monopoly; and still others created a state insurance fund to compete with private carriers.[18] California chose the third method by adopting the New Zealand model.

The way that this came about says something important about the Progressive movement and the antipodean linkages. In 1911 the California legislature adopted the new liability principles, voters endorsed the concept in a constitutional referendum, and the governor appointed a board of commissioners to implement the law. However, A. J. Pillsbury, the commission chairman, considered the law defective. He and his colleagues spent the next two years designing a better system. Functioning more as a commission of inquiry than as an administrative agency, the board gathered official reports and private studies, interviewed experts, traveled to the East Coast to consult, and carried on an extensive correspondence. Members were particularly troubled by the weaknesses they perceived in the insurance industry, which then had little experience in underwriting industrial accidents. They also feared that the large, well-established companies would conspire to charge uniform high rates and that the prospect of huge profits would attract "wildcat, fly-by-night, cut-rate concerns."[19]

Their investigation revealed that New Zealand had developed a system to avoid these hazards. When that colony adopted the new compensation principles in 1900, the Government Life Insurance Office, which had been competing for business with private underwriters for three decades, opened an accident branch. Pillsbury and his colleagues examined the colony's ten years of experience of underwriting employers' risks and they concluded that a similar program in California would provide employers and workers alike with the highest performance standards in the new field of accident insurance. Employers would benefit from reasonable premium rates because private firms would have to compete with a state office operating essentially as a mutual company, and injured workers, whether covered by a private or a state policy, would benefit from the example of an efficient and impartial handling of claims by the state office. "We borrowed the idea from New Zealand," Pillsbury reported, "but we dressed it in garments better suited to the industrial and political situation in California. . . ."[20]

The "New Zealandization" of the California workmen's compensation system is a dramatic example of the power of an appointed commission. Pillsbury and his colleagues had no mandate, legislative or popular, for their actions. Their instructions were both clear and simple—implement the 1911 law. They chose not to. Instead, they constituted themselves as an investigative body with powers to recommend. Because the legislature met only every second year, they had time to seize the initiative and to arm themselves with expert knowledge. By the time the legislature reconvened in 1913, they knew exactly what they wanted, and they knew more about employer liability systems than did anyone else in Sacramento. When they proposed the adoption of the New Zealand approach, they dealt from a deck stacked in their favor. Despite the determined power of the insurance industry's opposition, the Pillsbury commission had an irresistible combination of facts, arguments, and evaluations with which to win over legislators to their views.

New Zealand solutions to rural problems also influenced California legislators, though the borrowing process was selective and took almost three decades. When they took office in 1891 the antipodean Liberals made land reform a central feature of their program. As it took shape their program had three goals: opening land to small farmers, reducing the cost of rural credit, and creating work for the jobless. The Liberals discouraged both large estates and absentee ownership by tax policies and they intervened even more directly by acquiring properties, sometimes by compulsory repurchase, for subdivision and lease on attractive terms to small farmers. The government then supported these and other settlers with cheap developmental loans and educational services, and through a village settlement program it moved unemployed workers to rural areas, where they could supplement their farm income by seasonal labor.

The New Zealand program quickly attracted attention in Australia, where some states adopted the village settlements concept, and in the United States, where in the West, especially, reformers argued that land monopoly inhibited both settlement and democracy. California, it was reported, would be "much further advanced in population and general development" if the state had broken up "the great Mexican grants among actual settlers." The United States had a choice. "It must either . . . lend itself to the purposes of the monopolist . . . or it must give itself unreservedly to the interests of the people, to their social well-being and elevation, and to their political emancipation. . . ."[21]

Ely, Lloyd, Lusk, and Parsons, among others, all linked closer settlement with democracy and progress. That same linkage seems to have pervaded the "many hundreds of letters" received by the U.S. consul in New Zealand "from all classes of citizens—doctors, lawyers, legislators, would-be immigrants, farmers, and nearly all kinds of social reformers."[22] And William Smythe, as we have seen, made antipodean ideas a central feature of his campaign to "New Zealandize the West," though it should be noted that he made land taxation no part of his program to bring about closer settlement.

Though these ideas made some headway in reform circles, Smythe quickly encountered resistance from those suspicious of state efforts to help "timid fledglings" take up land even when they were so ignorant of farming that they required "instruction on digging fence posts or planting potatoes." Sturdy, self-reliant men were needed for farm making, declared the *Los Angeles Times.* Australasians should not be surprised when outsiders treated their village settlement schemes as a joke.[23]

And so New Zealand ideas languished until the election of Hiram Johnson as governor in 1911. Though Johnson came to office with little knowledge of or interest in agricultural problems, his advisers gradually convinced him to balance his urban concerns with rural ones. In 1912 Simon Lubin, an affluent Sacramento reformer, persuaded Johnson to appoint a committee to investigate farm conditions, particularly the plight of migratory and other agricultural workers; the next year he appointed Lubin's uncle, Harris Weinstock, to the American Commission on Credit and Cooperation, which was instrumental in the creation of the Federal Farm Loan Board in 1916; and in 1915 he appointed Weinstock, Chester Rowell, and David Barrows to a study committee that recommended the creation of a State Colonization and Rural Credits Commission. This was the forerunner of what became in 1917 the State Land Settlement Board. Significantly, it was headed by Elwood Mead, an irrigation expert and professor at the University of California who had recently returned from eight years in Victoria, Australia, where he had been chairman of the State Rivers and Water Supply Commission.[24]

As in Australasia, the California Land Settlement Board had a mandate to deal with land monopoly by bringing about closer settlement. It adopted essentially the same strategies. The state purchased large estates, subdivided and improved the properties, and then resold it to farmers on generous credit terms. The board also sold bonds so that it could lend money for housing, livestock, and implements, it supplied the new communities with agricultural experts, and it promoted the formation of agricultural cooperatives. Participants in the scheme, said Mead in 1920, "ought to have the same economic independence and the same reason for confidence that they can become land owners that was felt by farm laborers of the past when he could go west and homestead 160 acres or that is felt in Australia and New Zealand under their generous land settlement laws."[25]

Neither in California nor elsewhere in the United States did rural reform programs include the use of taxation to discourage absentee and monopoly land holdings. This is not to say that Americans ignored this feature of antipodean liberalism. On the contrary, they took a lively interest in this as well as other aspects of the tax question, but they differed widely on the meaning and utility of Australasian models.

Many commentators, such as Lloyd and Parsons, saw the New Zealand system of graduated taxes on incomes as well as land as evidence of the antipodean determination to prevent extremes of wealth and poverty. They hailed the colony as a country with neither millionaires nor tramps. However, it did not necessarily follow from their endorsement that they believed the United States could, or should, seek economic democracy through the same means. Others, such as the heirs to the La Follette insurgency in Wisconsin, emphasized the goals of fairness and efficiency. They believed the income tax to be more equitable than the personal property tax, especially in making business corporations bear their fair share of the revenue burden. Still others were attracted by the Australasian practice of giving local communities the authority to devise their own systems of taxation. This appealed to advocates of "grass-roots democracy," especially to those advocating home rule privileges in municipal charters and to single taxers.[26]

Quite without justification, single-taxers found Australasian tax policies particularly attractive. Although land taxes contributed only a tiny fraction of colonial revenues, the system of levying only on the unimproved value of real estate seemed to embody Henry George's central principle and was therefore seen as the harbinger of the spread, worldwide, of the single-tax concept. Three elements combined to reinforce that interpretation. First, New Zealand had enacted the unimproved land value tax principle in 1879, before George had published his *Progress and Poverty*, which suggested to his disciples a universality of understanding of modern problems. In fact, the idea came to New Zealand primarily from John Stuart Mill.[27] Second, in common with many other early observers of colonial liberalism, American single-taxers linked colonial prosperity to colonial reform, in their case the taxation of unimproved land values.[28] While that policy may have stimulated capital investment, better times in the Antipodes as in America rested much more fundamentally on the international improvement in the terms of trade for agricultural exports. Third, and much more credibly, colonial legislatures gave local taxing authorities a choice between levying on improved or unimproved land values. On both sides of the Tasman, as single-tax publications so avidly reported, the trend was toward relieving capital development from taxation. However, while this encouraged American single-taxers to believe that the system would soon be adopted universally, in the colonies pragmatism rather than ideology prevailed. To be sure, Henry George attracted a large following among settlers, but there was never a time that excise, customs, and other sources of revenue would be abandoned in favor of a tax on land alone.[29]

Still, American interest was such that the Colorado legislature sent three senators to Australasia in 1899 to investigate and report. When they returned they praised colonial tax policies, expressed their hope that "the people of Colorado and other States will take advantage of the experience of the nations of the antipodes [by remedying] the evils of their revenue laws," and recommended the adoption of three constitutional changes: empowering the legislature to abolish personal property taxes, including those on business firms; instituting a state-wide tax on land values; and adopting home rule taxing powers based on "the Australasian system for local needs." Colorado voters rejected these propositions by margins of more than two to one in a constitutional referendum in November 1902.[30]

The idea of empowering citizens to decide how real estate was to be assessed for revenue purposes also appealed to American proponents of "direct democracy," many of whom were not single-taxers. They saw the antipodean tax referendum system quite differently—as an important first step toward giving voters greater control over all aspects of public policy. For the same reason they applauded the periodic referenda held in New Zealand on the liquor trade. Beginning in the early 1880s, each general election for members of parliament gave taxpayers an opportunity to express their preferences, choosing between maintaining the number of existing licenses to sell alcoholic beverages in the electorate, reducing the number of licenses, or abolishing licenses altogether. With the enfranchisement of women in 1893 and the expansion of the referendum to include all voters, not just taxpayers, many electorates, especially suburban ones in the larger cities, voted themselves dry and for a time it appeared as if national prohibition would eventually prevail. Even though that did not happen (the terms and requirements of the referendum favored the liquor industry and public opinion in any event gradually turned against prohibition), for a time the New Zealand example acted as a powerful incentive to American advocates for both direct democracy and temperance.[31]

Those movements, in turn, were also linked to the worldwide effort to extend the vote to women. Both the attainment of voting equality with antipodean men and with it the prospect of abolishing "demon rum" in the colony attracted the enthusiastic attention of American reformers. They touted the New Zealand example as positive proof that their goals were within grasp, took added inspiration from the extension of the franchise to Australian women, and urged New Zealand leaders to write about their experiences and to attend international meetings as ways to encourage women from around the world to campaign even harder for the suffrage and allied causes.[32]

Much of what was said and written about the antipodean experience fell into two categories. In the first, the approach was overwhelmingly defensive and documented the argument that enfranchising colonial women had not brought the catastrophic consequences so confidently predicted by its opponents. No, family life had not been destroyed; no, women had not voted as their husbands or brothers directed; no, women had continued to nurture their children, provide moral environments for their families, and comfort and support their husbands; no, women had not become masculine; and no, giving women the vote had produced no vast upheaval in antipodean political life and institutions. On the contrary, family life continued, women voted independently on the issues and the moral qualities of the candidates, femininity remained intact, and evolution rather than revolution best described the pace and character of legislative reform.[33]

The second line of argument was positive rather than defensive and applauded the accomplishments directly attributable to bringing women into the political system. Three themes predominated. The first dealt with the enactment of legislation on behalf of children, which was seen as the special political sphere of mothers. In addition to educational reforms, it included laws abolishing child labor and requiring that learners be paid, raising the age of sexual consent, establishing juvenile courts, and even suppressing juvenile smoking. The second dealt with legislative changes in the status of women in general and of wives in particular and included the abolition of the Contagious Diseases Act, the compensation of slandered women without their having to prove special damage, the opening of the legal profession to women, reform of the divorce laws to give wives parity with husbands both in causes for action and in property settlements, and a law requiring a male testator to make suitable provision for his wife and family. The third theme stressed the broader contributions of women to the antipodean reform movement by pointing to their efforts on behalf of the establishment of pensions for the aged, asylums for alcoholics, and compensation for injured workers, improvements in the industrial code, and the prohibition of the opium trade. As Katherine W. Sheppard, a leading figure in the New Zealand W.C.T.U. and president of the New Zealand Council of Women, put it in 1908, "Let it suffice now to say that never in the history of our Colony has there been so much attention given to legislation of an humanitarian character as since women possessed the Suffrage."[34]

American reformers echoed her message. "For the results of conferring the ballot upon working women," Jane Addams declared in 1908, "we can now look . . . to Australia and New Zealand, where the legislation in which women have borne their share is beginning to attract the attention of thoughtful men and women in all civilized lands." She did not find it "strange that the legislation of those countries on matters involving the care of infant life, the wages and hours of women factory workers, the limitation of the work of children, and juvenile-court legislation, is in many respects in advance of anything we in America can yet boast." Her explanation was simple: reform came more easily where women had the vote and representation. "Our sponsors," she noted somewhat ruefully, "rarely penetrate further than some outside lobby."[35] In fact, American women were not as powerless to promote change as Addams argued or as her own career so eloquently demonstrated. But not having the vote certainly complicated the task in the United States and helps to explain why American reformers turned so readily to the successes of foreign women to make their arguments.

Such was the case with Jane Addams's Hull House colleague, Julia C. Lathrop, who in 1912 became chief of the newly created Children's Bureau in the U.S. Department of Labor. She brought to her position a degree from Vassar (1880), nine years of experience in Rockford business, twenty years of social work at Hull House, including eleven years of distinguished service as a member of the Illinois Board of Charities, and practical training in the political arts in the struggle to establish a juvenile court in Chicago and a probation law in Illinois.[36] At the bureau Lathrop immediately set about organizing what she called a summer "Baby-Saving Campaign" designed to reduce the incidence of infant mortality in 109 American cities and towns. In 1914 she had a member of her staff, Etta R. Goodwin, prepare a report on the "New Zealand Society for the Health of Women and Children: An Example of Methods of Baby-Saving Work in Small Towns and Rural Districts."[37]

The pamphlet summarized the principles and programs of the organization, popularly known as the Plunket Society, which had been set up by Dr. Truby King in 1907 to improve public health, primarily by educating mothers in sound methods of child care and domestic hygiene. Although the New Zealand infant mortality rate was already one of the lowest in the world, King believed that it was still too high and that "a generally diffused knowledge . . . of infant requirements and maternal duties would . . . increase the strength and vitality of the rising generation." Between 1907 and 1912 the colonial infant mortality rate dropped from 8.9 to 5.1 percent, meaning that a baby born in New Zealand was more than twice as likely to survive as one born in New York City.[38]

These results had been achieved through a combination of voluntary and state programs. Local Plunket committees set up health clinics staffed by visiting nurses trained in infant and maternal care, distributed education literature to expectant mothers, and placed syndicated health columns in daily and weekly newspapers. The government supported these efforts in a variety of ways: by registering births and certifying nurses and midwives, by operating maternity and infant hospitals, by distributing free pamphlets on baby care, and by subsidizing the Plunket Society.[39]

Although obviously impressed by these antipodean achievements, Julia Lathrop shrewdly refrained from urging the "exact reproduction of the New Zealand organization" in the United States. Rather she saw the Plunket Society report as a stimulus "in working out whatever methods are practicable locally for securing the same results. . . ." Nevertheless, she soon became convinced by the success of programs in both Australasia and Great Britain that local efforts for the "protection of maternity and infancy" needed state and federal funding to be effective. It took money to set up, staff, and maintain child-care clinics, publicize the services offered, and conduct educational campaigns. Julia Lathrop realized that goal in the Sheppard-Towner Act of 1921, the year she retired from the Children's Bureau.[40]

At first glance it may seem curious that Americans should also have paid some attention to colonial antitrust policy. After all, by United States standards, New Zealand faced no comparable problems. Nevertheless, those Progressives most troubled by the concentration of business power took comfort in both antipodean rhetoric and policy. They found colonial denunciations of monopoly especially congenial. Though mostly directed at large estates, these attacks also spoke to the larger questions of economic democracy. "The great curse of New Zealand," a politician declared in 1891, "is the variety of its monopolies," and John Ballance argued that "it is for the people to say whether the land . . . shall be widely distributed, or whether it shall be held by a privileged number." He cared little "for the mere capitalist. I care not if dozens of large landowners leave the country. For the prosperity of the colony does not depend on this class." In short, the Liberals believed that "the rights of the people—which with us is the Government"—had to take precedence over the interests of private business.[41]

New Zealand's policies also appealed to American reformers both for their simplicity and for their effectiveness. Reduced to the essentials, the Liberals combined two approaches: in the case of a flour-milling syndicate, the government threatened to reduce the protective tariff unless prices came down; and in insurance and coal, the government set up its own enterprises to compete with private firms. "There are no Trusts in New Zealand," the *New York Times* reported. "If a corporation shows signs of becoming too rich and powerful, or if it becomes too greedy, the Government steps in and either by reducing duties or by establishing an opposition State concern, selling the same goods at low prices, destroys the Trust."[42]

Not all American reformers applauded, however. Though he had noted the absence of "trusts, Standard Oils, and 'Systems' " in his 1906 report and had even declared that there "never can be in New Zealand any Coal Trust nor any manipulation of the coal market, nor any coal shortage to rig stocks, nor robber prices for coal, because the government owns and operates great coal-mines for the Common Good," by 1911 Charles Edward Russell saw such state enterprises as ineffectual shams. The state coal mines produced too little to drive down prices; the government built too few rental homes to break the housing market; and the state fire insurance office operated "a little," but "not enough to offend the capitalists."[43]

Russell's was very much a minority view and reflected his hostility to state socialism. Many other observers favored public ownership as a matter of principle, not necessarily as an antitrust technique but because they believed that all natural monopolies should be owned and operated for the public benefit. And so they saw state enterprises in the Antipodes as endorsement of policies they hoped to see adopted in the United States. Thus post office savings banks appealed to some reformers, primarily those concerned with the needs of people in small towns and rural communities.[44] Others noted the construction of state rental houses with approval, but must have realized that the American need was to replace slum tenements with cheap, sanitary, safe apartments. The models for that approach came from Europe rather than Australasia.[45] American insurance reformers approached underwriting differently as well, concentrating primarily on state regulation rather than state competition in the fire and life fields, though the New Zealand system had some influence in workmen's compensation, as we have seen, and may have had some influence on the development of state life insurance programs in Wisconsin and elsewhere.[46] Commentators also praised the operation of the state trustee office in New Zealand, observing as Russell did that "there is to be in New Zealand no looting of estates through incompetent or dishonest trustees, no inheritances wasted by bad investments; but every man can feel that when he dies, his accumulations, great or small, will be perfectly secured for his family."[47]

Of much greater interest to Progressives than these manifestations of state intervention was the broad question of public ownership and operation of both the transportation system and most types of utilities—electricity, telegraph, and telephone. Several considerations most impressed them about state ownership in Australasia. First, they saw it as a vehicle for national progress and prosperity. "Carefully, conscientiously considering the question of national progress from its social and moral bearings, as well as financial," said the Rev. J. M. Peebles in 1903, "I am thoroughly convinced that the interests of communities would be infinitely better conserved by Government ownership . . . than through private ownership—an ownership often so intensely, madly selfish and over-reaching as to be actuated by no higher principle than might makes right. New Zealand prosperity 'commends' itself . . . to the intelligent classes of every clime and country." Similarly, the editor of the *Independent* predicted three years later that "One of these days the National Government will own the railroads and telegraphs and telephones and other public utilities, as the little colony of New Zealand is setting us the fullest example."[48]

Second, along with Lloyd many reformers applauded what he called the "ideal of democracy," which he saw as the operation of railways "for service, not for profit." The New Zealand strategy was simple: once operating and interest costs had been recovered, "we reduce charges as rapidly as profits increase," an official reported. Moreover, the colonies used new construction to open land to small farmers rather than to enhance the wealth of large estate holders; in times of drought or other emergencies they reduced freight rates to help graziers shift livestock to other areas or to bring in fodder and even water; and railroads carried children to and from school free of charge.[49]

Third, reformers drew scathing comparisons between Australasian and American railroads. They emphasized the quality of service in the colonies, the low rates for both freight and passenger service, and particularly the absence of abusive discrimination, secret rebates, profiteering, and corruption. "The true friends of our great Republic," declared Benjamin Flower in 1903, "feel humiliated at the spectacle of the United States . . . remaining a prey to predatory bands who are acquiring annually millions upon millions of dollars that rightfully belong to society or the nation at large." By contrast, "New Zealand is awakening the admiration of intelligent patriotism and lovers of free government. . . ." As he saw it two years later, "The question that our people must settle . . . is . . . whether the railways shall own the government and make it more and more an instrument for the enrichment of privileged classes and giant corporations. . . . New Zealand points the way." Paul Kennaday agreed. "The lesson for us," he wrote in 1910, was that New Zealand railways were "a permanent productive asset." The "corrupting hand of the railway magnate" had disappeared.[50]

American advocates of public ownership did not rely exclusively or even overwhelmingly on Australasian experience to make their case. They probably drew even more heavily on European models, partly because the history there was longer and the evidence richer. Nor, of course, did they make much headway in reaching their goals, at least in the short term. The strength of the organized opposition aside (and that was the main difficulty), they failed to make many converts either in American legislatures or in the public at large. Notwithstanding the vastness of the literature they produced, the reach of their organizational network, or the vigor of their systematic advocacy of public ownership from classroom, press, and pulpit, one senses even if one cannot prove that reformers mainly preached to believers. Nevertheless, their interest in antipodean practices provided them with powerful reinforcement to their commitment to change.

Much the same can be said of the admiration many commentators—whether academics or journalists—expressed for various aspects of Australasian labor policy. As with the public ownership question, there too was confirmation of the emergence of colonial societies with advanced ideas about human needs and relationships. They found antipodean solutions to unemployment both innovative and effective without necessarily arguing that they were transferable to the United States;[51] they applauded colonial construction cooperatives on road and rail projects, seeing them as attractive alternatives to the American gang-labor system and as important first steps toward labor autonomy and brotherhood;[52] they took a keen interest in antipodean shopping laws because they limited retail hours, gave clerks a half day each week for their own use, and allowed female assistants to sit when not waiting on customers;[53] and they endorsed laws requiring that all wages be paid in cash, thereby liberating workers from exploitation at the company store.[54] In addition, as the next two chapters will argue, Australasian models shaped the American debate over the working conditions for women and the resolution of industrial disputes. In effect, the Antipodes provided Americans with some of the most important elements in their reform agenda.

5 *Maximum Hours, Minimum Wages*

Australasia had a direct and tangible influence on several aspects of the American effort to legislate improved working conditions. American reformers had a long list of demands. Stated generally, they wanted the work place to be safe and healthy, they wanted to restrict the length of the working day, and they wanted to raise wage rates to levels closer to the value added by workers. Trade unionists shared these goals, but in most instances they sought to achieve them through collective bargaining rather than through legislation. However, on some issues, reformers and trade unionists joined forces. These goals—factory and mine legislation, the abolition of child labor, and the regulation of female labor—were ones in which Australia and New Zealand were either legislative pioneers or more advanced than most other countries. The Antipodes provided Americans with both legislative models and demonstrable accomplishments. Along with several European countries, they also provided evidence on which to build a police-power rationale supporting the constitutionality of state regulation. Foreign models were important in the effort to regulate female labor but of marginal significance in the regulation of general working conditions and the abolition of child labor. There are several reasons why this should have been the case.

The Antipodes had relatively little to teach Americans about the problems of industrialization. After all, manufacturing was much further advanced in both scale and technology in the United States than in Australia and by American standards barely existed in New Zealand. If guidance were needed on problems of industrial health and safety, Americans could learn far more from Europe, where conditions were more comparable and where scientific and statistical research had been carried out for generations. New Zealanders may have been appalled by what they saw as sweatshops in the Dunedin garment industry, but

Chicagoans or New Yorkers would have found colonial working conditions far superior to what they knew at home.[1]

Moreover, Australasians drew their ideas from the same reform currents as did Americans, currents that had been coursing through the modernizing Western world for more than two generations. The concept of factory and mine regulation was as old as Benthamite England and had crossed the Atlantic in the antebellum decades and had been taken to the Antipodes with the colonists. So too had the principle of the eight-hour day. In time, reform goals in America no less than in Australasia had become more comprehensive, drawing on scientific as well as humanitarian principles. Thus the establishment of minimum standards of ventilation, lighting, sanitation, and safety, together with their enforcement by state inspectors, became concerns shared by trade unionists and reformers alike as the relationship between working conditions and public health became better understood and the combination of technology and rising national wealth made improvement both feasible and affordable. There was no reason for Americans to look to the Antipodes for new approaches to old and well-understood problems.

Nevertheless, New Zealand in particular and New South Wales and Victoria to a lesser extent provided American reformers, labor leaders, legislators, and industrial commissioners with what might be called, if the word is not too extravagant, inspiration. The Antipodes were widely touted as utopias and there is ample testimony—from Edward Tregear, United States consuls, and various government agencies—that Americans had an insatiable appetite for information about Australasian labor legislation. The underlying assumption was that there was a direct correlation between the industrial codes of Australia and New Zealand and living conditions, which were more pleasant and harmonious than those in either Europe or America.[2]

Judging by the sheer volume of words written about the labor laws of Australia and New Zealand, one can almost visualize Americans groaning under an avalanche of information. For example, the United States Bureau of Labor and some of the state labor bureaus devoted more space to antipodean laws in the Progressive period than to the laws of any other foreign country. Indeed, of the thousands of pages published, perhaps as many as a third and certainly a quarter dealt with Australasian legislation. Generally, these bulletins published the statutes with little or no commentary. However, these sources of information were supplemented by lengthy analyses by such federal and state investigators as Victor S. Clark and Harris Weinstock; by consular reports, which apparently circulated widely; by published legal briefs on labor cases; and by articles, books, reviews, and speeches by literally dozens of scholars, journalists, and reformers, ranging from John R. Commons to Frank A. Parsons.

The impact of this flood of words, whether direct or indirect, cannot be measured, but there were clearly three crucial messages: that industrial conditions could be significantly ameliorated through legislative intervention; that success required effective enforcement; and that such reforms promoted rather than inhibited national progress and prosperity.

Not that these concepts came as a revelation to Americans. The practical among them knew just as clearly as did William Pember Reeves or Edward Tregear that there could be a world of difference between the appearance and the substance of reform. Legislative loopholes and weak enforcement were universal complaints.[3] But what the Australasian labor codes seemed to demonstrate was that the combination of comprehensiveness in regulating every aspect of the work place and effectiveness in policing the code were feasible in a well-governed society; that the combination could be achieved without wrecking an economy; and that they explained (at least to those disposed to so believe) the superior quality of antipodean life.

Rather similar considerations apply to the struggle to abolish child labor. Americans had little need to look to the Antipodes for guidance on this question. Although New Zealand and some of the Australian states had laws and enforcement programs much in advance of what American legislatures had created, American concern with the employment of children dated back to the antebellum period. Reformers could thus draw on an indigenous tradition and it was generally, though by no means universally, conceded that the state had a legitimate interest in child welfare.[4]

Moreover, this was an issue on which Progressives, some employers, and labor leaders could agree. Ideally, regulation should reflect changes in public attitudes toward children. In contrast to earlier times, by the late nineteenth century, people had come to place a much higher value on the lives of children. Or at least the middle class could better afford to be humanitarian and was more inclined to impose its values on the lower orders, who could least afford the luxury of restricting child labor. Regulation should also reflect changes in economic conditions, particularly the new industrial system, which had greatly exacerbated the exploitation of children. Moreover, some employers, especially the largest and most efficient corporations, saw the abolition of child labor as a way of eliminating what they considered to be unfair competition. It was often the case in some industries that the leading firms employed only adults, provided superior working conditions, and paid higher than average wages. A prohibition on the employment of children, these firms believed, would make labor costs more equal.[5]

For very different reasons, therefore, Progressives, unionists, and some employers sought to raise the minimum age of employment, to lower the maximum hours that children could work, to abolish night and hazardous work for children, and to extend these regulations to as many types of employment as possible. By 1917, most states had adoped some or all of this program and Congress had excluded the products of child labor from interstate commerce. However, the Supreme Court struck down the congressional ban in 1918.[6] Despite this setback as well as the considerable lack of uniformity from state to state, the accomplishments were substantial. Progressives could take satisfaction from having muted "the bitter cry of the children," which had rung too insistently and painfully in their ears. Labor leaders, moved more by practical than humanitarian considerations, could take some satisfaction from having brought about a modest but salutory reduction in the labor supply. For as they well knew, the employment of children depressed adult wages, inflated the labor market, and increased unemployment. And employers, though not successful in abolishing child labor in interstate commerce until the New Deal, obtained some relief, especially in northern, midwestern, and western markets.

The struggle to protect female employees by limiting the length of the working day and week and by prohibiting the employment of women at night drew more directly from the antipodean experience. But even in this field Australia and New Zealand provided Americans with neither basic regulatory principles nor new ideas so much as with inspiration and demonstrated success. In part, that was because the Antipodean colonies provided legislative models generally too far ahead of American public opinion to be acceptable.

For example, the New Zealand Employment of Females Act of 1873 and its subsequent amendments specified working conditions such as American reformers could only dream of. The law imposed the eight-hour day, prohibited work after six o'clock in the evening, after two o'clock on Saturday afternoons and on Sundays, and required the installation of lunchrooms to make sure that workers had a rest period. Overtime was permitted but strict limits were set. Workers were entitled to a specified number of paid holidays. By 1894 the rules applied to all industrial establishments employing two or more workers.[7] To be sure, effective enforcement did not come until the nineties, but the basic concepts of the female labor code seemed utopian by American standards.

The case of Massachusetts, one of the most advanced of the states, provides an instructive comparison. In many ways it was far ahead of Australia and New Zealand. The serious struggle to regulate female labor came much earlier, in the 1840s, and Massachusetts was a pioneer state in the creation in 1869 of a Bureau of Labor Statistics, a major agency in providing a scientific basis for the industrial reform effort. After a full generation of agitation, the Bay State finally passed a ten-hour law for women in 1874. However, longer work days were authorized to allow one short day each week, and initially employers could be prosecuted only if they "willfully" violated the law. Not until 1890 did Massachusetts prohibit work after ten o'clock at night and not until 1907 was work prohibited after six o'clock in the evening. Even then, the law applied only to textile mills. A similar pattern can be seen in regulating the work week. Not until 1892 was the maximum reduced from sixty to fifty-eight hours, and not until 1908 was there a further reduction—to fifty-six hours.[8] That was still eight hours more than the New Zealand maximum.

Antipodean and American approaches to restricting the hours of employment in mercantile establishments were also quite different. In New Zealand, for example, the reform effort began as early as 1867, almost a generation before Americans became seriously involved with the question. Moreover, from the outset the New Zealand objective was not only to limit the working day and week but also to restrict the number of hours that an establishment could be open for business. The principles of "early closing" and half-holidays to offset the extra hours worked on the one evening a week stores could remain open were always central. The New Zealand goal was also to protect all female workers. In America, by contrast, the focus was only on restricting the number of hours that could be worked and initially only on protecting minors. And as in factory regulation, the American maximums were higher than the New Zealand ones (commonly sixty hours as compared to fifty-three and a half hours). The New Zealand approach was also more comprehensive, requiring rest and lunchrooms, setting minimum standards of light and ventilation, and even stipulating that assistants were to be provided with chairs. In Massachusetts, by contrast, the 1900 law covered only hours, and retail interests were sufficiently powerful initially to secure an exemption from regulation for their busiest season, the month of December.[9]

There are a number of reasons why American reform goals and accomplishments should have lagged. Some were practical, some were ideological, and some were constitutional. It may have been true, as Charles McCarthy asserted in 1904, that Wisconsin legislators were constantly discussing Australasian reforms,[10] but it is difficult to detect any direct borrowing from Antipodean labor codes. At most, it seems likely that American reformers were buoyed by Australian and New Zealand accomplishments. Perhaps they even saw them as targets worthy of emulation. But when it came to designing their own restrictions on the employment of women, the practical among them knew that they had to work within American political, economic, and constitutional contexts.

These contexts were very different from the ones faced by reformers in the Antipodes, especially New Zealand. At the practical level, economic competition between manufacturers operating in different states and hence under different labor codes was a crucial reform consideration. Any proposals that had the potential for making manufacturers in one state uncompetitive in regional or national markets were bound to be regarded with suspicion by employers and employees alike.

This problem was demonstrated most forcefully by the passage of the maximum-hour law for females in Massachusetts in 1874. By 1880 textile manufacturers were complaining that they had been made uncompetitive. A survey of the six New England states conducted by the Massachusetts Bureau of Labor Statistics disproved the claim. It demonstrated that Massachusetts mills were at least as productive as mills elsewhere in the region and that labor costs were fully competitive despite the shorter working week. Textile workers then used the report to secure ten-hour laws in most of the region. By 1887 all of the New England states except Vermont had enacted legislation protecting female workers, though in Connecticut, New Hampshire, and Rhode Island the laws were unenforceable, and in Maine there was no restriction on overtime. For the moment, at least, Massachusetts reformers were able to protect their hour law by producing the semblance of comparable reform throughout the region. Over the longer term, all of New England enacted real rather than paper standards, and there was no turning back. But by that time the complaints of Massachusetts textile manufacturers had come true. The lower and even nonexistent labor standards in the southern textile industry had made New England firms uncompetitive, and they had either to go out of business or relocate in the South.

Ideological considerations played no less a role both in slowing reform and in limiting objectives. Opposition came primarily from two groups, employers and labor leaders. Many businessmen and conservatives fiercely fought state regulation on economic and philosophical grounds, seeing in the trend the ultimate demise of the free marketplace. In their view, the state should leave enterprise totally free to pursue its own self-interest. Likewise, workers should be left in total freedom to accept or reject the offered conditions of employment as they deemed in their best interest. In this way the best interests of society at large would be best served. Adam Smith and laissez faire were the best guides to individual as well as legislative conduct.[11]

Many labor leaders were equally troubled by the demand for state regulation of working hours, though not always for the same ideological reasons. The most radical of them believed that such reforms would only perpetuate capitalism and hence wanted no part of state paternalism; the more conservative would have agreed with Samuel Gompers, the president of the American Federation of Labor, who saw regulation as "another step to force working men to work at the behest of their employers, or at the behest of the state, which will be the equivalent to . . . slavery." Gompers, of course, spoke primarily for craft workers, the so-called aristocrats of the labor movement. Rightly or wrongly, they believed that their special skills gave them leverage in the labor market and that they could achieve more and more quickly through collective bargaining than through state regulation.[12]

In any event, though this spectrum of attitudes was certainly known in Australia and New Zealand, extremes of either the right or the left were generally outside the mainstream of antipodean thought. At most, they slowed rather than prevented reform, though in time they provided the ideological basis for criticism of state socialism.[13] In the United States, by contrast, these attitudes proved more powerful and durable. Reformers faced stronger constraints than did legislators elsewhere.

More important in the short run were the constraints imposed by the Constitution of the United States. Some state courts, interpreting the "taking" clause of the Fourteenth Amendment, which declared that no state shall "deprive any person of life, liberty, or property, without due process of law," soon began to declare the regulation of working hours unconstitutional on the ground that it deprived employees of the freedom to contract. In this way judges "protected" women against legislative interference.[14]

The first such ruling came in the *Ritchie* case in Illinois in 1895. Florence Kelley, the state's chief factory inspector and the prime mover behind the struggle to abolish sweated labor, exploded in anger when she learned of the court's decision. She believed that such judicial activism—what Justice Oliver Wendell Holmes was later to denounce as the incorporation of Herbert Spencer's *Social Statics* into the Constitution—imperiled the very survival of constitutional government. She realized better than her associates that it was imperative to devise ways to persuade judges to adjust their thinking to modern social and economic conditions.[15]

As a practical matter, the *Ritchie* decision placed all hour laws under a constitutional cloud and the question remained unsettled until 1908. In the meantime, eight new states began to regulate female labor, and Congress and some legislatures even began regulating male labor as well. Even so, the question could hardly have been more confusing. The Massachusetts Supreme Court had upheld the validity of the state's hour law in 1876; the Illinois court had reached just the opposite conclusion in 1895; and only three of the twelve laws then on the statute books were enforceable. Inevitably, many legislatures hesitated to enter so controversial a field of regulation; factory inspectors frequently hesitated about enforcing the laws for fear that the statutes would be tested in the courts; and judges marched in opposite directions, some following the Massachusetts court in upholding regulation, others following the Illinois precedent by declaring hour laws unconstitutional.[16]

The police powers of the state and the categories of occupation to which they applied were the central questions. Until these issues were settled, enforcement was either spasmodic or nonexistent. For example, the United States Supreme Court upheld a Utah mining statute in 1898 on the ground that the state had police powers to protect the health and safety of workers by restricting the number of hours that they could work underground. Despite that clear affirmation, in 1899 a Colorado court declared a similar law unconstitutional.[17]

In the meantime, many states and municipalities had imposed hour restrictions on public contractors, in effect establishing the eight-hour day for workers paid indirectly from tax dollars. The Supreme Court upheld such arrangements in the case of *Atkin v. Kansas* in 1903. However, the decision did nothing to clarify regulations applying to working hours not involving public funds.[18]

Nor was there much to be learned about the constitutionality of basic regulatory principles from the decisions reached in the transportation industry. Beginning in 1890, states had begun to limit the number of hours railroad men could work without having a rest period. Congress itself adopted the concept in 1907, requiring that trainmen have ten hours' rest after sixteen hours' work; dispatchers had to be rested after nine hours' work. Though the courts eventually sustained these regulations, the basis for the decisions came primarily from concern for the safety of the traveling public rather than from the idea that railroad workers should be protected from excessive hours. That is, the constitutional basis for regulating hours in any save exceptional occupations, especially where either workers or the public were at hazard, remained clouded.[19]

The crucial test came in 1905, when the Supreme Court, by a five to four decision, struck down a New York statute limiting employment in bakeries to ten hours a day and sixty hours a week. In effect, the majority in *Lochner v. New York* distinguished between miners and bakers, declaring that baking bread was not a hazardous occupation and that employers should be free to offer and workers to accept a working day and week as long or as short as was mutually agreeable.[20]

Two of the four dissenting justices saw the situation very differently. Justice John M. Harland argued that baking, like mining, was hazardous and that the police powers justified interference with the liberty of contract. Justice Holmes took an entirely different position. He believed that most Americans did not view the regulation as a deprivation of liberty. In his view, the economic theory grafted onto the Fourteenth Amendment by his colleagues ran counter to "the traditions of our people and our law." In short, laissez-faire was not enshrined in the Constitution.[21]

The *Lochner* decision confirmed what Florence Kelley had recognized in the *Ritchie* case almost a decade earlier—that eighteenth-century concepts of liberty could not satisfy contemporary social needs and that judges had to be educated to a modern awareness of the world of work. That task fell to Louis D. Brandeis, the Boston lawyer, and Josephine Goldmark, his sister-in-law and organizer of the National Consumers' League. They devised the so-called sociological brief to prove the constitutionality of the 1903 Oregon maximum-hour law by replacing the usual legal arguments with evidence on the impact of industrial life on women. The strategy succeeded. In 1908 the U.S. Supreme Court upheld the law in *Muller v. Oregon*, and the Russell Sage Foundation began underwriting additional research so that even more effective briefs could be circulated wherever they would do the most legislative and constitutional good.[22]

The *Muller* decision had a stunning impact on the hour-law movement. In the nine years before America's entry into the First World War, thirty-nine of the forty-eight states passed laws restricting the working hours of women. The list included twenty-one states that entered the field for the first time or that, in the case of Illinois and Wisconsin, enacted their first enforceable laws. Particularly noteworthy was the trend toward extending the regulations to more and more categories of workers, and a few states prohibited night work in designated occupations. While standards generally fell far short of what reformers had accomplished in Australia and New Zealand, the trend was nevertheless clear.[23]

Noteworthy, also, was the support given by organized labor. In California, for example, the state Federation of Labor was the principal force behind the reform effort. After a hard-fought struggle culminating in a stormy legislative session in 1911, labor leaders succeeded in getting a law much in advance of the American norm. Maximum hours were shorter and more occupations were regulated than in most other states.[24]

Labor's strategy was clear. It well knew that in California, as elsewhere, it would be difficult if not impossible to regulate the working hours of males. Even if the legislature could be persuaded to enact such a law, the *Lochner* decision in New York made it clear that the Supreme Court would countenance such regulations only in such demonstrably hazardous occupations as mining. What Californians did was to borrow the Massachusetts strategy. They knew that if they could restrict working hours for females, in many instances they would reduce working hours for males as well. That was the predictable result in all those establishments, such as factories, which could not remain open once the female employees had completed their eight-hour day.

The effort to abolish night work, a fundamental feature of the antipodean laws, was much less successful in the years from 1909 to 1917 and, even when accomplished in a handful of states, the standard set—no night work between ten o'clock in the evening and six o'clock in the morning—was much less restrictive than the Australasian codes.[25] The difficulty reformers had to overcome was primarily constitutional. The New York Court of Appeals had struck down a night-work law in 1907 on much the same grounds as set out in the *Lochner* decision two years earlier. States could not restrict the freedom to contract. But with the *Muller* decision as a clear indication that sex differences justified differential legislation, New York enacted a restrictive night-work law in 1913. Its constitutionality was sustained two years later. However, unlike the *Muller* decision, *People v. Charles Schweinler Press* did not release a flood of night-work laws. Indeed, not even a legislative trickle followed, suggesting that American legislatures had already reached the limits of politically feasible regulation.[26]

Although reformers had no way of knowing, as it turned out, the Brandeis technique, used so effectively in securing the regulation of work hours, proved to be of less benefit in securing minimum wages for women. Here the connection with antipodean principles and models was both powerful and direct, but in the long term it proved useless. That was not because many reformers found them flawed, although the labor movement rejected the concept with as much vigor as it had endorsed hour regulation. Rather it was because the sex-differences argument, which had worked so well in the hour cases, was thrown out of court as preposterous and absurd in the wage case.

The concept of legislating minimum wages for women was well established in Australasian and British practice by 1911 when the first American state, Massachusetts, gave serious consideration to the question. In New Zealand wage setting had begun as early as 1895 through the system of compulsory arbitration. This approach proved unattractive to most Americans. Nor were they much attracted to a second New Zealand approach, specifying wage rates by statute, though this was the concept adopted by Utah in 1913 and by a few other states later. The statutory idea was New Zealand's solution to abuses in the garment and millinery trades. Unscrupulous employers hired juveniles as learners who exchanged their labor for free training. After a year or so they were discharged and their places taken by other young people. The New Zealand law stipulated that juveniles had to be paid a specified minimum wage from the first day of employment and that apprentices had to be paid on a rising scale bringing them in their last year of training close to the wages earned by journeymen. The New Zealand correspondent of the *New York Times* commended this solution to sweated labor to the attention of American trade union organizations.[27]

Most American reformers rejected both of the New Zealand models in favor of the system devised in Victoria in 1896 and later copied by South Australia, Tasmania, Queensland, and Great Britain. Wages were set not by arbitrators or legislators but by administrative boards. So-called "living wages" were the goal and employers benefiting from tariff protection had to pass along some of the resulting profits to their workers in the form of higher wages. The system had the advantage of flexibility, it was especially beneficial to unorganized workers, and it did not deprive them of the right to strike for higher wages.[28]

It is difficult to say why it took American reformers so long to take up the question of minimum wages. After all, for more than a decade there had been a steady stream of information on and commentary about antipodean labor codes. Although some of these reports had been critical, especially on the compulsory arbitration question, the general tenor had been favorable and some of it enthusiastic. Nevertheless, one is struck by the fact that the concept was virtually ignored in the reform press until 1908.[29] Even then, the issue was virtually dormant for another three years, when it burst onto the reform scene as an idea whose time seemed suddenly to have arrived.

What appears to have happened, although this is purely inferential, is that the seeds of reform were slow to germinate. When they did, it was because important reform organizations took up the crusade. The seeds were undoubtedly planted by Lusk in *Our Foes at Homes* (1899), by Lloyd in *Newest England* and *Country without Strikes* (1900), by Reeves in *State Experiments* (1902), by Parsons in *The Story of New Zealand* (1904), and by Clark in "Labor Conditions in New Zealand" (1903), "Labor

Conditions in Australia" (1905), and *The Labour Movement in Australasia* (1906). The concept of minimum wages seems then to have passed into academic and official circles and from there into the mainstream of Progressive reform.

John A. Ryan, a professor of moral theology at St. Paul Seminary in Minnesota, was a crucial figure in the movement. In 1905 he published a long philosophical discussion of the "living wage" in the *Catholic University Bulletin.* The following year he published *A Living Wage: Its Ethical and Economic Aspects,* a popular account of the 1891 papal encyclical on labor. The volume was reissued in 1910 with an introduction by Richard T. Ely, and again in 1915. What Ryan did in these and other writings was to put the minimum-wage question on the plane of high morality and to stress the ethical idea that there were levels below which wages should not be allowed to fall. Though resting on religious rather than humanistic premises, it was essentially the Reeves position: "If industries cannot prosper without the sweating of women, children, and men, and without bringing in their train the evils of the Old World, well, we should do better to get on without them."[30]

Ryan's view, with its emphasis on a living wage, gradually took hold in official and reform circles. The *Massachusetts Labor Bulletin* explored the question in December 1906, partly through an extended quotation from Parsons's *Story of New Zealand,* and in 1908 J. Ramsay MacDonald, the British labor leader, published an extended analysis of "Arbitration Courts and Wages Boards in Australasia" in the *Contemporary Review,* a periodical with a substantial American readership. Significant, too, was an article by Alice Henry, the Australian reformer, in the *Outlook* in which she described how the Australian wage boards were requiring employers to pass along tariff benefits to their workers.[31]

If the decision actively to seek minimum wages for women and minors was slow in coming, 1910 was the decisive year. In January, Florence Kelley argued that wage boards could have averted the strike then raging in the garment industry. The Women's Trade Union League was now actively committed to reform. So, too, was the National Consumers' League, which proposed a ten-year campaign for minimum wages. The National Conference of Charities and Correction also took up the cause following an address by John A. Ryan to its annual meeting in St. Louis in May. Ryan apparently made converts both there and in the readership of the *Survey* following an extended article he published there in September.[32]

Three state legislatures, Massachusetts, Minnesota, and Wisconsin, responded to these modest pressures and took up the minimum-wage question in 1911. In Massachusetts, the State Federation of Labor led the effort; in Minnesota, Ryan drafted the proposed legislation; in Wisconsin, a Milwaukee Republican, Carl Stern, introduced the proposal at the instigation of the State Consumers' League. "The minimum wage board is doubtless the most striking invention in governmental forms which has come to us from the new commonwealths of the South Pacific since the Australian ballot," declared the *Survey* in February 1911.[33]

To some extent, the "living-wage" question in America became entangled with immigration restriction just as it had in Australasia. In both Australia and New Zealand, reformers tried to protect the higher standards of living and working conditions from the influx of what they considered "undesirables"—primarily Asians, but also Europeans who might become a charge on public and private welfare resources. For fifteen years, declared the *Independent* in 1911, "Australia has successfully administered a minimum wages law, and by means of it has prevented the sinking of white labor to the Chinese standard of living. . . . The experiment is . . . not visionary, not academic. It has been proven workable by practical people in a practical land."[34]

An American Progressive, Paul U. Kellogg, tackled this sensitive question in January 1911 with a proposal that there should be a minimum-wage law for immigrants. Until newcomers had resided in the United States for five years, he suggested, they could not be hired for less than a living wage, say $2.50 a day. Kellogg appreciated that Americans notions of freedom of contract made it difficult to accept wage boards, but he was confident that his proposal would both protect the wages of American workers as well as prevent the exploitation of immigrants.[35]

Kellogg's idea attracted the attention of Arthur N. Holcombe, an instructor at Harvard and chairman of the special committee on minimum wage boards of the National Consumers' League.

He thought that Kellogg had provided "a substantial basis for practical proposals" for protecting "an American standard of living." Not that Holcombe wanted to close America to immigrants. That, he argued, would not be justified "until we have tried and failed" to establish "a living wage to all those who are now here."[36]

Acutely aware that any minimum-wage laws would have to "run the gauntlet of the American courts," Holcombe nevertheless urged reformers to "study the dissents of yesterday in order to learn the law of tomorrow." With Justice Holmes, he believed that Spencer's *Social Statics* could be read out of as well as into the Fourteenth Amendment. The only way to find out what was "concealed in the bosoms of our judges" was to pass wage laws and then test them in the courts.

Holcombe was particularly optimistic about Wisconsin's approach to the constitutional issue. Based on the analogy of regulating the use of property "affected with a public interest," the law created an industrial commission with broad powers to investigate, ascertain, and classify oppressive occupations and to fix a living wage for each. "If the police power of the state can reasonably be construed to cover the protection of the community against the evil results of employment at starvation wages," he predicted, "the bill will withstand the process of judicial review."

But as the *Independent* accurately observed, the problem was not exclusively constitutional. "To a large proportion of American voters such legislation will seem socialistic or paternalistic. . . . The objectors will not be found exclusively in the ranks of the larger employers of labor. Conservatism in these matters is deeper and more obstinate in the minds of farmers, shopkeepers, grocers, butchers, bakers, schoolmasters, ministers, doctors and lawyers than it is among the great corporation directors." While that notion may once have been true, declared the *Independent*, it no longer described the American scene. The "ignorance of . . . small property owners of the actual industrial conditions in this and other countries seriously threatens to send America to the rear among progressive civilized nations." The editor believed that the "time has come when the civilized world must pay living wages, . . . even if we have to go without . . . costlier entrées in our after-theater champagne suppers."[37]

The Massachusetts solution to this political problem borrowed from the successful British strategy of appointing a commission to investigate and recommend. A distinguished panel representing all segments of opinion was selected. It included the president of Simmons College, Henry Lefavour; a woman with many years of service on the state board in charge of juvenile reformatories, Elizabeth Gower Evans; a leading attorney and a 1912 Democratic candidate for statewide office, George W. Anderson; a Boston wool merchant and later a Democratic congressman, Richard Olney; and the president of the United Textile Union, John Golden. Anderson, Evans, and Golden had close ties to Louis Brandeis.[38]

Their report, filed in January 1912, was based on a careful study of working conditions. The commissioners found that most women worked out of "dire necessity" rather than to add to their family's "comforts or luxuries." Although some firms paid good wages, many did not. This tended to push the general rate for women below a "living wage." The low-paying firms were either exploiters or parasites. Thus the commissioners took the Reeves view that the state should intervene "to prohibit uncivilized conditions [by setting] a certain sort of social and economic standard." Even if the minimum made a particular firm "less profitable, this must always be balanced against the general good." As the *Independent* noted: "In the political economy of today there is no more fundamental principle than that every industry must meet its own costs, including the cost of maintaining its labor force in unimpaired health and efficiency."[39]

The commissioners recommended a complex system for establishing minimum wages for women and minors. There was to be a minimum wage commission authorized to organize a wage board for any industry in which the wages of a substantial number of women were less than sufficient "to supply the necessary cost of living and to maintain the worker in health." Each board was to have at least eighteen members representing employers, employees, and the general public. It required a two-thirds majority of the board to establish the minimum wage rate, but the commission was not bound by the recommendation.[40]

The Massachusetts legislature accepted the general principle of minimum wages but created a weak, cumbersome system. The mandatory feature, by which employers would have been required under penalty of fine to pay at least the minimum rate, was dropped. Instead, firms that failed to pay the recommended scale were to be exposed in the press. Moreover, recommended wage rates were to reflect not only the cost of living but also the financial condition of the industry. The measure went through the lower house unopposed and through the upper with only one dissenting vote.[41]

For so controversial a measure, the legislative process was also swift. The great textile strike in Lawrence no doubt gave urgency to the wage measure. At issue in that confrontation—the most serious Massachusetts had yet seen—were wage cuts following the statutory reduction in the work week. The minimum-wage law was widely believed to be an effective method of preventing industrial conflict. As Elizabeth Evans noted, that had been the Australian experience. "Strikes occur in women's trades, and it is probable that . . . they will occur more frequently; and any measure . . . to correct abuses by peaceful means is to be welcomed."[42]

If Massachusetts had provided an imperfect model, it had nevertheless established a precedent other states were quick to follow. In the next year, 1913, eight other states enacted minimum-wage legislation. More important, five of them (California, Minnesota, Nebraska, Oregon, and Wisconsin) rejected the Massachusetts approach by stipulating that wage rates were to be based solely on the cost of living and by making the failure to pay the minimum rate or more a punishable offense. In addition, Ohio enacted a constitutional amendment authorizing the legislature to establish wage boards, although nothing was done during the Progressive period to implement the amendment; and in several other states, including Connecticut, Illinois, Indiana, Michigan, New York, and Pennsylvania, legislatures took minimum-wage laws under serious consideration.[43] All of this legislative activity was accompanied by a widening public debate of the issue. For a time it appeared as if minimum-wage laws would soon become the American norm.[44]

In New York, for example, Democratic Governor William Sultzer actively campaigned for reform. "We must now convince employers," he declared, "that any industry that saps the vitality and destroys the initiative of the workers is detrimental to the best interests of the State and menaces the general welfare of the Government." Sultzer's idea was that "Starvation and destitution caused by underpayment cannot be distinguished from starvation and destitution caused by war in draining the vitality of a people."[45] This emphasis on health for working women and on their ability to raise healthy children was crucial. It was the basis of the sex-difference argument that had been used so effectively in establishing the constitutionality of the laws regulating the working hours of women.

The reform was debated primarily in academic journals and in liberal magazines of relatively limited circulation. The scholarly publications included the *American Economic Review;* the *American Labor Legislation Review;* the *Annals* of the American Academy of Political and Social Science; the *Journal of Political Economy;* and the *Papers and Proceedings* of the Minnesota Academy of Sciences. Articles, editorials, reports, and summaries also appeared in a wide range of periodicals, some obscure, some better known. Included were the *American Review of Reviews; Atlantic Monthly;* the *Bulletin* of the City Club of Philadelphia; *Catholic World; Chautauquan;* the *Debater's Handbook; Forum; Hearst's Magazine; Life and Labor,* a magazine edited by Alice Henry, an Australian expatriate; *Literary Digest; Living Church; Nation; Outlook;* the *Proceedings* of the American Federation of Labor; a report by the Social Survey Committee of the Oregon Consumers' League; and *Survey.* Considering the paucity of discussion previously, this coverage reflected a remarkable upsurge in scholarly and popular interest.[46] Two themes stood out in the discussion: the extent to which foreign experience with minimum-wage regulation provided a useful guide to American reformers and the advantages and disadvantages of regulating wage rates.

The spectrum of reform protagonists also ranged widely from such well-known activist academics as Matthew B. Hammond and John A. Ryan to the British Fabian socialist Sidney B. Webb. All agreed that wage regulation should be adopted but disagreed about the meaning and significance of the foreign experience. For example, Mrs. Glendower Evans acknowledged the success of wage regulation in Australia and New Zealand. However, she did not think it possible to "argue from them to other countries." Henry Rogers Seager, an economics professor at Columbia University and president of the American Association for Labor Legislation, agreed with her that the antipodean systems had worked well, as did Hammond, but they were convinced that these laws were instructive for Americans. Established standards had not in fact become the maximum-wage levels, a matter of concern to American workers, and Victorian manufacturers had not suffered in interstate commerce, a matter of concern to American businessmen.[47]

Sidney Webb argued that the Victorian experience was conclusive. During the sixteen years that wage boards had been operating, wage and employment rates had risen significantly, while hours of employment had declined. Moreover, the legislature had reconsidered the experiment on five separate occasions and in each instance had voted to continue regulating wages. Webb also believed it significant that the system had been steadily expanded to cover more and more industries. Both employers and workers had requested these extensions. The result had been increased industrial productivity and a necessary step in Victoria as well as in Great Britain toward the prevention of national degradation.[48]

Perhaps the most persuasive advocate was Hammond. A professor at Ohio State University and a member of the Ohio Industrial Commission, he was probably the foremost American expert on wage laws, having visited Australasia to make a detailed investigation. His assessment was both realistic and judicious. Wage boards had virtually wiped out sweated labor in Victoria, though not at the cost of destroying the industries themselves. On the contrary, Hammond reported that manufacturing had probably expanded as rapidly in Victoria as in most countries. At the same time, industrial disputes had become rare in the regulated industries, in part because the debates in the wage boards had helped management and labor to understand each other's problems and needs. Nor did Hammond place much credence on the assertion that regulation would reduce all wages to the minimum level. He knew of no evidence to support this in Victoria, but reported that in New Zealand, where the Arbitration Court set wages, most workers (51 to 61 percent) received more than the minimum rates.

It was possible, Hammond supposed, that some workers would lose their jobs because they were not worth even the minimum wage. However, the number was so small that it ought not to be used as an argument to prevent reform. On the matter of productivity, Hammond found the evidence in Australia and New Zealand inconclusive. In some, but not all, industries, higher labor costs had stimulated investment in machinery and other laborsaving devices and this had increased output. Other employers commonly complained, and labor leaders heatedly denied, that workers had conspired to restrict production. Hammond rejected this allegation as irrelevant to the discussion of wage regulation. Such complaints were heard in countries that did not have wage boards. To the extent that there was any truth in them, the cause lay in the extension of trade unionism.

Finally, Hammond reported that Victorian employers and workers unanimously favored retention of the wage-board system. That both sides complained about the administration of the law, Hammond took to show that wage inspectors were both conscientious and fair. In Australia, the only issue at dispute in wage regulation concerned method rather than principle: workers favored and employers opposed replacing wage boards with a federal arbitration court. In short, Hammond provided a cautious, factual, and well-reasoned endorsement of the Victorian system. Though he acknowledged that similar results had been obtained in other Australian states and in New Zealand through compulsory arbitration, he rejected that model for the United States, believing the overwhelming majority of Americans to be fundamentally opposed to the New Zealand system.[49]

John Bates Clark, another leading economist and academic reformer, was similarly concerned with the consequences of minimum-wage laws rather than with the question of whether they should be enacted. That he took for granted. Unlike Hammond, he thought unemployment would result. This would require society to make appropriate adjustments. In Clark's view, such a price was a reasonable cost of reform.[50]

A very different analysis appeared in the *Living Church.* There it was argued that minimum-wage laws to prevent women having to turn to vice to support themselves was the wrong approach to the moral problem of prostitution. In many states this vice question figured prominently in the minimum-wage debate. The writer in the *Living Church* argued that reform should begin with a system of minimum wages for men. Then women, whether single or married, could remain at home. If for some reason a woman had to be employed, she should receive the necessary training to be a skilled worker and hence paid enough to keep her from prostitution. Those incapable of skilled work should be placed in domestic service, an occupation that would provide both a home environment and an opportunity to acquire domestic skills. Removing the supply of unskilled women from the labor market by these means might force some businesses to the wall, but if the only way to get cheap shoes was to feed cheap girls "into a machine" that turned them out "broken in spirits, in health, and in morals," then, the writer declared, "let us all go barefoot."[51]

It is significant that these and other advocates of reform necessarily argued from a defensive position. They were responding, of course, to a series of claims asserting either that the experience of foreign countries was worthless or that in one way or another minimum-wage laws were pernicious. At the most general level, critics denounced reform because it would reduce incentive and self reliance. More specifically, opponents quoted Edward Aves, the investigator sent to Australasia by the British government to report on the systems of wage regulation, to the effect that neither Australia nor New Zealand offered industrial conditions in any way comparable to those in the United States. "The propaganda . . . now under way with so much enthusiasm suffers from too much dogmatism," argued James Boyle in the *Forum.* "It assumes that wherever the principle has been tried it has been successful, and it insists that the same remedy may be applied everywhere, to all sorts and conditions of wage-earners."[52]

Boyle's attack must have infuriated reformers, partly because he used highly selective evidence to buttress a series of assertions and partly because it appeared in a highly respected magazine. For example, he argued that wage laws were unnecessary because American workers had already obtained through strikes and collective bargaining more than could be obtained through wage boards. As proof he pointed out that organized labor was just as vigorously opposed to minimum-wage laws, especially for men, as it was to compulsory arbitration. In any event, what may or may not work on a very small scale in the Antipodes was an impossibility in "such a vast and varied country, industrially, as the United States!"[53]

With President Woodrow Wilson and Samuel Gompers, Boyle also believed that the minimum rates set by wage boards would soon drag all earnings down to that level. He cited no evidence to support such a conclusion beyond the fact that the California Federation of Labor opposed wage regulation. Boyle was not above quoting Victor S. Clark's 1903 and 1905 reports on Australia and New Zealand to the effect that the wage laws were experimental and inconclusive. He asserted that the recent political reverses suffered by the Labour party in some of the Australian states and the unrest among militant trade unionists demonstrated growing dissatisfaction with state regulation. While he thought that something should be done to prevent the gross exploitation of American workers, such problems were so unusual that they should be dealt with on an exceptional rather than a general basis. Concluded Boyle, "so extraordinary has been the recent extension of the State into activities and functions heretofore considered as belonging to the individual domain, that dogmatism in opposition to a general legal minimum wage would be as unwise as dogmatism in advocacy of it is now unwarranted."[54]

What was so extraordinary about this upsurge in public interest in minimum-wage regulation from 1911 to 1913 was that it declined even more quickly. Barely a handful of articles appeared in 1914, though the Industrial Commission of Ohio did publish a substantial bibliography on the subject. The only article to extend the discussion appeared in the *Journal of Political Economy.* H. A. Millis, an economist at the University of Kansas, provided a careful evaluation of the Victorian and British experience and offered three new conclusions. Wage boards had encouraged unionization because workers were represented on the tribunals. Employers who paid good wages had been protected against undercutting by the less scrupulous and less competent. Regulation had checked petty abuses by employers, though it had not necessarily prevented fraud where employees had a choice between being thrown out of work and winking at the falsification of the wage records.[55]

Two explanations for the apparent decline in public interest are possible. The outbreak of war in Europe may have diverted attention from reform, though that seems improbable since the decline was already evident before the outbreak of hostilities in midsummer. More probable is the fact that because most legislatures met biennially in odd-numbered years, reformers were waiting until 1915 to resume their campaign. If that were the case, then it means that the flood of articles in 1913 did not so much reflect an upsurge in public interest as a campaign contrived to create the illusion that there was a widespread demand for reform.

Confirmation of this strategy began to appear early in 1915. The *Catholic World* published John A. Ryan's summary of minimum-wage laws in its January issue and his publisher brought out a new edition of his 1906 work on the "living wage." Moreover, in February the *Survey* published six articles setting out the case for wage regulation. Written by Florence Kelley, Louis D. Brandeis, Matthew D. Hammond, John A. Hobson, N. I. Stone, and Howard B. Woolston, the articles were republished in pamphlet form by the National Consumers' League, the reform organization most actively involved in the campaign. This was followed in April by the publication of "Minimum-Wage Legislation in the United States and Foreign Countries" by the United States Bureau of Labor and Statistics as a separate issue of its *Bulletin*. A volume of more than three hundred pages, the report combined an extended analysis with the texts of the various statutes. More than a third of the analysis was devoted to the Australian and New Zealand systems. Clearly, the volume was designed as a handbook for lawmakers intending to propose wage regulation at the forthcoming legislative sessions. From all appearances, reformers seemed to have every reason to be confident that they would be at least as successful in 1915 as they had been in 1913.[56]

Nevertheless, a constitutional cloud hung over the minimum-wage question. Reformers must have been jubilant in 1914 when the Oregon Supreme Court upheld the constitutionality of the wage law passed the previous year.[57] But the employer who had been prosecuted for failing to pay his workers the prescribed rate had refused to accept the decision and had appealed to the United States Supreme Court. Although the case had been argued in 1914, no decision had been rendered by the opening of the 1915 legislative season and there was no way to predict what the ultimate outcome would be. All that could be said with any certainty was that the justices were clearly troubled by the case and that the arguments pleaded in favor of the constitutionality of the law had somehow failed to produce a decisive majority to uphold.[58]

Especially disconcerting to reformers must have been the fact that the brief had been prepared by Brandeis and Goldmark, who had followed the strategy used so successfully in the *Muller* case in 1908. They had argued the case on sociological grounds, seeking to demonstrate that women and minors, by reasons of sex and age, were deserving of special constitutional consideration. As mothers of the race and as workers in an unusually weak bargaining position women needed the protection of minimum-wage law. The brief followed the now-established pattern of summarizing the sociological argument and buttressing the reasoning with statutory and scientific testimony culled from all over the world. Included in the *Stettler* brief were no fewer than 369 extracts from reports and other publications. Inevitably, because Australia and New Zealand were the pioneers in wage regulation and because so much had been written about their experiments, Brandeis and Goldmark played the antipodean evidence for all it was worth. They quoted extensively from the legislation as well as from the commentary of reputable observers. And just as inevitably, they put the best possible connotations on their evidence. Thus William Pember Reeves was quoted as an expert witness on wage regulation, but not identified as the author of the New Zealand legislation and thus as someone whose testimony might be brushed aside as self-congratulatory special pleading. Rather he was described as the Director of the London

School of Economics, the post he held when the brief was prepared.[59]

Brandeis and Goldmark presented a series of propositions that, they argued, provided a sound basis for affirming the constitutionality of wage regulation. They admitted, of course, that the constitution protected the liberty to contract. But that protection was not absolute and could be abridged where the evil of low wages threatened public health, safety, or morals. The first proposition, therefore, was that the Oregon legislature had determined that the evil was of sufficient magnitude to justify state intervention. The second proposition was that Oregon had chosen a reasonable remedy. The act was not arbitrary and it was directly related to the objectives sought. The third proposition declared that even if the justices had doubts about either the wisdom or the efficacy of wage regulation, they should nevertheless not interfere.

The brief tried to make it difficult for the Supreme Court to challenge these constitutional propositions. To have done so would have been to deny not only the existence of the wage evil but also the right of the legislature to make reasonable efforts to deal with it. "Can this court say that the Legislature of Oregon, knowing local conditions, . . . supported by the Supreme Court of Oregon (supposed also to have some special knowledge of local conditions), . . . was so absolutely and inexcusably mistaken in their belief that the evils exist and that the measures proposed would lessen those evils, as to justify this court in holding that the restriction upon the liberty of contract involved cannot be permitted?"[60]

With the issue unresolved in the courts, reformers, far from harvesting a bountiful legislative crop in 1915 as anticipated, accomplished little. Only two states, Arkansas and Kansas, enacted minimum-wage laws. Both followed the Oregon wage-board model rather than the Massachusetts or Utah systems, which relied on either public exposure or rates fixed by statute.[61] That the movement had lost rather than gained momentum was further confirmed by the paucity of public discussion. After April, virtually nothing on the subject appeared in the academic and reform periodicals, and in the following year, 1916, so little was published about the minimum-wage question that one might have supposed that the reform movement had been an illusion.[62]

But obscured from the national discussion—though not from the local press—was a powerful and well-organized effort to prevent the enactment of wage legislation. The groups and strategies involved varied from state to state. In some states, trade union leaders actively opposed reform as they had done in California; elsewhere, chambers of commerce, associations of manufacturers and merchants, and even workers purporting to speak for women formed the organized core of resistance. And everywhere, opponents borrowed their tactics from reformers, demonstrating that they too could put together massive studies and assorted foreign testimony to demonstrate that wage regulation was as much to be feared as welcomed. This was an effort best carried out in legislative corridors and hearing rooms rather than in the national press.[63] In Ohio, for example, delaying tactics succeeded. Although voters had overwhelmingly endorsed a constitutional amendment supporting minimum-wage laws for men as well as women, the legislature made only a half-hearted effort to act. That was because it decided instead to instruct the Industrial Commission to conduct a full-scale inquiry. By the time it was completed the reform momentum had collapsed.[64]

Of importance, too, was the fragile and narrow base on which the reform movement built. It would not be too much to say that in California, for example, the minimum wage was pushed through almost singlehandedly by Mrs. Katharine Philips Edson, who was actively associated with the State Bureau of Labor Statistics and who succeeded in getting Governor Hiram Johnson to support an Oregon-style measure. In the face of powerful opposition from the trade union movement, especially in San Francisco, chambers of commerce, and other business organizations, she rallied the Federation of Women's Clubs throughout the state and succeeded in passing a constitutional referendum endorsing the concept of minimum wages. It was not to be supposed that a reform depending so heavily for enactment on the enthusiasm of one person could easily sweep the country.[65]

Of greater significance, perhaps, was the constitutional question. Advocates and opponents alike were awaiting the outcome of the *Stettler* case, which had been pending before the Supreme

Court since 1914. So long as constitutional uncertainty remained, the reform effort was necessarily hampered. But a definitive answer could hardly have been slower in coming. The case was reargued in 1916, this time with Felix Frankfurter replacing Brandeis in pleading the constitutionality of the Oregon law, but again no decision was handed down.[66] It was not until 1917 that the court gave a verdict. At best, all that could be said was that the court's position was necessarily ambivalent. For although it sustained the constitutionality of the Oregon minimum-wage law, it did so only because the court was deadlocked four to four. Brandeis, who had joined the court the previous year, did not participate. Under the court's rules, an evenly split vote let the lower court's decision stand, but it also meant that a definitive decision had yet to be made. While it could be claimed that the Brandeis abstention really meant that a majority of the court favored minimum-wage regulation, it seemed probable that one justice who had voted in favor of hour regulation had voted against wage regulation. This meant that it was highly unlikely that the Oregon law could be tested again in the Supreme Court, but it also meant that the minimum-wage laws in the other states were vulnerable to constitutional challenge.[67]

This constitutional uncertainty virtually paralyzed the reform movement. Between 1917 and 1923, only six minimum-wage laws were passed: Arizona (1917); the District of Columbia (1918); North Dakota, Puerto Rico, and Texas (1919); and South Dakota (1923). But as a practical matter, most of the seventeen laws on the statute books in 1923 were a dead letter. In California and Wisconsin, for example, the industrial commissions avoided enforcing wage regulation until the constitutional question had been definitively settled, and in Minnesota opponents obtained an injunction and effectively prevented enforcement until 1918, when the state Supreme Court declared the law constitutional.[68]

The Supreme Court finally settled the question in 1923, more than a decade after Massachusetts had enacted the first minimum-wage law. At issue was the constitutionality of the 1918 District of Columbia law.[69] By that time, the composition of the court had greatly changed. Only two justices who had participated in the *Muller* hour-regulation case in 1908 were still on the bench—Oliver Wendell Holmes and Joseph McKenna—and only two other justices—James C. McReynolds and Willis Van-Devanter—had also voted on the *Stettler* case in 1917. New were Chief Justice William H. Taft and Justices Pierce Butler, Edward T. Sanford, and George Sutherland, all of whom had joined the court since 1920. Louis D. Brandeis was also new, but because he had been actively involved in the minimum-wage movement, he did not participate.[70]

Felix Frankfurter, who was to join the court in 1939, prepared the brief on behalf of the district wage board and pleaded the case before the court. An active member of the National Consumers' League, Frankfurter adopted the Brandeis strategy of pleading that women were deserving of special constitutional consideration. His brief demonstrated that Congress had held extensive hearings and had heard considerable testimony about English-speaking countries to the effect that wage regulation was an effective method of providing women with the special protection that their sex needed. In essence, though modified to deal with the congressional legislative history of the measure and to demonstrate that minimum-wage laws had been in successful operation in Australasia for more than a quarter century, the brief followed the one prepared by Brandeis for the *Stettler* case in 1914 and adapted by Frankfurter when he had represented Oregon before the Supreme Court in the rehearings in 1916 and 1917.[71]

Supporting briefs were also filed by California, Kansas, New York, Oregon, Washington, and Wisconsin. They repeated the Brandeis line of argument: the exploitation of female workers was a grave and proven evil; regulation was required to protect women and through them the future of the race, and the means chosen by Congress and many state legislatures to deal with the evil were reasonable and appropriate. As Justice Holmes observed: "The means are the means that have the approval of Congress, of many States, and of those governments from which we have learned our greatest lessons."[72]

Five of the eight justices—Butler, McKenna, McReynolds, Sutherland, and VanDevanter—rejected the Brandeis-Frankfurter theory of the Constitution and found wage regulation an unwarranted interference in the freedom of women to contract. Particularly offensive to the majority was the idea that women were entitled to a living wage even if their labor was worth less than the prescribed amount or if an employer or industry would be driven out of business by the required scale. Such regulations fell within the constitutional proscription against laws depriving persons of their property, without due process of law. Such a "taking" of private property was, in its nature, uncompensated and hence unconstitutional. In short, the majority rejected the Reeves principle that employers who could survive only by exploiting their workers should be put out of business.

Holmes, Sanford, and Taft dissented. As usual in such cases, Holmes tried but failed to convince the majority that they should not confuse their personal economic preferences with the question of constitutionality. "The criterion," he wrote, "is not whether we believe the law to be for the public good." The evidence presented, particularly from the efforts made in Australia, Great Britain, and a number of American states, demonstrated conclusively to Holmes that many reasonable men believed that wage regulation was a proper and effective method of protecting women. Holmes himself did not like the method chosen, and he especially disliked the use of arbitration courts, but that was not the question at issue.[73]

The adverse decision in *Adkins v. Children's Hospital* seemingly routed the minimum-wage reformers. Within four years, the Arizona, Arkansas, Kansas, Puerto Rico, and Wisconsin statutes had been struck down, and in California and Minnesota enforcement through the courts was plainly impossible, for if challenged, their statutes would also have been declared unconstitutional. Only the Massachusetts system was not vulnerable; compliance was voluntary rather than compulsory. Even there, however, the state supreme court weakened the statute by ruling that newspapers could not be obliged to publish the names of firms that paid less than the minimum wage. However, since most newspapers did not object to publishing the names of noncomplying firms, the ruling did not seriously interfere with the system.[74]

As it turned out, the *Adkins* decision proved more of a theoretical than a practical setback to the reformers. To be sure, no new laws were passed except in Wisconsin, where the legislature tried to shift from the "living wage" concept to one forbidding oppressive, inadequate, and unreasonable wages. In many states, industrial commissions and wage boards continued to function, often achieving voluntary compliance with their recommendations.[75] At first glance, this may seem surprising. However, it was very much in keeping with what might be called the "Herbert Hoover" spirit of the twenties, in which the federal government actively promoted fair business practices and welfare unionism. Thus paying living, nonoppressive wages was seen by "responsible" employers as a demonstrable sign of public enlightenment. Not all employers were either responsible or enlightened, of course. But that was a problem for the New Deal era and for the second great wave of minimum-wage reform.

Three things stand out in the Progressive effort to regulate the wages of women and minors. First, the papal encyclical of 1891 ultimately triggered American concern. Father Ryan, between 1906 and 1915 the most important figure in the reform crusade, popularized the moral question of "living wages," and he was joined by other priests and by Catholic action groups. Together with such organizations as the Young Women's Christian Association, the National Consumers' League, the American Association for Labor Legislation, the Women's Trade Union League, and the Federation of Women's Clubs, Ryan and his associates marshalled the forces of reform.[76] Second, in almost every state that seriously considered minimum-wage legislation, commissions of inquiry into wages and working conditions provided an essential strategy in mobilizing public sympathy and support, though opponents sometimes used investigation as a delaying tactic.[77] Third, at both the legislative and judicial levels, antipodean models and extrapolation from antipodean experience were skilfully—if not in the end successfully—used to persuade legislators to regulate wages and to convince judges that such remedies were sanctioned by the Constitution. Even if ultimately the judicial strategy failed, Reeves's principle of a minimum standard of treatment below which no civilized country should fall became a widely accepted article of American democratic faith.

Increasingly after 1906 and most especially after 1911, few Americans questioned the idea that humanity or morality or sound business required minimum standards. Where disagreement existed—and then, as now, it powerfully inhibited reform—it was over means rather than ends. Should the achievement of minimum standards be left to the persuasive force of public conscience manifesting itself through private voluntary action? Or was it appropriate—even allowing for the American emphasis on political freedom, private initiative, and self-reliance—to have the state intervene in wage matters to protect employers and employees alike from their own worst selves?

Given Australasian political traditions and the virtual absence of constitutional impediments to social and economic reform there, it was relatively easy for New Zealand, the Australian colonies, and later the Commonwealth of Australia to plunge into the thickets of what at the time was dubbed "state socialism." In doing so, and quite fortuitously and unconsciously at first, these countries provided working if small-scale legislative examples of solutions to modern problems. It was inevitable, since American reformers had similar goals, that they should seize on the purported antipodean achievements and try, as critics complained, to "New Zealandize" America.

6 The Compulsory Arbitration of Labor Disputes

Of all the measures adopted at the Antipodes in the Lib-Lab era (1891–1911), the one attracting the most American attention was the New Zealand solution to labor warfare, the Industrial Conciliation and Arbitration Act of 1894, which gave the state the power to impose and enforce settlements. Although foreign observers concentrated on the concept of "compulsory arbitration," the law contained many voluntary principles and was intended, in fact, to make state intervention unnecessary except in the rarest of instances.[1] Reduced to its essential provisions, the statute created a three-stage mechanism for resolving conflicts between labor and capital. Throughout the process, only those associations of employers and employees who voluntarily agreed to be bound by the law could be compelled to abide by the terms of an award. That is, the statute combined voluntarism with compulsion.

The first stage provided for the ordinary process of private collective bargaining. For example, a carpenters' union in any community could negotiate a contract with a local association of builders. They could agree on any or all aspects of employment, ranging from wages and hours to such matters as the ratio of journeymen to apprentices and safety rules. Once an agreement had been reached, the document had to be filed with a registrar. The parties were then bound by its terms. Failure to comply was punishable by fines. In enacting the law, parliament anticipated that the overwhelming majority of employers and workers would reach these kinds of voluntary agreements.

In some instances, however, it was predicted that the parties would fail in their private efforts to hammer out a contract. The second stage in the resolution process could then be invoked. Either side could take the dispute to a regional conciliation panel made up of representatives elected by labor and capital. They selected an additional person to serve as an independent chairman. The board brought the parties to the bargaining table and heard their testimony and arguments. At its discretion, the board could also visit work places, the better to understand the issues in contention, and question owners, managers, and workers alike. So informed, the board then recommended detailed terms of agreement. If accepted by the union and by the employers' association, the board registered the document, which then became binding on both sides in exactly the same way as if it had been negotiated independently through collective bargaining. In the meantime, neither side could take direct action: employers could not lock out their employees; workers could not withdraw their labor. These arrangements were similar to the voluntary mediation systems in Massachusetts, New York, some of the Australian colonies, and some European countries.

What was different and caught the interest of foreign observers was the third stage of the process, a court of arbitration empowered to settle disputes and compel compliance. It, too, had three members: one represented associations of employers; a second, associations of employees; the third, a Supreme Court judge, who presided. This panel accepted cases at the request of either side of an unresolved dispute by holding hearings, at which testimony, both oral and written, was taken, along with oral and written arguments. Interested third parties could be heard. The court could compel witnesses to attend and documents to be submitted, and it could even appoint a board to investigate the issues and make recommendations. The arbitration court then rendered its decision, the majority opinion constituting a labor contract binding on all employers and employees in a particular industry and district. As a practical matter, the judge held the balance of power; whenever the other two panelists disagreed, his views prevailed.

The statute incorporated several innovative principles. First, its author, William Pember Reeves, then minister of labor but later New Zealand's representative in the United Kingdom, director of the London School of Economics, and chairman of the board in London of the National Bank of New Zealand, sought to bring only responsible parties to the bargaining table. To obtain the benefits of his system, associations of employers and employees had to be formed and register themselves. In doing so, they made themselves legally liable in their corporate capacity should they break the terms of an award, whether achieved privately, through the conciliation process, or through the Arbitration Court.

Second, the act encouraged both conciliators and arbitrators to proceed in whatever manner would best serve the system's objective, to end the war between labor and capital. If the parties to a dispute agreed, either or both could be represented by legal counsel, but hearings were not to be formal trials of the issues strictly bound by traditional rules of either evidence or procedure. Rather, the objective was the search for just solutions, which reflected colonial standards of fairness and were acceptable to both sides.

Third, Reeves recognized the overwhelming power of capital and its sometimes utter determination to bend labor to its will. He sought to bring about a more equitable balance by encouraging unionization. Once organized, workers could, if necessary, take their grievances to the Arbitration Court. The mere threat of compulsion, he supposed, would put so much pressure on employers that they would accept trade unions as a fact of modern industrial life and would therefore engage in good-faith collective bargaining. That achieved, industrial cooperation would follow without resort, except perhaps in exceptional instances, to either state conciliation or state arbitration. In short, he designed a remedy for strikes and lockouts he never intended or expected to be invoked.[2]

It would be no exaggeration to say that this antipodean model dominated the American debate over labor relations for almost three decades, from the 1890s to the 1920s. Whatever the protagonists may have thought about the policy choices they debated, however, it would also be no exaggeration to say that at no time was there any serious possibility that the New Zealand remedy would be enacted into American law. Though the debate lingered on into the twenties, early on it became so ritualized that no one said anything fresh and there was no meeting of minds on what to do about industrial warfare. On each side, spokesmen merely reiterated their basic arguments, supplementing them from time to time with new evidence from the Australasian record. Simply put, they spoke past rather than to each other.

Not only did the debate fail to produce a genuine dialogue on so vital a question, it might even be said that it did more harm than good. For it may have diverted discussion from other, more viable approaches to labor-management relations. After all, Americans made little headway in resolving this problem between the Homestead Strike in 1892 and the Steel Strike in 1919. Meanwhile, labor disputes cost the economy millions of hours in lost output, even more millions of hours innocently disrupted on the sidelines of these labor battles, and hundreds of lives snuffed out, mostly by capital's intransigence. The horror of the Ludlow Massacre in Colorado in 1913 captures the ultimate futility of the debate, for Ludlow underscores the American failure to deal with the fundamental issues.

Simply stated, the antipodean solution was designed as a method of promoting union recognition and collective bargaining—reasonable American objectives, surely well within the boundaries of traditional American approaches to problems. The New Zealand law encouraged capital and labor to deal with each other by confronting and resolving the issues between them. If they could not, the state stood ready to help, first through conciliation, then through arbitration. These remedies became available only after the parties had failed to agree privately. Looked at in this way, the compulsory principle must be seen as a red herring.

Americans—labor, interested observers, the public at large—did not understand Reeves's intent; they allowed themselves to be speared on the issue of compulsion versus voluntarism. And so they needlessly wounded themselves over a full generation of futile debate and costly labor wars. Not until the Wagner Act in 1935 were there the beginnings of a resolution. The irony is that Americans then embraced the compulsory principle—not arbitration, to be sure, but compulsion nevertheless—by requiring management to concede union recognition and engage in good-faith collective bargaining when a majority of workers voted to organize.

The concept of forced settlements was not new to Americans when New Zealand enacted that remedy in 1894. It had been considered as early as 1878 in the aftermath of the Great Railroad Strike,[3] but the antipodean law attracted little attention until

1899, when Henry Demarest Lloyd returned from Australasia with the first detailed account of the experiment and quickly began laying out the parameters of the labor-relations debate that was to continue for the next two decades.

Lloyd set out to "New Zealandize" America, by which he did not mean swallowing each and every antipodean experiment whole, but rather adapting colonial models to American needs and wherever possible pushing the reform effort far beyond what the little Pacific country had achieved.[4] Thus he enthusiastically embraced its approach to industrial problems while urging his fellow citizens to fashion their own legislative remedies tailored to American conditions, institutions, and procedures. Nevertheless, in praising New Zealand's success—the abolition for all time, he supposed, of disruptive warfare between capital and labor—he polarized American thinking about industrial relations by framing the policy choices narrowly: either compulsory arbitration as the solution of final and peaceful resort, or a continuation of barbaric mayhem based on a laissez-faire system of might over right.

Reduced to its essentials, Lloyd's support for state intervention rested on several basic propositions drawn from his preconceptions reinforced by his antipodean observations. Over the next twenty years these lines of argument sustained the American drive for compulsory arbitration. Whether in editorials, articles, books, book reviews, speeches, conferences, sermons, field reports from the Antipodes, testimony before investigative bodies, or interscholastic debates, these propositions appeared over and over. They also sustained legislative efforts in at least nine states, ranging from Massachusetts, New York, and Pennsylvania in the East, Texas in the Southwest, Illinois, Minnesota, and Missouri in the Midwest, to Colorado and California in the West.[5]

First and probably foremost, Lloyd declared that New Zealand had achieved lasting industrial peace. In the six years since the system had gone into operation, lockouts and strikes had become a relic of the past. To be sure, in the beginning both capital and labor had been suspicious of state intervention, but experience with the new system had quickly taught them that owners, workers, and the public at large all benefited. Though the parties in conflict gave up some freedom of choice, that loss had been more than offset by the advantages of continuous employment and sustained profits. Neither capital nor labor wished to return to "the bad old days."[6]

Until 1908, when for the first time some serious difficulties appeared in the New Zealand system, American supporters of compulsory arbitration had little difficulty sustaining Lloyd's first proposition, that a method of achieving industrial peace had finally been achieved. Both Victor S. Clark, reporting to the U.S. Bureau of Labor in 1904, and Harris Weinstock, reporting to the governor of California even as late as 1910, confirmed the earlier accounts of antipodean success as well as the assessments that neither employers nor employees wanted to abandon the system, even though both Americans questioned the suitability of the New Zealand concept under American economic and political conditions. As the journalist Florence Finch Kelly had reported in the *Craftsman* in 1906, the "final clinching argument" was that compulsory arbitration "works." She pronounced it "a practical success." Similarly, Weinstock interviewed scores of colonial critics, who, he reported, knew little of foreign conditions. "When these were pointed out," he told the governor, "I do not recall one who was finally willing . . . to exchange [New Zealand conditions] with those prevailing in Europe and America."[7]

These affirmations of success drew powerful reinforcement from reports that the Commonwealth of Australia and some of the individual colonies had followed New Zealand's lead by adopting their own systems of compulsory arbitration. This export of a solution to industrial warfare from one side of the Tasman Sea to the other was the more impressive to Americans because it followed careful investigation and evaluation of New Zealand's results. The most enthusiastic and optimistic Americans believed that it was only a matter of time before the antipodean system would become universal in the western world.[8]

Second, by arguing that New Zealand had shown the United States a way out of its industrial chaos, Lloyd also appealed to America's noblest aspirations. The colony had substituted a rational and peaceful process for the old order of naked force, whether dynamite, Gatling guns, and thuggery or martial law, starvation, and eviction. The choice was simple: a civilized remedy or barbarism.[9] This appeal to the American heart evoked a powerful response, partly because fellow citizens were conscience-stricken about the chaos resulting from conflicts between capital and labor, and partly because it was so easy to draw harrowing comparisons between the tranquillity of colonial industrial life and the brutality of American conditions. In a commentary on the Great Anthracite Strike in Pennsylvania in 1902, Lloyd himself had set the tone when he declared that America had become habituated to "the sight of blood on its daily bread," while the antipodean colonies had fashioned "easier, wiser, and wealthier" forums for the peaceful resolution of conflict. Americans built armories; Antipodeans built courtrooms.[10]

Lloyd's supporters enthusiastically rang the changes on this theme. Frank Parsons, the Boston reformer, for example, contrasted New Zealand's quiet hearings with America's "shooting, eviction, dynamite, assassination, kidnapping, torture, [and] pitched battles. . . ." New Zealand had "cured the chronic war of industry." The colony had "made more progress toward Industrial Harmony and Economic Freedom than any other country in the world."[11]

Frank E. Smythe, the apostle of irrigation, echoed Lloyd and Parsons in the West. He, too, wanted to "New Zealandize" America, either as a Congressman in Washington or as California's governor in Sacramento. He formulated a broad reform program directed mainly at solving farm problems, but he also supported the concept of arbitrating labor disputes. A recent San Francisco strike, he thought "a blot on the history of California. Thousands of men were idle for weeks. The children of some of them no doubt suffered the pangs of hunger. Assaults were committed and blood was shed." Why should strikes have to be settled "by those two grim arbiters, the Depleted Bank Account and the Empty Stomach?" That was "barbarism."[12]

Others agreed. Charles Francis in New York City, president of a printing firm, proclaimed "Strikes are War! War is Hell!" They sometimes threw the nation into industrial convulsion, shaking it from end to end. "Is that civilization?" he asked. Such conflicts were "a fight for the mastery by one class over the other . . . for the sake of pecuniary and selfish advantage."[13] And in

Philadelphia Rabbi Joseph Krauskopf declared that there was "a state of war between capital and labor. . . . May we . . . soon learn that there are nobler and surer ways of settling trade disputes than by wars against classes by strikes and lockouts, by bullets and by bombs, by intimidation of employers and by starvation of employees. . . . Arbitration courts are our only hope for industrial peace. Ours is the solemn duty to turn that hope into reality."[14]

Edward Tregear, a colonial official who published many articles in American reform journals and who corresponded with many American reformers, used similar images. "Arbitration will one day eliminate injustice from industrial strife," he predicted, just "as arbitration will some day sweep away that other form of war which now bases its arguments on the method of rending tender and beautiful human bodies with the eloquent shell and logical bayonet."[15]

Third, Lloyd also argued that it was no longer possible in the modern industrialized world to view labor-capital conflicts as private matters best left to the protagonists to settle for themselves by whatever means they could find. As a socialist, he put great emphasis on the virtues of brotherhood, cooperation, and harmony in human affairs, and he believed that the collective interests of the community had to take precedence over the private and often selfish interests of either corporations or unions. These private interests had to be subordinated to the greater needs of society, which had a legitimate claim to the uninterrupted flow of goods and services as well as to economic and social tranquillity. With the beginning of the twentieth century and the interdependence of modern life it was no longer possible to allow owners and workers the freedom to engage in private warfare; the stakes had simply become too high. Civilization was at risk.[16]

Most supporters of the system of compulsory arbitration repeated Lloyd's emphasis on society's stake in social harmony. The activist priest who led the American "living wage" movement, John A. Ryan, saw the New Zealand concept as "a triumph of justice and social order over injustice and economic anarchy. How long," he implored, "will the practical American people allow the warring factions . . . to afflict the community with senseless and costly strikes? Even if capital and labor should be left to their own folly and obstinacy, . . . the public should not be compelled to suffer with them."[17] Smythe wanted to know why "a few employers and workingmen [had] any moral right to imperil the welfare of the entire State [or] to inflict wanton injuries upon their own families? If so, why do we restrain men from committing suicide? Why do we compel them to support their wives and children?"[18]

The editor of *Arena*, Benjamin O. Flower, followed the same line in 1904 in calling for a law to "protect the public at large . . . from the inconvenience and suffering which follow . . . during such periods as the great coal-strike . . . legislation which would also render impossible such spectacles of lawlessness . . . as recently witnessed in . . . Colorado."[19] Francis argued that the adoption of the New Zealand plan would be "a lasting monument in the social organization of the 20th Century."[20] And Hugh H. Lusk, a former colonial politician and attorney who came to the United States in the 1890s and who joined Lloyd's reform circle, urged the compulsory system on Americans because it would establish "the principle that society is charged, for its own protection, with the duty of seeing that justice is done to all classes, . . . even to the extent of discouraging the growth of riches in one class to the degradation of others."[21]

The "living wage" movement drew particular inspiration from this appeal to human values, pointing to a New Zealand precedent. "It is impossible for these girls to live decently on the wages you are now paying," declared the judge in a case involving a new match factory, whose owners had argued that they could not afford to pay more until the enterprise was securely established. "It is of the utmost importance that they should have wholesome and healthsome conditions of life. The souls and bodies of the young women of New Zealand are of more importance than your profits, and if you cannot pay living wages it will be better for the community for you to close your factory. *It would be better to send the whole match industry to the bottom of the ocean, and go back to flints and firesticks, than to drive young girls into the gutter.* My award is that you pay what they ask."[22]

The president of the Australian Court of Conciliation and Arbitration, Justice Henry Bournes Higgins, brought the same message to Americans in 1914. He reported a universal growth in "the value of human life" and thought it "too valuable to be a shuttlecock in the game of moneymaking and competition." The "injurious strain of the contest" should be "shifted from the human instruments."[23]

Finally, Lloyd reported that compulsory arbitration, by bringing New Zealand industrial harmony, had promoted so much economic expansion that the colony had become the "most prosperous country in the world." By every measure, the antipodean experiment had to be counted a resounding success. Employment, output, investment, profits, and living standards had all risen sharply since the adoption of the new system. The United States, Lloyd predicted, would reap similar rewards as soon as it, too, became "a country without strikes."[24]

Such a vision appealed powerfully to the ambitious American growth ethic. Those who wanted state intervention in industrial affairs embraced it enthusiastically. Economic growth and prosperity went hand in hand with industrial harmony. Supporters cast their arguments in a variety of ways. In San Diego, Smythe asserted that compulsory arbitration would "enhance the prosperity of manufacturers, of workingmen, and of the . . . community," while in Boston, Conrad Reno, the organizer of a League of Industrial Courts, told readers of the Hearst newspapers that "Strikes and lockouts and boycotts often . . . entail losses aggregating millions of dollars. If such disputes were averted, the annual production would be much larger. . . . This increase in wealth would constitute an additional fund, out of which larger dividends to capital and higher wages to labor could be paid, without raising the price to the consumer."[25]

Additional confirmation came from all sides. Tregear told American readers that "capital seems to thrive and grow fat in a marvellous way," reinforcing Lloyd's description of colonial capitalists as "wingless birds" who, far from taking flight, chose to remain "to share the prosperity." Similarly, the Columbia political scientist, A. S. Johnson, praised Reeves's two-volume study, *State Experiments in Australia and New Zealand* (1902) and pronounced the Lib-Lab program a success because "Capital is increasing, manufactures are thriving. . . ." In 1910 Weinstock confirmed the rise in investment and wealth, but also reported a decline in tax rates. Compulsory arbitration, Lusk asserted in 1912, had brought New Zealand "an economic success far greater, in proportion to the numbers of its people, than that of any other national community in the world."[26]

These interwoven arguments were also best summarized by Lusk, who declared that this "great social and economic experiment . . . has substituted peace and good feeling for industrial war and bitterness; it has converted a large majority of its bitterest opponents into supporters; it has steadily, and with amazing rapidity, increased the production of the colony and the wealth of all classes of its people; and, finally, it has so impressed the people of the countries nearest to it, . . . that they are one by one adopting its provisions for themselves. Such is the record. Of how many legislative experiments yet tried for the benefit of society can as much as this be said?"[27]

Few new arguments in favor of compulsory arbitration came over the years. None added much to the debate. Both Reno and John Bates Clark, the Columbia economist, made industrial harmony an essential condition for American producers if they were to seize and hold international markets against British, French, and German competitors. "If law is to rule," Clark declared, "if democracy is to succeed and become permanent, if our country is to be rich, contented and fraternal and is to have its vast strength available in the contest for the prizes of a world-wide commerce, a system of authoritative arbitration is inevitable."[28]

If these two commentators saw compulsory arbitration as a system for promoting private enterprise while at the same time defending the public interest, the British economist and lecturer, J. A. Hobson, saw it as a "half-way house to socialism." The growing concentration of capital, he predicted, would increase strikes and lockouts and thus demands for state intervention. The public would see the essentially "social" character of private industry, and "no theoretic objections to socialism" would hold off demands that the public, "for its security and convenience," be protected from the "fights of rival producing interests." The "consumer-citizen of modern industrial states" would eventually seek the "experimental shelter" of the New Zealand system.[29] That was a fresh perception, but it was not one likely to carry much weight in the United States except perhaps among some groups, such as Christian and Fabian socialists.

Noteworthy in all of these arguments was the almost complete absence of significant voices claiming to speak for either capital or labor. Those who did, such as the dry-goods merchant Weinstock, the printer Francis, or even the secretary of the Association of Western Manufacturers, Walter Fieldhouse, spoke either for themselves or for minor business constituencies. Similarly, few unions or their leaders supported the compulsory principle, the main exceptions being the Electrical Workers and the Iron, Steel, and Tin Plate Workers, both fragile organizations with small membership rosters.[30]

Rather, the advocates of the antipodean system came overwhelmingly from those who would not be directly affected by what the sociologist Nicholas Paine Gilman labeled the "legal regulation of labor disputes" rather than "compulsory arbitration."[31] They came from the ranks of reform journalism—Flower, Lloyd, Lusk, Smythe, and Julius Wayland, the Kansas editor of *Appeal to Reason*; the social gospel clergy—Russell H. Conwell, Krauskopf, Ryan, Josiah Strong; social scientists—Richard T. Ely, Clark, Hobson, Gilman, Johnson, Paul Kennaday, Parsons, H. L. Wayland; labor bureaucrats—F. N. Johnson (Minnesota), Charles McCarthy (Wisconsin), Charles H. Myers (Maryland), Thomas P. Rixey (Missouri), James T. Smith (Colorado); and citizen-activists—Stanley Bowmar, a single-taxer, Theodore Gilman, a Wall Street banker, and Reno, all of whom presumed to speak for the public interest and most of whom saw state interventionism as the most effective way to deal with America's economic and social problems.[32]

Their ranks also included a few politicians, such as Edward P. Costigan of Colorado, Henry J. Allen of Kansas,[33] John Lind of Minnesota, and William A. Stone of Pennsylvania, but most legislative efforts appear to have been headed by minor figures, which helps to explain why the compulsory idea made so little progress. Indeed, despite the "tons of newspapers . . . sodden" with "New Zealandizing" arguments, or the "oceans of atmosphere stirred" up, as one opponent complained,[34] an effective constituency for the antipodean plan never emerged in the United States, either in Congress or in state houses.

Why that was so has several explanations. Taken together they tell us some important things about reform in America. Neither capital nor labor accepted the concept of compulsory arbitration as a solution to their differences; other critics expressed serious reservations about the constitutionality of forced interventions in labor-management relations: ideologues from both the left and the right flatly rejected New Zealand's "state socialism" either as an unwarranted invasion of human freedom or as a cruel capitalistic hoax designed to prop up an evil, exploitive system; and throughout the extended debate, opponents systematically challenged the veracity of Lloyd's proclamations of New Zealand's achievements, along with his assertions that the experimental system would work in the United States. Although these opponents spoke with many voices rather than with a single one, and although they shared no common perspective on labor-management relations, they succeeded in frustrating the reform effort.

These attacks put Lloyd and his successors so much on the defensive that they ended up spending more of their energies trying to dispel criticism than in promoting their cause. In effect, these critics waged a war of attrition. Over the long term, the reformers lacked the will to survive. Their hope that the antipodean solution to industrial warfare would find an American home as it had in Australia certainly survived into the 1920s, but the vitality of their effort had been drained and even the most devoted supporters of the compulsory principle probably accepted, though reluctantly, the fact that the New Zealandization of labor relations had died a slow but certain death.

The attack on compulsory arbitration can be summarized succinctly. Most capitalists opposed the system as another unwarranted and undesirable example of state intervention. As a spokesman for the National Association of Stove Manufacturers put the case: compulsory arbitration "is opposed to the principles of individual liberty. . . . There is no law that can compel a man to work if he does not want to, nor prevent a man closing down his works if he elects to do so."[35]

Organized labor joined employers in denouncing the New Zealand system though often on very different and much more complex grounds. Martin Fox, speaking for the iron moulders, declared that there is "something about the idea of compulsion that is repugnant to American conceptions of liberty of action, and it's not difficult to conceive a case in which working men would be compelled to work under conditions or for wages that were obnoxious to them." Charles B. Spahr wanted to know how the state could "make any man except a criminal work against his will? Would dissatisfied workers be sent around in chain gangs?" The machinists agreed, describing the system as "the absolute enslavement of the wage workers." The strike weapon "would be stricken from our hands, and we would become subject to the Court's charity." Samuel Gompers said the same thing when he argued that an arbitration award, no matter how unfair or unjust, would compel employees to work under penalty of either fine or jail, neither of which was "one jot removed from slavery."[36] Though not always stated explicitly, these arguments rested on the protections against slavery and involuntary servitude guaranteed in the Thirteenth Amendment to the Constitution.

On several other grounds, too, labor opposed compulsion. For example, Gompers and others saw the antipodean idea as a not-so-subtle scheme by labor's enemies to subvert trade unionism, partly by allowing the state to intrude between employers and employees, partly by depriving unions of control over their own affairs, partly by exposing individual members as well as union treasuries to court-imposed fines, and partly by creating "made-to-order unionists," men "who have not fought the battles of labor, who have little or no interest in the trade union ideal, to whom class solidarity means nothing and wages and hours everything."[37] Even when well-intentioned, any system of compulsory arbitration would necessarily weaken the labor movement and thus make it harder to achieve industrial harmony and justice through effective collective bargaining between parties of roughly equal power. Moreover, the "paternalism which the system necessarily exercises dwarfs rather than develops individual character and initiative. It would not harmonize with the progressive ideas for the Western Hemisphere."[38]

However, some spokesmen admitted that compulsory arbitration might be acceptable in two instances—where a very large firm so dominated a particular industry as to make negotiated contracts impossible—and in some public services, transportation and utilities, for example, where the public interest transcended the private interest of labor no less than capital.[39] But these were exceptional circumstances and barely affected the overwhelming antagonism of organized labor to the compulsory idea.

Powerful opposition came from the American right, too. It drew its inspiration, of course, from deeply held philosophical opposition to state interventionism, but it drew its ammunition primarily from abroad, mainly from antipodean critics of compulsory arbitration and the English and Scottish press, which gave credibility to colonial complaints. On the whole, conservative criticism contributed more heat than light. If it did little to elevate the quality of a debate, it was primarily responsible for keeping the Lloyd forces on the defensive and thus helped delay any resolution to the labor-management crisis.

The main source for this opposition was *Australasia Old and New* (London, 1901) by James Grattan Grey, an Irish-born Australasian journalist.[40] His and several other accounts challenged the Lloyd assessment on many crucial points: New Zealand was either bankrupt or soon would be, the level of taxation and the size of the national debt were frightening and dangerous burdens on colonial enterprise, industrial harmony had not been achieved at the Antipodes, the Liberal ministry in New Zealand had belatedly realized the folly of its industrial experiment and was about to abolish it, and the arbitration system had sapped colonial character and vitality. Many of these assertions had no basis in fact; nor could the subjective assessments be verified. Lloyd and others struggled to set the record straight. To their sorrow, they learned that in journalism truth rarely overtakes disinformation.

No, the New Zealand premier had not admitted that the "plan is a failure" and that "the abandonment of compulsory arbitration is 'imperatively necessary in the interest of industrial peace.' " Yes, the colony was indeed prospering, investment was increasing, and taxes were declining. Yes, the antipodean system did "conciliate" and it did "arbitrate." It was not "perpetrating a mere farce, ... sanctioning hypocrisy and delusion." No, the concept was not "inimical to the principle of the open shop. . . ." Nor did it support "men who are not skillful and do not care to be industrious." No, the system was not a "ghastly failure," and New Zealanders had not become devitalized, degenerate, and sapped of their initiative.[41] These and similar charges diverted public discussion from the potential benefits of adopting the New Zealand system.

Critics from the left were no less devastating. They, too, rested their arguments on ideological assumptions, but their attacks had a surer factual basis. For example, Julius Wayland in Kansas, an early and enthusiastic supporter of the Lib-Lab program, soon came to regret his endorsement, concluding that New Zealand's state socialism was a "capitalist fake" designed to prop up an evil system and deprive workers of their just rewards. The editor of the *Nation* agreed, cautioning "sincere Socialists" against appealing "to the example of New Zealand as conclusive."[42]

Both anticipated Charles Edward Russell's attack of 1911. On a previous visit to the colony Russell had praised the arbitration system. "New Zealand had blazed the world's way. We had only to follow. No more strikes! . . . What a country! Joy be its portion and happy man be his dole that thought of arbitration boards to supplant brick-bats and night sticks!" Five years later he condemned the system as undemocratic, repressive, unworkable, and harmful. Disputes between labor and capital could never be stopped "so long as you retain the present organization of society."[43]

Russell and others supported the emergence of labor militancy in the South Pacific with its refusal to be bound by the system of conciliation and arbitration. These unions, mostly in mining and transportation, rejected state intervention. Instead they looked forward to bringing about the collapse of capitalism and the creation in its place of a collectivist, industrial democracy, Russell's "Co-operative Commonwealth."[44]

Their support for militant industrial unionism aside, these critics mounted a powerful challenge to the Lloyd assertion that a solution to industrial warfare had been devised. By 1907, when packinghouse workers struck for higher wages in defiance of the arbitration court, it was no longer possible to call New Zealand "a country without strikes." Clearly, many workers were restless and dissatisfied, in part because the economy had turned downward and the arbitration court had become less willing than previously to grant wage increases.[45]

And so the American supporters of the antipodean system found themselves on the defensive from both the left and the right as well as from less biased critics, one of whom declared that the recent strikes "shriek aloud that the alleged remedy for industrial troubles is, so far, no remedy at all."[46]

From New Zealand, Tregear tried somewhat ingenuously to paper over these problems and reassure American supporters. He made several clever if not necessarily plausible points. First, he appealed for patience, asserting that the colony had never supposed that a perfect system could be created instantly. Second, he argued that the enactment of a law could no more abolish industrial conflicts than it could abolish burglary or murder. And third, he minimized the difficulties with the colonial system, trying to characterize them as "teething pains" rather than fundamental design flaws. From the New Zealand perspective, he may have been more right than wrong. But from the American perspective, he had unintentionally confirmed existing doubts about the efficacy of the antipodean idea, thereby making compulsory arbitration even more vulnerable to criticism than before.[47]

Academic assessments both helped and harmed the Lloyd campaign. Most observers confirmed the reports that the New Zealand system worked and that the overwhelming majority of employers, workers, and citizens alike did not wish to return to the conditions prevailing before 1895. However, almost without exception these analysts doubted the exportability of the antipodean concept to the United States. Mostly, they shared two perceptions. First, that the New Zealand economy was small, simple, and overwhelmingly agricultural and that what worked well there would probably not work at all in large, complicated, and industrialized countries. The fact that the system had been adopted in Australia did not prove that it would bring industrial peace to European countries or to the United States.[48]

Second, academics emphasized attitudinal differences between Americans and Antipodeans, which they also saw as fatal impediments to the success of the New Zealand experiment in the United States. Colonials willingly deferred to government, law, and authority, something Americans did only reluctantly. Americans were too individualistic, too much lovers of freedom, too lacking in deference to authority to allow a judge to dictate work contracts.[49]

Finally, some academics feared that a compulsory system of resolving labor disputes would dry up the flow of investment capital. Such a result could have a devastating impact on the development of the nation's economic infrastructure, particularly in the cities. These analysts also challenged the proposition that New Zealand's prosperity was best explained by the achievement of industrial harmony. On the contrary, they looked to external factors, primarily the fundamental improvement in the terms of trade for agricultural exports and the opening of European markets to New Zealand dairy and meat products.[50]

In short, for almost every Lloyd proposition there emerged a counter argument. Both cases rested on a recitation of purported facts along with emotional appeals. There were few shared perceptions, few shared premises. Instead of a genuine dialogue leading to agreements on some middle ground of compromise for resolving labor disputes, the protagonists cast the discussion in the form of a debate in which policy makers and the public alike had to choose between two incompatible and irreconcilable solutions: either compulsory arbitration in some American form or a continuation of the existing chaos.

In retrospect, it is clear that the Lloyd campaign suffered from three fatal flaws. First, though it tapped into a general American wellspring of desire for industrial harmony, the objective was so amorphous that it was virtually impossible to create at the essential levels of political activism the organizations capable of persuading state legislatures or the Congress to enact compulsory systems. Second, the parties most vitally affected by the New Zealand concept—capital and labor—vigorously opposed state intervention, though for very different reasons. Without their acquiescence, whether active or passive, it was unlikely that politicians would choose to lead where neither employers nor workers chose to go. Third, Lloyd and his followers were naive and paid the price: they mistakenly assumed that the American people would enthusiastically and expeditiously embrace the antipodean solution simply because it was "right." And so they failed, not only in securing a system of compulsory arbitration, which would probably have no more worked in the United States than it did in New Zealand, but also because they helped delay for almost a full generation the formulation of better methods of dealing with industrial disputes.

The fault was not entirely theirs, of course. Support for the New Zealand approach weakened at crucial moments by growing American interest in the Canadian system, which also involved the compulsory concept, but applied it in a more limited way—an obligatory cooling-off period when a dispute threatened, so that the facts at issue could be investigated and publicized. The pressure of public opinion, it was supposed, would force the contending parties to resolve their differences equitably for the benefit of themselves as well as the public. That was the solution Weinstock recommended for California in 1910 and the Commission on Industrial Relations recommended for the nation in 1915.[51]

Colorado, which had perhaps suffered as much as any state from labor wars, took up the Canadian idea in 1915 in the expectation that public opinion, "finally instructed and aroused by the proven facts of industrial life and the fair demands of human brotherhood, will eventually shape a new industrial order of peace based on justice." That hope soon proved illusory. Within a year, the governor urged the legislature to repeal the law; he argued that it had the opposite of its intended effect. Not only had it exacerbated industrial discord, it had also subjected workers to involuntary servitude.[52] This Colorado experience with a limited version of the compulsory principle raised additional doubts about the utility of the New Zealand plan. But in the interim, some American interest had been diverted from the Antipodes to Canada.

The Lloyd movement suffered from another crucial handicap. To win credibility for the proposition that industrial warfare could be abolished, the New Zealand solution had to be tested in the United States, preferably in a large, economically complex state. That never happened. Other antipodean ideas—minimum wages for women, agricultural credit schemes, village settlements, and systems for underwriting worker compensation plans, for example—were adopted, and some of them, American-style, spread from state to state, but that essential breakthrough never happened with the compulsory arbitration concept.

There was one exception, Kansas, in 1920 hardly a large and economically complex state. In that year the legislature created an industrial court and compelled certain "essential" industries and their workers to submit to compulsory arbitration if they could not resolve their differences. The governor claimed, perhaps accurately, though perhaps out of ignorance, that the law owed nothing to the antipodean model. It really did not matter. Capital, and especially labor, resisted, each for its own reasons. Constitutional challenges came almost immediately, confirming the concerns expressed from the very outset of the American debate. Soon, the U.S. Supreme Court struck down the statute, at least as it applied to the meat-packing industry, because it infringed on "the liberty of contracts and rights of property guaranteed by the due process clause of the Fourteenth Amendment." The Kansas legislature abolished the industrial court in 1925.[53]

That unfruitful episode put an end to further American efforts to implement the New Zealand scheme. However, the end had probably come much earlier, perhaps even by the time of Lloyd's death in the fall of 1903 and the loss of an energizing leader, but certainly by 1908, when a series of labor disruptions challenging the arbitration system gave the lie to the claim that the South Pacific colony was "a country without strikes." And the strike on the Waihi goldfield in 1912, with the Liberal government's resort to not only the militia but a naval force as well to maintain "law and order," confirmed American doubts about the utility of the compulsory idea.[54]

But there were further problems with the New Zealand model, only some aspects of which were appreciated at the time. The fact that American critics paid so much attention to the compulsory aspect of the antipodean remedy was not happenstance. They intuitively understood, without necessarily comprehending, that the parties to New Zealand disputes never engaged in either private collective bargaining or in good-faith conciliation. Rather, a pattern quickly developed which made a mockery of Reeves's intentions. The parties only walked themselves perfunctorily through the motions of either bargaining or conciliating. Ordinarily, both sides staked out absurdly unreasonable positions, which was not unusual in collective bargaining the world over, but the strategy was not to bring demands to the table so as to have points to concede in the give-and-take of negotiation. Rather, the demands were intended to make bargaining and conciliation impossible, thereby forcing the dispute on to the arbitration court docket. Employers associations and trade unions simply chose not to deal with each other, preferring to take the easy way out by leaving decisions to a supreme court judge. As a consequence, the Australasian colonies never developed histories of responsible leadership in industrial relations. Americans noted this trend as early as 1905, when the *Nation*, for example, reported that compulsion had become the rule rather than the exception and that the arbitration court in New South Wales had a thirteen-year case backlog.[55]

Little noticed, too, was the fragmentation of the New Zealand labor movement. Reeves certainly succeeded in promoting unionization, but not in the form he intended. Instead of large, strong unions counterbalancing the power of capital, the system enabled workers in even the smallest establishments to register themselves as separate bargaining units unaffiliated with either regional or national unions. These unions lacked the muscle to bargain effectively and therefore looked routinely to the arbitration court to give them what they were powerless to negotiate for themselves. Reeves and New Zealand learned that reform, no matter how well intentioned, does not always do good or produce the predicted results.

It would be a truism, of course, to say that the New Zealand model was an idea whose American time never came. Throughout the long debate from 1895 to 1925 the weight of evidence, argument, and policy preference opposed the adoption of the antipodean experiment. Whether from capital or labor, Left or Right, from the academy or the general public, Americans distrusted compulsion in industrial relations. Though Lloyd and his acolytes thought they detected a conspiracy to block the

"New Zealandization" of America, the truth was probably very different; Americans were simply highly selective, accepting some antipodean programs while rejecting others. To be sure, compulsory arbitration attracted and probably held considerable support in the United States, but never enough and never in the right places to translate the principle into law. Meanwhile, Americans inched painfully and ever so slowly in their own time and in their own ways, through welfare capitalism, for example, toward a very different method of achieving industrial harmony, the principles laid out in the Wagner Act.

But if the New Zealand version of the compulsory concept failed in the United States, it also succeeded, though in an ironical and quite unfruitful way. For the antipodean idea took sufficient hold that it framed the American debate over industrial relations and for three decades diverted the American people from other, more effective ways of ending the chronic warfare between capital and labor. Such can be the power of ideas, even those whose time never comes.

Part 3
THE INTERNATIONAL CONTEXT

7 *American Progressivism and the World of Reform*

The Progressive era, spanning the decades from the 1890s to the 1920s, can be seen as a great watershed period in American history. Primarily at the state and local levels, but at the federal level as well, public policy shifted toward government intervention in economic and social affairs and away from the concept of laissez faire.[1] This trend moved the United States down the road toward the modern welfare state, the characteristics of which include the mixed economy, the manipulation of economic activity through monetary, tax, and other techniques, government regulation of business, the use of natural resources, and the environment, and a broad range of welfare programs, from aid to dependent children, food stamps, and public housing to farm subsidies, social security, and unemployment insurance. While many of these interventionist techniques came with New Deal responses to the Great Depression and Fair Deal and Great Society responses to postwar conditions, their origins lay at least a generation earlier in the Progressive effort at the turn of the century to reconstruct the American democracy.

The Antipodes contributed in significant ways to that first phase of the transformation of the Republic from a laissez-faire to an interventionist society. Initially, from the early 1890s to about 1905, Australasian reform programs served two principal though interconnected and overlapping Progressive constituencies. For well-educated, middle-class or patrician activists, whether reformers on the left whose motivation was Christian socialism and other forms of idealism—clergymen, journalists, social workers, or bureaucrats—or public-spirited citizens troubled by the "crisis of democracy"—club women, settlement-house workers, academics, socially conscious businessmen—the Antipodes provided convincing proof that dedicated men and women could so reshape public policy as to abolish human misery and repression, deprive the "interests" of their control of the Republic, and return America to its true path, the pursuit of a more perfect society.

These perceptions of colonial reform combined a heady mix—an inspiring hope that it was not yet too late to redeem the Republic, a conviction that the Antipodes had devised brilliantly workable strategies for solving the world's problems, and that with even greater effort and devotion to the reform cause, the highest of American aspirations would, in due course, be realized. From the cynical perspective of the 1980s, that may seem like a highly romantic vision of the American future, but considering the depth of reform concern in the 1890s and beyond, it was an understandable and powerfully felt need to discover a basis for believing that all was not yet lost and that "the world's last best hope" still had time in which to redeem itself.

And so the Lloyds, Flowers, Parsonses, Smythes, and their kind took both heart and inspiration from what they either saw or learned about the antipodean experiments, trumpeting colonial achievements and arguing that models for America's redemption had been found. As Smythe said in 1905, Lloyd "furnished a text for innumerable speeches and writings." They seemed "very likely to bear fruit in the future institutions of the State. More than any other man, he educated our people on the subject of New Zealand."[2]

This inspirational, optimistic, and sometimes romantic enthusiasm drew other Americans into what might well be called a cottage industry of interest in things antipodean. For the most part, these newcomers came to Australasian models with fewer preconceptions and greater skepticism, but with an equally powerful determination to put whatever they learned to either personal or reform purposes. In this second phase, extending from about 1905 into the 1920s, three distinct responses to and uses of colonial reforms can be identified.

Academics constituted an important set of these newcomers Defined as labor economists, they taught college courses, wrote scholarly articles and books, published texts for classroom use on a wide range of public-policy questions, including the compulsory arbitration of labor disputes, factory regulation, minimum-wage and maximum-hour legislation, the abolition of child labor, workmen's compensation, and social insurance, and some of them, such as John R. Commons and Matthew B. Hammond, moved freely in two worlds, the academy and the bureaucracy.

Unlike the Lloyds, Lusks, Parsonses, Smythes, and similar observers, whose writings and speeches encompassed the whole range of antipodean reforms, from labor and land laws to old-age pensions and votes for women, most academics showed less interest in the comprehensiveness of colonial interventionism than in specific measures, ordinarily because the topics lay within their fields of specialization. Thus John Bates Clark and Nicholas P. Gilman concentrated on the compulsory arbitration of labor disputes; Matthew B. Hammond, H. W. McCrosty, H. A. Millis, and John A. Ryan made the minimum-wage question their cause; and Henry Rogers Seager paid particular attention to both the living-wage and social-insurance issues. Only Richard T. Ely and James E. Le Rossignol, both of whom visited New Zealand, showed a broad interest in antipodean social and economic experimentation. Even so, Ely told Helen Page Bates in 1915 that "New Zealand has not accomplished the wonders that men like H. D. Lloyd thought that it had, but it has done nevertheless great things," and he told E. C. Franklin that the American people "have an insatiable appetite for lectures on that far away country."[3]

More important, though many academics enthusiastically embraced such concepts as minimum wages for women and pensions for the aged, in general they approached the Australasian democracies with considerable scholarly detachment. Unlike Lloyd and others, they refused to embrace colonial programs as if they provided solutions to all that ailed America. While many of them readily acknowledged the success of antipodean reforms, thereby helping to give the lie to much of the criticism circulating in conservative Anglo-American circles, nevertheless they seriously questioned the exportability of most of these programs to the United States. For example, they confirmed that the compulsory arbitration of labor disputes had brought a considerable measure of industrial peace to the colonies, but they doubted that America could also become "a country without strikes" by adopting the antipodean system.

In effect, academics treated "New Zealand fever" with a strong dose of skepticism, thereby shifting attention from Lloyd's effort to "New Zealandize America" to a case-by-case analysis of selective proposals they judged suited to American conditions, institutions, traditions, and, above all, needs. As that more limited approach took hold and gathered momentum, the reform agenda also shifted from one borrowed whole from the Antipodes to one determined pragmatically by Americans and driven by an American rather than a colonial reform timetable. Thus, although the question of adopting a system of abolishing lockouts and strikes through the compulsory arbitration of labor disputes continued to be debated into the 1920s, as we have seen, there was never a time, and certainly not after Lloyd's death in 1903, that the colonial solution would win sufficient American support to be adopted.

Instead, serious reform focus shifted to other Australasian ideas, such as child and maternal care, rural credits, village settlements, workmen's compensation, state life insurance, minimum-wage and maximum-hour legislation, and old-age pensions. But Americans pursued these causes serially rather than in a comprehensive rush, clearly picking and choosing from the range of Australasian experiments and just as clearly trimming their reform sails to the winds of public opinion. Not that they held back from pursuing causes in which voters showed little initial interest—after all, most reformers, whether of the Lloyd stripe or academics like Ryan, put great stress on educating the public. Nevertheless, they proved shrewdly adept at gauging sentiment and then riding the crest of the wave of opinion as far as it would carry them.

That was certainly the case with rural credit and village settlement programs, which Smythe had pushed in 1902 but which took more than a decade to achieve either in Sacramento or Washington. And significantly, the reform impetus came primarily from investigatory commissions rather than from reform journalism. That was also true with maximum-hour legislation and even more so with the living-wage and workmen's compensation issues.

But if the New Zealand virus proved more selective than Lloyd and his acolytes both expected and wished, the "New Zealandizing of America" went a good deal further than has been previously realized. The Antipodes, more so New Zealand than

Australia, helped propel the United States toward the modern welfare state.[4]

Bureaucrats, politicians, and foundation workers constituted a second important set of observers of Australasian reforms and transmitters of information, ideas, assessments, and recommendations. The virus of "New Zealand fever" transmitted by Lloyd and his circle infected both legislators and officials in several ways. On the political side, some legislators, such as James W. Bucklin of Colorado, persuaded their colleagues to establish a tax reform commission and direct it to visit Australasia and bring back recommendations. Similarly, Harris Weinstock persuaded the governor of California to appoint him a labor commissioner to tour the world in search of solutions to industrial warfare, and in California, Massachusetts, New York, and Oregon, legislatures established commissions of inquiry on diverse issues ranging from rural credits and factory conditions to old-age pensions and workmen's compensation. All looked abroad, particularly to the Antipodes, for legislative or regulatory models.

Bureaucrats also became involved, primarily as gatherers and disseminators of reform information. Since the army of Progressivism marched on information, the growth of the bureaucracy in the late nineteenth century, staffed by experts and funded at unprecedented levels, was a crucial new factor in the reform equation. Officials functioned in two ways.

First, some agencies commissioned investigators to go out into the field to observe and report. That was the case with A. J. Pillsbury and the California Industrial Accident Board, and Victor S. Clark, who wrote two substantial reports on conditions in New Zealand and Australia for the U.S. Bureau of Labor and who subsequently transformed his data into a doctoral dissertation at Columbia University.

More important, public and private agencies responded to legislative and public demands for information by publishing and distributing scores of reports and bibliographies. Federal and state bureaus of labor were clearly the most important, especially on questions of child labor, factory and mine regulation, industrial safety, hour and wage questions, labor relations, and workmen's compensation. But other agencies became involved as well—municipal and state research bureaus, legislative libraries, federal and state departments of agriculture, municipal and state branches of the National Consumers' League, the League's New York headquarters in reprinting articles and legal briefs on questions of concern to working women, the Russell Sage Foundation as underwriter of both the research and the publication of works on these issues, the U.S. Children's Bureau, the American Academy of Political and Social Science, the American Association for Labor Legislation, the National Civic Federation, and such periodicals as the *Chautauquan*, the *Proceedings of the National Conference on Charities and Corrections*, and the *Survey.* Librarians joined in by collecting Australasian documents and reports and by compiling and publishing bibliographies on Progressive issues. State universities also became involved, partly through their teaching activities, including extension courses and lectures, and partly through their library acquisition programs.

The third set of responses to the idea of the Antipodes as the world's economic and social laboratory involved commercial as well as reform considerations. Progressive periodicals along with journals on the left—ranging from the *American Fabian, Appeal to Reason, Coming Nation, The Commons, Everybody's, Independent, La Follette's,* and the *Nation* to the *National Post, Out West, Public, Single Tax Review,* and *Wayland's Monthly* all devoted considerable space to Australasian affairs. Other weeklies and monthlies, such as *Atlantic Monthly, Contemporary Review, Forum, Hearst's Magazine, Lippincott's, Nineteenth Century, North American Review, Pearson's Magazine, Review of Reviews,* or *Twentieth Century,* carried only occasional articles on the Antipodes. They did so less out of a commitment to reform than to a desire to maintain circulation by supplying their readers with what editors judged to be interesting stories.

Some accounts were simply second-hand reports by Americans with no personal knowledge of the Antipodes, such as Jane Addams, Florence Kelley, or Frank Parsons, but many others came from colonists, ranging from O. T. J. Alpers, John Christie, H. G. Ell, and Henry Bourne Higgins, who were journalists, jurists, or reformers, to William Downie Stewart, Edward Tregear, Robert Stout, and Sir Joseph A. Ward, who were officials or politicians. Both groups contributed to the flow of antipodean ideas and information reaching the American public.

Whether as writers for newspapers or for periodicals, American visitors also contributed in significant ways to this same transmission of antipodean intelligence. The most noteworthy, of course, was Henry Demarest Lloyd, who though a reformer of considerable private means expected to make money from his articles, books, and speeches about Australasian affairs. So, too, did Charles Edward Russell, the famous muckraker. Unlike Lloyd, he had to make his living from his writing, but like Lloyd, he too chose subjects combining reform with commercial considerations. They took him to the Antipodes twice, first in 1906 and again in 1911. Out of those two visits came a dozen political articles for *Everybody's*, *Coming Nation*, and the *National Post*, as well as a couple of travel pieces for the *Twentieth Century Magazine*.

Even the *Los Angeles Times*, a conservative newspaper with a strong anti-union bias, judged antipodean affairs to be sufficiently important to its readers to send a journalist, Allen Kelly, to Australasia to write a seventeen-part feature series with the general title *Under the Southern Cross* for its Sunday editions. Accompanied by his journalist wife, Florence Finch Kelly, who also wrote about New Zealand for the *Craftsman* and the *Independent*, as well as in her memoirs, Allen Kelly reached the South Pacific with some strongly held preconceptions about colonial society. In particular, he shared his editor's reservations about colonial state socialism in general and the influence of organized labor in particular. That skepticism came through in his first essays, but over the weeks a subtle change occurred as he became persuaded that New Zealand liberalism had produced considerable benefits to colonial society and that trade union leaders had behaved responsibly and positively in public affairs. No such change of attitude came when Kelly crossed the Tasman Sea to Australia, where he made much of what he saw as the adverse influences of unions in economic and political affairs. But those reports, some of which were comparative, reinforced his favorable assessments of New Zealand labor leaders, politicians, and reforms.

Other newspapers, most notably the *New York Times*, retained stringers in Australasia and published regular reports on antipodean affairs. In these ways as well as through telegraphic reports mainly funneled through London, the American press maintained a steady flow of information about colonial developments.

Similar commercial considerations influenced the editorial policies of book publishers. Only a few American and English houses brought out books devoted to Australasia: Henry de R. Walker's *Australasian Democracy* (1897), Lusk's *Our Foes at Home* (1899) and his *Social Welfare in New Zealand* (1912), Lloyd's *Country without Strikes* and *Newest England* (1901), Grey's *Australasia Old and New* (1901), Reeves's *State Experiments in Australia & New Zealand* (1902), Parsons's *Story of New Zealand* and the abridged edition, *Politics in New Zealand* (1904), Clark's *Labour Movement in Australasia* (1906), Guy H. Scholefield's *New Zealand in Evolution* (1909), Anthony J. St. Ledger's *Australian Socialism: Historical Sketch of Its Origins and Developments* (1909), Rossignol's and Stewart's *State Socialism in New Zealand* (1910), Siegfried's *Democracy in New Zealand* (1914), and Frances Norene Ahl's *New Zealand through American Eyes* (1918). Over a two-decade period, this was not a substantial output, almost half the authors were colonials rather than Americans, and although many of these titles attracted wide newspaper, magazine, and journal attention, none became best sellers. For example, Lloyd complained to his publisher about the modest sales of his two books, though Reeves reported that American sales helped within a few years to put his two-volume work out of print.[5]

Three other kinds of commercial books probably had a larger American circulation and influence. College textbooks in the emerging social science disciplines and the helping professions—economics, political science, sociology, and social work—reached a whole generation of students, familiarizing them with the leading policy questions of the day and informing them about antipodean programs. Similarly, many commercial houses brought out trade books, sometimes as separates, sometimes in series, such as the *Citizen's Library,* devoted to Progressive issues ranging from rural credit and development, votes for women, and the public ownership of utilities, railroads, and transit systems to industrial conciliation and arbitration, old age pensions, and workmen's compensation. These sorts of books often combined several functions. On the living-wage question, for example, they supplied data on American conditions, examined the effectiveness of foreign solutions, and advocated reform. Such works circulated widely through sales, lending libraries, and among college students through being adopted as texts or as sources for research papers. Money could be made as well in publishing debating handbooks, manuals supplying contestants with arguments on both sides of major questions, usually in the form of extracts from the literature, supplemented by bibliographies listing the leading articles, books, and public documents debaters could consult.

It is important to note that in the Progressive years forensic contests attracted large audiences in high schools, normal schools, colleges, and universities. Debates were already taking on a characteristic American earnestness and seriousness. Unlike such exercises elsewhere in the English-speaking world, where levity and wit and audience involvement gave debates a sporting rather than an intellectual quality, in America faculty coaches had already become part of the forensic organization. The debate circuit required that subjects be selected well in advance, to give participants ample time to prepare themselves with convincing factual arguments. Adequate preparation required more than consulting the manuals and library holdings; the most determined also wrote away for data and ideas—to Lloyd, for example, or to the U.S. consul in New Zealand.[6] Information, not flights of rhetoric, was the stuff of these battles. Commercial publishers, particularly the H. W. Wilson Company in New York, met these needs not only by publishing manuals but also by reproducing stenographic transcripts of the constructive and rebuttal speeches in particular debates, along with bibliographies.[7]

The topics for these debates were the great issues of the progressive years—direct democracy, graduated income taxes, conservation of natural resources, social insurance, and the labor movement, for example, as well as such topics as world peace and the independence of Ireland. These highly organized events exposed audiences and debaters alike to both sides of these questions, of course, but students who might otherwise have remained ignorant of economic, political, and social issues—young men and women from rural backgrounds at high schools no less than urban sophisticates at Chicago or Harvard—acquired a larger knowledge and understanding of worldwide reform trends. So exposed, a whole generation of young Americans came to voting age more sensitized to these questions than would otherwise have been the case.

This outcome obviously fell far short of what Lloyd and Parsons had hoped for from their campaign to "New Zealandize America," but in the larger sense they succeeded better than they knew when they died in 1903 and 1908, respectively. It was still too soon for the virus of "New Zealand fever" to have brought many tangible results. The United States still showed few signs of rushing headlong to either adopt or improve on antipodean reform models. Nevertheless, over the longer term it did borrow a good deal in specific solutions (minimum wages, rural credit, state underwriting of industrial accident risks, and village settlements, for example) and it did borrow reform concepts (security for the aged, care for babies and mothers, and reform of industrial relations).

Most important of all, the Antipodes gave Americans ways of looking at "the crisis of democracy" and bringing them to a modern acceptance of the idea of state interventionism as a way to deal with their problems. Looked at in that way, Parsons's view that New Zealand was "the birth place of the 20th century" and that "What is history in New Zealand is prophesy for the rest of the world" accurately foreshadowed what lay ahead for America. Much more slowly than in the Antipodes and slowly even as compared with western Europe, the United States did in its own time and in its own way come to embrace welfarism. Whether for good or ill, Australasian liberalism contributed much to that process, whether in particulars or in underlying attitudes toward state interventionism.

This is not to suggest that the Antipodes had a primary role in the transformation of the Republic. That would be absurd. Nor is it to suggest that the Antipodes had an exclusive role. That, too, would be no less absurd. On the contrary, as academic and other observers were quick to point out, the Australasian colonies were too small, too rural, too sparsely peopled, and much too undeveloped to offer Americans more than a limited range of reform concepts and models. Moreover, they noted as well that colonial attitudes toward government and colonial political institutions and traditions did not mesh easily with American customs and mores. In addition, partly through the tug of Old World ties running backwards to the very beginnings of colonization and partly through the presence of millions of European immigrants and their native-born children, transatlantic influences did much more to shape American Progressivism than did transpacific ones. After all, commercial links to the colonies were both recent and modest and the number of colonists who had emigrated to the United States could be counted, figuratively speaking, on the fingers of a single hand.

But to say that is also to emphasize that the reform currents moving the United States toward the mixed economy and the complex welfare apparatus we know today were part of a worldwide interventionist phenomenon. Undeniably, American Progressivism rested heavily on indigenous forces—domestic perceptions of economic, political, and social problems seemingly unique to America, especially in the largest cities, and the presence of constitutional, ethnic, political, religious, rural, social, and urban considerations and values of crucial importance to how, when, and in what ways Americans would act to reconstruct their society. However, crucial though these indigenous factors were to American progressivism, they operated within a much larger framework moving the developed world—Europe, the Americas, southern Africa, and Australasia—along the road to welfarism.

The great paradox of the Age of Progressivism was that the most fundamental of these forces moving the world toward state interventionism came from a growing disenchantment with capitalism. By the closing decades of the nineteenth century, Adam Smith's "simple and obvious system of liberties" was falling into disrepute. The free market seemed not to be producing the benefits even its most devoted apologists claimed for it. This perception was not confined to the "lower orders," though small farmers, miners, clerks, domestics, and the unskilled had the most powerful reasons for dissatisfaction. But paradoxically, ordinary folk were considerably better off than they had been even a century earlier. In that sense, capitalism had increased national incomes and had improved standards of living.

However, the rhetoric of capitalism had taught people to expect much more from the free market than it seemed capable of producing, year in and year out. The wild ups and downs of the economy in the second half of the nineteenth century jeopardized continuity of employment and income and seemed to put those goals as far out of reach as ever. Even if it was still widely accepted that in the older sense the poor would always be with us, concern grew that a totally new kind of poverty was on the increase, poverty with its roots not in individual defects—laziness, alcoholism, feeblemindedness, or illness—but in what we would now call structural defects in the economic system. Some kind of corrective action seemed imperative.

The demand for state intervention was not confined to working people and their sympathizers. Businessmen everywhere were deeply troubled by problems emerging within the capitalist system itself. These concerns included excess capacity with the resulting fierce struggle for markets at home and abroad, the impetus to cartelization and other forms of collusion, sharp business practices, inequities in the availability of credit, a squeeze on smaller firms, and rising costs of entry to the market place. In the abstract, capitalists both large and small much preferred a system in which market forces alone determined success or failure, but in the practical world and on particular questions they too were drawn to government as arbitor, regulator, and promoter. That is, for reasons of self-interest, capitalists themselves retreated from laissez faire. The trend was worldwide.

This was particularly evident in the agricultural sector, where for many farmers the returns did not seem commensurate with the risk and effort, especially as compared with rewards in the commercial, financial, and industrial sectors. Like workers, farmers sought income and security, though there were collateral issues, varying from place to place, broadly concerned with the "quality of rural life." Again, the crucial causative force appears to have been a failure of expectations. The market system was not living up to its promise; and this disenchantment was exacerbated by the presumption that the world owed farmers, above all others, a favored place in the sun. Government interventionism appeared to many farmers to be the method best calculated to achieve that goal.[8]

In short, the origins of the modern welfare state can be traced to a profound crisis in late nineteenth-century capitalism. Failures of performance sapped confidence in the system and exposed it to political interference. That businessmen themselves frequently led the charge simply underscores the argument that a broad consensus existed for the modification of free-market principles.

The growing fear of the left intensified the trend. It produced a siege mentality in business and encouraged the politics of cooption as a strategy for survival. The most dramatic example, of course, is Bismarck's Germany, where the counterattack on socialism brought massive restraints on employers and foreshadowed welfare programs that were to become commonplace on both sides of the Atlantic over the next century.

The paradox in all this should not go unnoticed. For all the talk about the failures of capitalism, it was the success of the system that made the interventionist state possible. By the closing decades of the nineteenth century, the prodigious productivity of the market economy provided the essential resource base for a significant increase in government activity. It was not until then that policy makers could dare to think that they could have a consequential impact on everyday affairs. They could now raise sufficient revenue to finance their programs, and business could now absorb whatever additional burdens—regulatory costs, for example—that might be imposed.

If affluence made the interventionist state financially possible, human arrogance made it thinkable. Abstractly, human beings since the eighteenth century had believed in their capacity to exert substantial control over their world, but it was not until the closing decades of the nineteenth century that this confident belief in the power of reason began to shape public policy in ways leading to the modern welfare state. The achievements of science and technology obviously had a powerful influence on interventionist thought. It was not difficult to suppose that if men could devise ways to vulcanize rubber, perform surgery under anesthesia, mass-produce steel, or transmit messages by undersea cable, they could deal effectively with social and economic questions.

To do that, they had to develop a knowledge base about human behavior and relationships, the analytical methods to investigate the causes and consequences of social and economic problems, and the scientific principles on which to ground public policy. What is so significant about the emergence of the social sciences is that from the outset they were heavily biased to problem solving. There was no point in studying society unless the knowledge acquired could be applied. That is why these new disciplines attracted men and women who were interventionist by inclination or who became so through their training. Moreover, the social sciences supplied journalists, clergymen, legislators, and other reformers with essential information, ideas, and arguments. If scientific knowledge and theory could reduce infant mortality or increase industrial productivity, then there was surely no reason to doubt the human capacity to reduce poverty, disease, or unemployment.

Finally, a fundamental change in the nature of political life led to rising demands for state interventionism. It manifested itself earliest in New World countries but was everywhere evident in the decline in deference to traditional leadership and in the rising claims on government by spokesmen for farmers, workers, petty businessmen, women, and other powerless groups. More than the democratization of politics moved public affairs in this direction, though that was clearly important. Important as well was the rejection of the primacy of the market as the arbiter of the outcomes of life. Poverty or unemployment or slum housing or rack renting or sweated labor or land monopoly or inequalities of wealth were no longer automatically accepted as the inevitable human condition. The immutable natural order came under attack as distinct, organized interest groups began formulating their agendas of expectations and demands. Increasingly, the art of politics became populist in the sense that elections hinged on putting together coalitions of interest groups. Political survival depended on catering to their demands. Politicians had to act in new ways. They had to articulate the interests of their constituents; they had to demonstrate responsiveness. Not that all politicians were swept up by this tide. There was still a place for the resisters. They could block, delay, or, as a last resort, modify any particular demand, but over the long term, Progressivism everywhere meant the new politics of activism.

To summarize: the worldwide impetus to reform had its causes in dissatisfactions with capitalism, in the accumulation of resources sufficient to finance interventionism, in the presumption that human problems had rational causes and were therefore solvable by rational solutions, in the decline in political deference, and in the erosion of the politics of passivity.

What common elements can be identified in the programs by which countries began moving in the Progressive years toward the modern welfare state? A useful first approach can be found in the traditional categories of land, labor, and capital, though not all reform components fit perfectly within this framework.

The universal land issue was income and security. In some places, particularly in New World countries, there was in addition the problem of monopoly, which manifested itself in attacks on alien, absentee, or corporate ownership, or simply in complaints about the concentration of holdings in the hands of a few. The most common objective in these cases was the creation of opportunities for the landless, but there was also talk of land nationalization based on the ideas of Alfred Russel Wallace and what might be called income equalization through taxation—the theories of John Stuart Mill and Henry George. In general, the significance of these issues lay not so much in the legislation they inspired as in the way they shaped attitudes toward state intervention and strengthened demands for programs responsive to rural needs. Both the Mexican and Russian revolutions also spoke powerfully to land issues, but the compulsory repurchase of large holdings in New Zealand was more important as a symbol of government concern than as a solution to landlessness. So was the 999-year lease of public land, which was a sop to nationalizers and survived only until tenants could muster enough political strength to force the government to offer them the right to buy a freehold title. Similarly, the progressive land tax placed an inconsequential burden on holders of large estates and did little to redistribute New Zealand's property.[9] The story was much the same in California, where the state's acquisition of ranches for subdivision into working farms never evolved beyond a few demonstration projects.

A much more important manifestation of the interventionist impulse was the attack on the problem of income and security through the subsidization of agriculture. The technique used in both the Old World and the New was the harnessing of science and education to the task of increasing the productivity of land and labor, the systematic improvement of processing techniques, and the investment of public funds in the search for and promotion of market opportunities. Especially in the newer countries, governments also subsidized agriculture by supporting the development of transportation networks. That is, farmers, processors, and merchants looked to the state for a variety of agricultural services. Departments of agriculture emerged to coordinate the effort and provide research facilities and demonstration projects to service and educate the farming sector. In the dairy and meat industries, for example, public health standards were imposed, and in international markets the diplomatic service acquired agricultural responsibilities. Everywhere the objective was the same: the income and security of farmers, as well as that of processors and distributors, was to be promoted by the state.[10]

To this trend must be added state efforts to increase the supply of rural credit. Methods varied from country to country. Nevertheless, a common theme can be identified. The universal starting point was the perception that capitalism produced a maldistribution of credit. Manufacturers and merchants had all the capital they needed and generally on attractive terms. Farmers, by contrast, were starved for capital, which was scarce, and even when it was available, the cost was excessive. Since bankers and lenders gave no signs of willingness to correct the imbalance, it behooved government to take corrective action, meaning that the rural sector had a legitimate claim for special treatment. In New Zealand that demand manifested itself in the government's borrowing on the London money market and granting state loans to farmers at rates substantially lower than commercial terms. In the United States the technique was quite different, but the purpose was essentially the same, a government system of credit collateralized by the farmer's crop—cotton or corn or wheat. By this means, it was hoped, farmers would obtain the funds to make next year's crop and might even have a surplus for reinvestment in capital improvements. In the meantime they would not have to dispose of their harvest at what were essentially distress prices. Comparable concerns shaped public policy throughout the world of agriculture.[11]

Similarities in the world of work are no less evident. As in farming, the common denominators were income and security. Everywhere involved in one way or another was a rejection of market forces as the sole determinant of the job contract and the interposition of the state between employer and employee. And as in farming, crucial presumptions underlay public policy. The first was the view that capitalism had failed to produce work for all those who offered their services and second, that capitalism had also failed, partly through the same oversupply of labor, to distribute national income in a defensible way. It was not just that too many workers lived out their lives on the margins of existence. From the Left there was also a challenge to the reward system based on the labor theory of value.

Corrective action throughout the world of reform followed broadly similar lines and usually involved some mix of humanitarian, practical, and ideological considerations. The abolition of child labor was a common goal. Given the gradual reformulation of the meaning of childhood in the nineteenth century, there were sound humanitarian and social reasons for keeping children out of the labor force. However, it is realistic and not necessarily cynical to say as well that the reform also reflected a practical response to the scarcity of adult employment. If the competition of children could be eliminated, there would be more jobs for their older brothers and sisters and for their parents, and child labor would no longer depress wage rates. Similarly, efforts to abolish night work for younger workers and women and to limit the length of the work week for them had humanitarian as well as practical resonances. In addition to health considerations, these restrictions affected adult male workers as well by abolishing the night shift in all manufacturing plants that relied heavily on young people and women. Presumably, output could be sustained only by building more factories, hiring more workers, operating longer each year, or by employing more men. The common characteristic of these laws was the categorization of the labor force by age and gender.

Other laws grew out of a concern for another aspect of security—safety and health. Hazardous occupations—mining and transportation, for example—were typically the first categories to be regulated. From that beginning the trend was usually toward comprehensive industrial codes that specified minimum standards in such areas as sanitation, ventilation, lighting, and safety. The most advanced legislation specified maximum hours for all workers rather than just for selected categories and the retail trade became subject to comparable comprehensive regulation.

The enactment of mandatory systems of workmen's compensation supplemented and strengthened these codes. The basic principle was that the employer became absolutely liable for all work-related injuries. Benefits were payable according to a fixed scale. This concept became as common in countries with a Roman law tradition as in those with an Anglo-Saxon legal heritage. Other considerations aside, these requirements gave employers a vested interest in job safety. The safer the operation, the lower the cost of doing business.

The Progressive era also saw considerable efforts to deal with the income side of the labor question by mandating minimum wage standards. The solution was both conservative and radical, conservative insofar as it neither altered the reward system nor redistributed national income, radical in that government intervened in the free market to guarantee workers a minimum level of welfare. As in the question of hours, the most common approach used the categorization principle to single out particular industries for regulation and women for special protection. They were the industries where exploitation was most rampant and where women had the least leverage. There were moral imperatives as well. Many reformers linked prostitution to poverty. It was also assumed that setting a wage floor beneath female workers would have a ripple effect on all employees. However, once established for one category of industry or worker, the logic of reform was to extend the minimum-wage principle to all occupations and all workers.

The third common line of intervention involved the resolution of disputes between labor and management. Three principal models can be identified: voluntary mediation, as in Massachusetts; compulsory investigation, as in Canada; and compulsory arbitration as the technique of last resort, as in Australasia. Whatever the method adopted, intervention rested primarily on the presumption that lockouts and strikes were no longer the exclusive concern of workers and owners. All disputes, though some much more obviously than others, affected the public interest. The state therefore had an obligation to promote harmony. There were other motivations as well, ranging from fear of capital's excessive power to fear of labor's potential for revolution. In most countries these systems of modifying industrial relations were probably of limited practical consequence. Much more important was the assumption by the state of new power and responsibility and the blurring of distinctions between the public and private sectors of the economy.

Perhaps the most useful way to examine the common elements in reform programs affecting capital is to start from the premise that the universal goal was the preservation and reformation of the market system rather than its overthrow and replacement by some other system, most notably a collectivist one. But this conservative objective rested on the perception that capitalism was working less than perfectly, that the system gave few signs of correcting itself, and that the state would have to mandate change if catastrophe were to be averted. This premise does not preclude active participation by capital in the reform process; nor does it preclude selective public ownership.

A major reform thrust, therefore, was the rationalization of business—an attempt to bring order out of chaos. It took a number of forms. Much of the labor legislation can be characterized in this way. By prescribing higher standards in wages and working conditions, the state favored the larger and more efficient firms, which were already in compliance or which could comply easily. Similarly, laws protecting consumers from spoiled meat, adulterated foods, or dangerous pharmaceuticals put many small firms at risk. And laws regulating retail-trading hours eliminated the competitive advantage of small, family-operated businesses over department and other large stores. To these measures can be added the enactment of codes proscribing sharp business practices, which if they did not necessarily favor the strong over the weak, at least sought order and stability in the market place.

Even the various approaches to the emergence of the very large firm fall into the same pattern. The problem was to find ways to obtain the benefits of bigness and rationality while at the same time leaving the doorway of opportunity open to smaller firms and newcomers.

Another way of making this point is to say that the state asserted its primacy over private capital. In effect, government subjected business to higher performance standards. That assertion found different expressions in different countries, but the underlying objective was similar. In the railroad industry, for example, and in utilities (gas, water, electricity) the technique was public ownership and operation in some countries but regulation in others. The common denominator was the idea that these services were so essential to the public welfare that society had to insist that they operate accordingly. In insurance, housing, and mortgage lending, some countries turned to state competition to force private underwriters, landlords, and lenders to reduce their charges and in that way to perform satisfactorily. Elsewhere, the same goal was sought through public regulation. Similarly, building codes set performance standards for property owners, and zoning laws subjected them to uses embodying standards of community welfare over private rights. Even the conservation movement, whether manifested in the preservation of recreational land or in the management of natural resources, reflected the same trend: the subordination of private claims to the larger public interest.

Finally, universality can be seen in programs dealing with problems of dependency. Throughout the world of reform, state intervention hinged on the perception that neither capitalism nor charity could deal adequately with the needs of the aged, the orphaned, the widowed, the disabled, the sick, or the unemployed. A few innovators aside, businessmen generally rejected responsibility for such problems, and charitable organizations—even if they possessed the will to respond—lacked the organization and resources to be effective. In the new economic order needs were far too massive for traditional solutions.

Perhaps more important was the revolution in the perception of dependency. In the emerging politics of the late nineteenth century, citizens began asserting claims on society as a matter of right rather than of charity. Responses to these demands varied from country to country. Most commonly, the state invoked the insurance principle, thereby rationalizing the creation of welfare payments on rights earned through contributions to the program, but in other systems legislatures looked to the general pool of revenue for funding. Rights lay in citizenship, not in premium payments. Either way, progressivism everywhere was moving toward the modern welfare state.

Stressing state intervention as the common response to the crisis of capitalism does not mean that the world of reform functioned exclusively on that single stage. On the contrary, enormous private efforts were simultaneously at work as people everywhere sought to order their lives and define relationships through voluntary organizations. Associations were formed or reconstituted to meet every need, from merchants to steelmakers, attorneys to medical doctors, historians to political scientists, farmers to meat packers, and from undertakers to underwriters.

Several points need to be made about this trend. First, although they were voluntary organizations, most of them were concerned with setting standards of behavior or performance. Membership conferred recognition and status, but it also brought with it obligations to act according to a code of conduct prescribed by the group, be it fair dealing, medical ethics, or the canons of scholarly objectivity. Second, the organizational trend was overwhelmingly linked to occupational, professional, and business categories—iron molders, engineers, mine owners—each of which defined for itself a set of interests that were at once both self-serving and supposedly of benefit to society at large. Third, it was then a relatively short step to the promotion of group interests through legislative intervention. The obvious examples are the licensing of architects, attorneys, barbers, doctors, and engineers and the regulation on grounds of health or safety of food processors, drug manufacturers, or railroads. In other words, the effort to achieve order through private means became in due course the vehicle moving societies everywhere along the road to the modern welfare state.

Obviously, much more could be said about the ways that countries responded in the 1890s and beyond to the crisis in capitalism, but these examples illustrate the common trends and underscore the similarity of the American experience to what was happening elsewhere.

Similarities also existed in the process of reform and underscore the parallels between American Progressivism and patterns of change elsewhere. Several approaches suggest themselves. First, the label Progressivism masks the universal transformation of liberalism as a philosophy and a program. At the birth of the American Republic and for some time afterward, liberalism here as elsewhere was a revolutionary and dynamic force for change. In the past, government had been a repressive and tyrannical instrument dedicated to the preservation and enhancement of the wealth and power of entrenched vested interests. The only way to alter the human condition, it came to be believed, was to reduce government to the barest essentials by enlarging to the greatest extent possible the domain of individual choice and freedom. Every aspect of life—association, religion, speech, behavior, commerce—had to be made absolutely free.

This nineteenth-century unleashing of individual ambition and energy had prodigious material results, which probably went far beyond what Adam Smith and his followers could possibly have envisioned. Evidence of progress piled up on every hand—burgeoning cities, factories, farms, and mines; vast railway networks, bridges flung across great rivers, and telegraph lines snaking across continents; and Western civilization and commerce carried to even the most remote corners of the globe.

But the costs of that progress were everywhere just as visible, whether in the gritty, black Salford slum of Manchester where my mother grew up, in the deathly mines of Arizona's copper collar, or in the mosquito-infested rice fields of Italy. By the late nineteenth century these conditions seemed to say that the newly invented system of liberalism had spun out of control, that the new freedom no longer pushed the boundaries of human potential outward. The overwhelming majority, it now seemed, were once more condemned, as they had been throughout most of human history, to the hard scrabble of survival on the margins of life.

Liberalism then took a 180-degree turn. In place of the classical concepts of freedom came a new orthodoxy, one utterly unrecognizable from the liberalism of the Founding Fathers or the Manchester school of economics. The goal of public policy remained unchanged; it was still a fundamental commitment to individual autonomy and dignity. But the means to that end were quite different. Decision makers now concluded that the world had become too complicated and too dangerous to be left to the efficacy of the "invisible hand" of the marketplace. What was needed was a new remedy, a new strategy. Though they had different names for it then—liberalism, state capitalism, state socialism—what they really had in mind is what we now call planning. In the private sector, that meant the application of scientific principles to the tasks of management with the objective of bringing rationality, order, and control to the world of business. In the public domain, it meant applying the same principles and techniques to the task of improving the quality of civic and individual life.

Progressivism in the United States, therefore, was the American version of this worldwide transformation of liberalism. It is easy to see the United States as a laggard in the development of the modern welfare state. One can cite the belated establishment of security for the aged or the failure to this day to create what looks like a "traditional" national health system. That is to miss several crucial points, however. For all of its fiscal and other problems, the social security system has evolved into a comprehensive and generous program comparable to what is provided elsewhere. And for most Americans, poor and rich alike, comprehensive medical care is provided at nominal or no direct cost to the patient. The system may not look much like what is provided in other countries, but appearances can be deceptive—General Motors spends more on health insurance than on steel.

More crucially for this analysis, these and other responses to the needs and problems of the twentieth century had their origins not in the crisis of the Great Crash of 1929 or the Great Depression of the 1930s but in the emerging new liberalism of the Progressive years. In the United States, as elsewhere, the decades from the 1890s to the 1920s were years in which reformers enunciated the basic principles of state interventionism, achieved some successes in implementing their ideas, and in those ways laid the ground for the more sweeping changes of the 1930s and beyond. That is, the catastrophic events of the Hoover and Roosevelt years are best seen as the precipitating crises leading to an accelerated thrust toward the modern welfare state rather than as the beginnings of the process bringing us down to the present.

From the founding of the Republic, the American reform tradition had continuously renewed itself from both internal and external sources. Drawing on their own perceptions and experience as well as on ideas from abroad, Progressives came to share with their counterparts in Europe and elsewhere fundamentally different notions from their predecessors of both the meaning of freedom and the proper role of the state in its guarantee. What they saw was profoundly shaped by their domestic reform tradition—whether Henry George or Edward Bellamy, to cite two homegrown critics and prophets—as well as by what they saw and learned about reform activity elsewhere, witness the very different careers but remarkably similar outlooks of Walter Rauschenbusch, Vida Scudder, or Jane Addams and Ellen Gates Starr.

The point is that the new interventionism knew no national boundaries or even political allegiances. It became the universal theme of the emerging twentieth century. And so everywhere the center of political gravity shifted, drawing conservatives no less than traditional liberals toward what has emerged as the modern welfare state. Political rhetoric notwithstanding, thereafter the terms of debate would be quite different: not laissez faire or interventionism, but how much interventionism, when, and in what form.

Second, the worldwide similarity of theory and practice demonstrates how crucially the trend toward the welfare state depended on the development of an international information network. This was not a new phenomenon. After all, the transatlantic flow of knowledge had been underway since the Age of Discovery and we are well aware of the importance of the Continental and Scottish Enlightenments in shaping American ideals.[12] What was new by the late nineteenth century was the massiveness and speed of the flow as well as the capacity to disseminate information on a scale previously unknown.

The first information revolution, to distinguish it from the computer revolution of our own times, also had both a technological and an institutional base. Trains, steamships, the telegraph and cable, the telephone and radio, typewriters and typesetting equipment, and inexpensive paper and high-speed presses allowed an increase in velocity and volume and a decrease in cost of the transmission of news and commentary, while the Universal Postal Union and the mass circulation of books, pamphlets, reports, magazines, and newspapers provided the public with easy access to information. At the same time, sharp reductions in travel costs, together with improvements in comfort, convenience, and speed, greatly increased personal and professional contacts across continents and oceans.

From the perspective of the present we can now see that this international information network emerged in a series of interconnected, overlapping stages. The first can be categorized broadly as educational, meaning either the traditional grand tour of the Old World or training at European universities. The point is too well known to require elaboration, but one must be struck by the number of Progressives whose careers in reform had their origins in that experience, just as one must be impressed by the linkages that flowed from that experience across the boundaries of time and space.

One example will have to suffice. John Bates Clark, a major figure in the development of the economics profession and in linking the "dismal science" to ethical considerations, studied at Heidelberg and Zurich as well as at Brown and Amherst. As professor of political science and history at Smith in the 1880s, he made his students aware of the social problems of the day and deeply influenced Vida Scudder, who in 1884 went to Oxford as a postgraduate student, where she attended John Ruskin's lectures. On her return she taught at Wellesley, where for thirty-seven years she exposed successive generations of young women to her Christian socialist views. In their turn, many of her students, together with some of her colleagues and others in her religious circle, became active in settlement house work and other reform activities.[13]

What one sees in these interconnected lives and the many others like them is the way in which the European educational experience shaped American perceptions of and responses to the crisis in capitalism and democracy. But one sees as well the basis of contacts abroad, familiarization with reform trends elsewhere, and the transmission of those concerns to others by teaching, writing, and example.

Broadly educational, too, as contributors to the information network was the proliferation of the organizations we associate with Progressivism. They ranged from the American Association for Labor Legislation to the World Peace Foundation, and from the Anti-Saloon League to the Women's Trade Union League. Many of these associations had important international links. That was as true of professional societies, such as the American Economic Association, whose *Review* published many articles on foreign reforms, as it was of political groups, such as the American Fabian Society, whose monthly magazine paid close attention to international trends, or the National Consumers' League, which had European branches.

These organizations were important not merely as conduits for the publication of information from abroad. They were also important through their annual meetings and conferences as forums for the exchange of data and ideas and for making personal contacts. Participants carried back to their classrooms, pulpits, libraries, settlement houses, unions, offices, legislatures, and other settings what they had absorbed. Typically, what had been gathered in this way then passed into the local information network through that myriad of community organizations so characteristic of America at the turn of the century—men's clubs, women's clubs, church clubs, literary clubs, and the like. Sometimes it seems as if the Republic consisted of study circles rather than states.[14]

If this first phase of the information revolution was overwhelmingly voluntary and generally unsystematic, the second was dominated by public agencies and by a more orderly effort to pursue particular issues. It is in this second stage that important other characteristics of the Progressive movement came into play, most notably the rise of the bureaucracy as a vital innovative force in public affairs, the allocation of significant amounts of tax revenues to the acquisition, analysis, and dissemination of information, and through these vehicles the shaping of the reform agenda.

The first point to be made about the public agencies established in the two generations after the Civil War is that their initial role was overwhelmingly educational and informational. This was true at both the federal and state levels—hence the Massachusetts Bureau of Labor Statistics, which under Carroll D. Wright's leadership, 1873–1888, remained exclusively an investigatory body. Wright carried the same philosophy—a belief in public exposure as an engine for amelioration—to the U.S. Bureau of Labor and to the National Convention of Chiefs and Commissioners of Bureaus of Statistics of Labor, over which he presided for nearly twenty years.[15]

But it must also be said that Wright's view of the proper role of these agencies masks a fundamental shift in the kinds of information reported over the years. In the beginning, only local conditions were investigated. By the nineties, however, readers found more and more space devoted to foreign reports. This trend gathered momentum with the opening of the new century. Mostly these accounts were scrupulously objective and factual. Nevertheless, the content had changed. While the older style of reports on foreign working conditions continued—wages, living standards, industrial health, and so forth—the emphasis now shifted to legislative interventions of various kinds. Foreign laws, not foreign conditions, dominated the pages.[16]

Drawn along in the wake of this shift in emphasis came a rising interest by officials, legislators, labor reformers, and the informed public more generally in an evaluation of these foreign interventions. How well did they work? Were there lessons for Americans in these distant programs? Did they provide models for solving American problems? Answers to these kinds of questions now began to appear in the reports of labor bureaus, sometimes summarized from the literature, including partisan accounts, but commonly also obtained by sending experts abroad to conduct investigations in the field. Such was the case with Victor S. Clark, who prepared monographs for the U.S. Bureau of Labor on conditions in Australia, Cuba, Great Britain, Java, Mexico, and New Zealand, and Harris Weinstock, who in 1910 reported to the governor of California on ways to deal with strikes and lockouts. Weinstock had spent fifteen months in Europe and Australasia. While these kinds of reports were primarily factual, they also crossed Wright's informational boundary line by providing assessments and interpretations of what had been observed abroad. Weinstock, for example, urged California to adopt the Canadian approach to resolving industrial disputes. Subtly, but nevertheless unmistakably, official reports began to take on an advocacy role.[17]

The trend was probably inevitable. As agencies came increasingly to be staffed by professionals, either trained in the academy as labor economists, such as John R. Commons, or on the job, as Victor Clark was, neutrality on reform issues was hardly to be expected, the more so since many of those who gravitated to these careers were interventionists by inclination.[18] Such was the case with Florence Kelley, Illinois's first factory inspector, or Julia Lathrop, another graduate of Hull House, who went on to a distinguished and activist career as head of the U.S. Children's Bureau.[19] Also noteworthy in this respect was the formation in 1915 of the International Association of Accident Boards and Commissions. Essentially sponsored by the U.S. Bureau of Labor, the association served as a clearinghouse for administrative and legislative questions in the field of workmen's compensation. That is, by its very nature the association was dedicated to improving industrial health and safety and to improving the system of compensating injured employees. That required members to assume advocacy roles and to draw on worldwide experience for techniques and models.[20]

These examples also underscore the transformation of the bureaucracy itself. Wright's older concept of a narrowly statistical and informational role had to give way as legislatures conferred regulatory powers on labor bureaus or created new administrative agencies, such as the Interstate Commerce and Federal Trade commissions. Knowing what we do now about the ways these agencies have grown and proliferated down to our own times, we too easily forget the creative way in which they used their power, at least in their early years. Initially, at any rate, the leading administrative and staff positions were filled by men and women blessedly free from a preference for bureaucratic jargon, and the time had not yet come when agencies recruited lawyers dedicated to picking regulatory nits. Instead, policy-making personnel believed that they could make a difference in improving the lives of those whom they served. They saw the emerging bureaucracy as a powerful engine for change and for good.

Two very different cases illustrate this point. The first is the celebrated Ballinger-Pinchot controversy. Factionalism, personal animus, and party politics aside, the dispute really boiled down to a quarrel over which group was more dedicated to conservation, land-use planning, and opposition to the "interests." The "winner" in the struggle, at least until the Ickes report in 1940, was Gifford Pinchot, whose Forest Service publicity juggernaut speaks directly to the argument about the power of the new bureaucracy to exploit the information revolution and thereby shape public attitudes toward the systematic management of natural resources.[21]

In a very different way, as we have seen, Julia Lathrop's career also demonstrates the power of information to shape events. Her influence on the Illinois Board of Charities came from her making herself more knowledgeable than her colleagues about institutional conditions, and her successful campaigns for a juvenile court and a probation law drew no less powerfully on her careful study of the issues. She was persuasive because she had armed herself with the facts. Those were the qualities that also made her so effective at the Children's Bureau. Her "Baby-Saving Campaign" not only reduced infant mortality but it also improved maternal health. And she achieved those goals with an initial budget of less than $30,000. By 1921 she had secured federal funding for state programs.[22]

But these public agencies had more than just dedicated personnel. Just as crucially, they had the financial resources to pursue reform goals. By today's standards their budgets may seem woefully inadequate. Nevertheless, money bought information and conferred the power to use it to shape the progressive agenda. For the first time on a significant scale there were funds to send senior administrators to conferences at home and abroad, to commission field reports from all over the world and on all manner of subjects, and most fundamentally to gather and disseminate information.

This was especially true at the federal level, though it is important to notice that many of the subjects of inquiry were matters of state or local rather than national interest. Such was the case with the massive two-volume study of European social insurance programs directed for the U.S. Bureau of Labor by I. M. Rubinow and published in 1911. The investigation helped lay the basis for state and federal workmen's compensation laws and, eventually, the social security system.[23]

Rubinow's career, one might add, sustains the common but now questionable view of the Progressive era as the age of experts. Born in Russian Poland in 1875, Rubinow came to the United States in 1893. After earning an accelerated baccalaureate at Columbia in 1895 he went on to receive a medical degree at New York University three years later. Radicalized by his experience of working with New York's poor, he gave up medicine to become a leading agitator for and authority on all forms of social insurance. To that end he became an expert actuary and statistician. At one time or another until 1919 he held positions in the federal and New York City governments, worked for a private insurance company, served as a consultant to various state workmen's compensation boards, chaired the rate-making committee of the casualty underwriters' trade association, helped draft the standard health insurance statute sponsored by the American Association for Labor Legislation, and became secretary of the social insurance committee of the American Medical Association. Along the way he managed to find time to take a doctorate at Columbia (he used sections of his European report on social insurance for the dissertation), published authoritative books on health and social insurance, and founded the Casualty Actuarial and Statistical Society of America.[24]

The extraordinary range of this career, which has been only partially summarized here, underscores the importance of the flow of information from abroad into the American reform milieu. Rubinow's New York experience taught him that voluntary organizations—settlement houses and charity groups—provided no enduring or satisfactory solutions to the newly emerging problems of dependency in the urban cauldron of slums around him—not for victims of age, accident, health, orphanhood, or widowhood. Only compulsory programs of social insurance, he came to believe, would provide the essential safety net of support suffering humanity as well as the working poor needed. And that, he concluded, could be obtained only with certainty, dignity, and self-reliance along the lines so effectively demonstrated by the European experience. That the remedies Rubinow so passionately advocated came so slowly says a good deal about the fiscal, philosophical, and constitutional restraints of the times. It also speaks to flaws in his own temperament and personality and his lack of the essential political skills. Experts may set agendas, but they do not always control timetables.

The American Commission on Credit and Co-operation, which President Woodrow Wilson established in 1913, also illustrates in a very different context much the same process by which foreign models found their way into the emerging American welfare state. Made up of American and Canadian experts, the commission traveled to Europe to investigate distant solutions to pressing domestic problems—the desperate shortage of capital for long-term development and security. The idea for such an investigation came from a Californian, David Lubin, half-brother to Harris Weinstock and Weinstock's partner in a prosperous Sacramento department store and mail-order house. Governor Hiram Johnson nominated Weinstock to the federal commission, which in due course recommended a national system of rural credits. Weinstock was particularly impressed by two European concepts: mortgages amortized over very long periods so as to enable small farmers to acquire land of their own; and the system of substituting land bonds for mortgages. Congress created a comparable program in the Federal Farm Loan Act of 1916. It established twelve regional banks, jointly financed by the government and farmer cooperatives, to grant long-term loans at lower than prevailing market rates.[25]

On a more limited scale, the states and their larger cities also created new agencies or expanded the functions of existing ones, often combining, as did the federal government, both informational and regulatory functions. And from time to time they too appointed *ad hoc* commissions to investigate and report on particular problems or proposals. Evident as well was the same impressive flow of information into and out of the bureaucracy as a crucial element in the process of reform.

Again, at these levels both staff and funding were crucial considerations.

Several common elements stand out. Typically, every major constituency came to have its own permanent agency—agriculture, health, housing, labor, mining, transportation, utilities, and so forth—and each according to its mandate publicized its activities in annual and special reports. In many instances they received additional currency through newspaper and magazine accounts. Not uncommonly, these agencies comprised an appointed board of part-time, perhaps unpaid, commissioners and a full-time, professional staff. Although the commissioners were often political appointees, members usually brought to their service considerable experience in the area of the board's jurisdiction and strong commitments to reform. Academic experts commonly served on these commissions. Matthew B. Hammond of Ohio State University, for example, served on several state commissions (the Industrial Commission, the Health and Old Age Insurance Commission, and the Coal Mining Commission). He also advised the U.S. Food Administration and the U.S. Anthracite Coal Commission and served on the War Labor Policies Board.[26]

Depending on the human mix, in some instances these commissioners set the reform agenda; in others, the professional staff had the political skills together with sufficient control of the flow of data through the agency to move the commissioners in whatever direction they chose. In the formative years, however, bureaucrats normally were not sufficiently entrenched—either through longevity of service or through rigid adherence to prescribed administrative routines—to exercise domination.

That was less true of the general information agencies created during the progressive years—the legislative and municipal reference bureaus and the state libraries. Charles R. McCarthy in Wisconsin, for example, had a sensitive ear to the currents of public concern and supplied legislative leaders with timely reports on reform models from all over the nation and the world. To some extent, of course, McCarthy simply responded to the political issues of the day, but one can also be impressed by how acutely he anticipated what politicians wanted to know. And it is important to notice that he had the staff and resources to gather the information and considerable leeway in deciding the issues to be investigated.[27] Librarians, both in state capitals and in Washington, were probably more reactive than anticipatory, but at both levels the flow of information (bibliographies and reports) was crucial in informing legislators in particular and the interested public more generally of worldwide reform trends.[28] The task was facilitated, of course, by the international system of exchanging public documents. A check of the holdings of state libraries for the Progressive period is testimony indeed to the scale of this international flow of information.

Several examples of this process illustrate this point. First, the case of Harry L. Russell, the distinguished agricultural scientist at the University of Wisconsin. Between 1894 and 1907, when he became dean of the College of Agriculture, he probably did more than any other person to transform the Wisconsin dairy industry through his campaign to eradicate bovine tuberculosis. Though only partially successful—farmers and legislators resisted some of the compulsory elements in his program—in 1901 he was instrumental in the creation of a Livestock Sanitary Board empowered to eradicate and control diseased animals. Farmers could choose between compensated slaughter or a state quarantine. The statute drew directly on Danish practice, the effectiveness of which Russell demonstrated through his own field trials. Significantly, what Russell was doing for the Wisconsin dairy industry others, including John McKenzie in the New Zealand Department of Agriculture, were also doing throughout the world of dairying.[29]

The second example takes us back to California and the Lubin-Weinstock connection. As we have seen, as early as 1904 David Lubin recognized the importance of market information in the rationalization of the production, processing, and distribution of agricultural commodities. The International Institute of Agriculture he established in Rome eventually became the United Nations Food and Agriculture Organization. Simon Lubin, his son, and Harris Weinstock, his half-brother, became active in rural reconstruction in California, taking up the cause of migratory workers, small farmers, and the landless, through a variety of schemes: the regulation of labor camps, village settlements, demonstration farms, agricultural education, rural credit, and marketing cooperatives. These programs drew on models culled from the international reform network, ideas that they disseminated through investigative commissions and agency reports.

But the army of reform marched on more, much more, than the information and leadership supplied by these public agencies. The world of progressivism drew even more powerfully from private efforts as well. The process can be separated into two broad categories.

First, commercial considerations sent a tidal wave of ideas and information through the marketplace of reform as publishers of books, magazines, and newspapers kept American readers abreast of international trends. In the four decades from 1890 to 1930, citizens were probably better informed about worldwide reform currents than at any time before or since. To be sure, much of the information appeared in periodicals such as *Arena* or the *Commons*, which had only limited circulations and which, in any event, spoke primarily to those already converted to the New Liberalism. Nevertheless, many of their readers were reform activists and exercised an influence in public affairs many times greater than their mere numbers would indicate, and some periodicals, most notably Wayland's *Appeal to Reason*, reached millions, partly through subscriptions and partly through reading clubs.

As we have seen, these vehicles played a significant role in informing Americans about antipodean reform, but the flow of news, analysis, and commentary about Australasia was minuscule compared with what appeared in other areas of the world, especially in Great Britain and Europe. In any event, most publishers took a highly selective view of Australian and New Zealand liberalism, partly because only a few programs seemed to speak directly to American needs. Moreover, there were greater affinities with the problems of industrialization and urbanization on the other side of the Atlantic, such as slums or unemployment, and with the rural problems of landlordism and marketing. Hence the American interest in British housing programs, French public health reforms, German social insurance arrangements, the Irish land question, or Danish farm cooperatives. Publishers also responded to immigrant hunger for information about the countries of their birth, including accounts of reform programs.

What might be called "noncommercial" but still private agencies also played an important informational role. They ranged from the American Academy of Political and Social Science, which published hundreds of articles on worldwide reform issues in both its *Annals* and *Supplements*, often devoting entire issues to particular questions, sometimes by reproducing conference proceedings, and the American Association for Labor Legislation, whose journal reflected international reform currents, to the Church Social Union in Boston, whose semi-monthly tracts served as an Episcopal forum for the issues of social justice and as a vehicle for spreading Christian socialist ideas, to *Life and Labor*, the magazine of the Women's Trade Union League, which was edited by Alice Henry, an Australian-born immigrant who reached Chicago by way of the English social reform movement and who was very much an internationalist.

The striking thing about these publications and so many others like them—the *Commons*, the journal published by one of Chicago's most famous settlement houses; *Chautauqua*, the magazine of the New York self-improvement organization and sponsor of lecture-circuit networks, including a series in Australasia; *Charities*, the proceedings of the Conferences of Charities and Corrections; or *Survey*, its successor—was just how much attention they paid to international reform trends. There is no way to measure their impact on Progressivism, of course. However, it is inescapable that they educated the reading public and enlarged the milieu of American reform in much the same way, as previously noted, that the high school and collegiate debating circuit drew thousands of students into familiarity with worldwide reform trends.

What is also clear is that this organized flow of information from abroad helped bring American Progressivism into rough conformity with the emerging patterns of state interventionism and welfarism elsewhere. The work of the Russell Sage Foundation, though obviously an exceptional organization, speaks directly to this point. Established in New York City in 1907, it quickly emerged as an influential reform clearinghouse through a combination of research and publication activities. Particularly important, as already noted in the analysis of the hour and wage issue, was its underwriting of the innovative strategy used by Louis Brandeis and his successors to persuade judges that the regulation of the working conditions of women came within the police powers of the Constitution. The foundation financed the preparation of the briefs with their proofs drawn from international experience, subsidized the National Consumers' League in the publication and circulation of these arguments to legislators, officials, and judges, underwrote the publication of *Survey*, edited by Paul U. Kellogg, a leading Progressive activist, and sponsored economic and sociological research, mainly on women's issues. A private organization it may have been, but the power of money and professional staff had its impact, just as it did in the emerging public agencies, though the foundation had a clear advantage in that it could take a much more overt advocacy role than could bureaucrats.

Placing the Progressive movement in this larger context of worldwide reform adds a useful new dimension to our understanding of both the substance and the process of change in America. It does not mean, of course, that Progressivism became a mere mirror image of British liberalism or German statism any more than Australasian reform simply aped foreign concepts and models. What it does mean is that reformers everywhere drew on common bodies of knowledge, perception, and technique, adapting what they learned to their own country's distinctive needs, institutions, and traditions. And what it means as well is that in the Progressive era the United States, in common with the rest of the developed world, underwent a great change in public policy, which carried the Republic inexorably toward the modern welfare state.

NOTES

PREFACE

1. New York, 1931.
2. Boston, 1952.
3. *Pacific Historical Review* 27 (August 1958): 221–237; *Journal of Modern History* 30 (September 1958): 227–235.
4. Ibid., 234–235.
5. The Turner chapters span pp. 47–164.
6. See, for example, his *Survey of British Commonwealth Affairs, vol. 2, pts. 1 and 2, Problems of Economic Policy, 1918–1939* (London, 1940, 1942).

CHAPTER ONE. THE MISSION OF THE AMERICAN DEMOCRACY

1. Philadelphia, 1817, p. 36.
2. Hennig Cohen, editor, *White-Jacket or the World in a Man-of-War* (New York, 1967), 150.
3. From "The Emancipation of Labor," in *Hints toward Reforms, in Lectures, Addresses, and Other Writings* (New York, 1850), 49–50.
4. Leslie Lipson, *The Politics of Equality: New Zealand's Adventures in Democracy* (Chicago, 1948), passim.
5. For an example of the uses of political influence, see R. C. J. Stone, "The Thames Valley and Rotorua Railways Company Limited, 1882–9; A Study of the Relationship of Business and Government in Nineteenth Century New Zealand," *New Zealand Journal of History* 8 (April 1974): 22–43.
6. On the monopoly question, see Frank Dillingham, "Antitrust Legislation in New Zealand," *U.S. Consular Reports* 289 (October 1904): 89–90; and "Tips on Trust Busting from the Antipodes," *New York Times*, July 6, 1906. For Charles Edward Russell's criticism of Australasian policies, "Reports Failure of Model Government," ibid., June 7, 1911.
7. Compare Graeme Wynn, "Conservation and Society in Late Nineteenth-Century New Zealand," *New Zealand Journal of History* 11 (October 1977): 124–136; and *National Parks of New Zealand* (Wellington, 1965), 9–10.
8. For example, although a chief conservator of forests had been appointed in 1885, it was not until 1913 that a Royal Commission recommended principles of scientific management and its advice was not adopted until 1919, when the State Forest Service was established. See W. J. Wendelken, "Forests," in Ian Wards, editor, *New Zealand Atlas* (Wellington, 1976), 100–101.
9. The best-known example is Peter G. Filene, "An Obituary for 'The Progressive Movement,' " *American Quarterly* 22 (Spring 1970): 20–34. See also

David M. Kennedy, "Overview: The Progressive Era," *Historian* 37 (May 1975): 453–468; and John D. Buenker, "The Progressive Era: A Search for a Synthesis," *Mid-America* 51 (July 1969): 175–193.

10. See, for example, Michael H. Ebner and Eugene M. Tobin, editors, *The Age of Urban Reform: New Perspectives on the Progressive Era* (Port Washington, N.Y., 1977). The ten original essays in this collection confirm Filene's concern over conceptualization and my own point that particularity can obscure rather than clarify. Individually, these are useful analytical pieces; collectively, it is hard to see what, if anything, is the common thrust of urban reform. Nor do the editors draw the separate essays into an overarching synthesis.

11. For an especially impressive example of the particularist approach, see Richard L. McCormick, *From Realignment to Reform: Political Change in New York State, 1893–1910* (Ithaca, N.Y., 1981).

12. Compare David P. Thelen, *The New Citizenship: Origins of Progressivism in Wisconsin, 1885–1900* (Columbia, Mo., 1972); David P. Thelen, *Robert M. La Follette and the Insurgent Spirit* (Boston, 1976); and Melvin G. Holli, *Reform in Detroit: Hazen S. Pingree and Urban Politics* (New York, 1969).

CHAPTER TWO. THE MISSION OF THE NEW ZEALAND DEMOCRACY

1. *Lyttelton Times*, March 23, 1894; *Speech Delivered by J. D. Connolly (United States Consul) on the Occasion of an Address Being Presented to the Hon. Wm. Jennings in Commemoration of His Being Called to the Legislative Council of New Zealand* (Auckland, 1893), 6; N. J. Napier, *The Mission of the New Zealand Democracy* (Auckland, 1892), 15. Alpers had emigrated from Denmark in the seventies. Journalist and poet as well as teacher, he later practiced law and was eventually appointed to the Supreme Court bench. His personal reminiscences, *Cheerful Yesterdays* (London, 1928), appeared posthumously. Connolly was a Californian of Irish background. He served as consul from 1889 to 1897.

2. Michael Turnbull, *The New Zealand Bubble: The Wakefield Theory in Practice* (Wellington, 1959).

3. See pages 4 and 13. She wrote under the pseudonym of "Femina." Her husband, a surgeon, a member of the Nelson Provincial Council, and a resident magistrate, opposed the feminist movement. The pamphlet attracted the attention of John Stuart Mill. She also corresponded with Clementia Taylor, the secretary of the London Emancipation Society. See Patricia Grimshaw, *Women's Suffrage in New Zealand* (Auckland, 1972), 12, 14–15.

4. *Otago Daily Times* (Dunedin), September 19, 1872; *New Zealand Parliamentary Debates* (cited hereafter as *N.Z.P.D.*) 28 (1878): 193, 479; *The Possible Future Development of Government in Free States* (Wellington, 1882), 8; *The Year Book of New Zealand, 1886–1887* (Wellington), 3.

5. *Lyttelton Times,* July 12, 1890, and September 29, 1891; Stout is quoted in the Right Hon. The Earl of Onslow, *State Socialism and Labour Government in Antipodean Britain* (London, 1893), 4–5.

6. *Otago Daily Times,* March 28, 1872; Robert Stout, "The Social Future of Labourers," reprinted in the *Hawke's Bay Observer* (Napier), July 25, 1918; J. C. Richmond, *Historical Illustrations of Communism and the Idea of Property* (Nelson, 1872), 4; C. W. Purnell, *An Agrarian Law for New Zealand* (Wellington, 1874), 4, 9, 13; *Lyttelton Times,* June 8, 1880; August 6, 1888; *Sweating System in Dunedin* (Dunedin, 1889), 16; *Appendices to the Journals, House of Representatives,* 1890, H.-5, p. vi.

7. C. W. Purnell, *Our Land Laws: What Should Be Their Basis?* (Dunedin, 1876), 5; *New Zealand Herald* (Auckland), June 5, 1871; April 15, 1873; *Lyttelton Times,* January 3, 1871; July 23, 1879; October 25, 1879; May 18, 1884; William M. Bolt, *Land and Labour* (Dunedin, 1882), 13; *Otago Daily Times,* June 28, 1873; March 19 and 21, 1883; newspaper clipping collection, Stout Papers (Alexander Turnbull Library, Wellington), undated and unspecified, but probably an issue in ibid., for 1873.

8. *Otago Daily Times,* July 19, 1882; March 19, 1883; "A Voice from the People," *Hard Times and Land Monopoly* (Auckland, 1884), 2.

9. *Lyttelton Times,* October 28, 1887, September 30, 1889, March 4, 1890; W. B. Sutch, *The Quest for Security in New Zealand, 1840 to 1966* (Wellington, 1966), 68–69; A. H. McLintock, editor, *An Encyclopedia of New Zealand* (3 vols., Wellington, 1966), 2: 796.

10. Keith Sinclair, *William Pember Reeves: New Zealand Fabian* (Oxford, 1965), 136, 138–139, 147–151.

11. Leslie Lipson, *The Politics of Equality: New Zealand's Adventures in Democracy* (Chicago, 1948), 19–26, 167–169.

12. Grimshaw, *Women's Suffrage in New Zealand,* passim.

13. A. R. Grigg, "Prohibition and Women: The Preservation of an Ideal and a Myth," *New Zealand Journal of History* 17 (October 1, 1983): 144–165. As compared with the 1890 election, the Liberals increased their percentage of the vote from 56 to 58 and their number of seats in the House from 31 to 51. See Lipson, *Politics of Equality,* 186.

14. *Lyttelton Times,* October 24, 1891.

15. J. D. N. McDonald, "New Zealand Land Legislation," *Historical Studies: Australia and New Zealand* 5 (November 1952): 195–211.

16. Quoted in André Siegfried, *Democracy in New Zealand,* translated by E. V. Burns (London, 1914), 108. On Reeves, see Sinclair's biography, especially chapters 1–7.

17. The industrial code is set out in an official publication, *The Labour Laws of New Zealand* (Wellington, 1903).

18. See two articles by James Holt, "The Political Origins of Compulsory Arbitration in New Zealand: A Comparison with Great Britain," and "Compulsory Arbitration in New Zealand, 1894–1901: The Evolution of an Industrial Relations System," *New Zealand Journal of History* 10 (October 1976): 99–111;

and 14 (October 1980): 179–200; and Sinclair, *Reeves,* 105–116, 151–153, 203–213.

19. R. T. Shannon, "The Fall of Reeves, 1893–1896," in Robert Chapman and Keith Sinclair, editors, *Studies of a Small Democracy: Essays in Honour of Willis Airey* (Auckland, 1963), 127–152; Sinclair, *Reeves,* especially pp. 214–245.

20. R. M. Burdon, *King Dick: A Biography of Richard John Seddon* (Christchurch, 1955), 1–106 passim; W. H. Oliver, *The Story of New Zealand* (London, 1960), 148–160.

21. Frank Parsons, *The Story of New Zealand: A History of New Zealand from the Earliest Times to the Present . . .* (Philadelphia, 1904), 279–289, 367–397 passim; William Pember Reeves, *State Experiments in Australia & New Zealand* (2 vols., London, 1902), 216–241.

22. Hugh H. Lusk, *Social Welfare in New Zealand: The Result of Twenty Years of Progressive Social Legislation and Its Significance for the United States and Other Countries* (New York, 1913), 126–163, 198–238 passim.

23. N. M. Chappell, *New Zealand Banker's Hundred: A History of the Bank of New Zealand, 1861–1961* (Wellington, 1961), 161–276 passim.

24. The Seddon quotations are from *N.Z.P.D.,* 95 (1896): 624, and W. B. Sutch, *Poverty and Progress in New Zealand: A Re-Assessment* (Wellington, 1969), 151.

25. The summary of social reform is drawn from Sutch, *Poverty and Progress,* 168–186, the revised edition of his 1942 Penguin Special, *The Quest for Security in New Zealand, 1840–1966* (Wellington, 1966), 82–96, 141–164, and from his *Women with a Cause,* 2d ed. rev. (Wellington, 1974), 70–99.

26. Siegfried, *Democracy in New Zealand,* 96.

27. Parsons, *The Story of New Zealand,* 715.

CHAPTER THREE. THE ANTIPODES THROUGH AMERICAN EYES

1. *Independent* 71 (August 17, 1911): 367–370.

2. "Social Experiments in New Zealand," *Outlook* 49 (April 7, 1894): 620–621.

3. For Lloyd's early contacts, see Fred W. Boys, Robert Stout, Edward Tregear, and Henry Latchford to Lloyd, September 1, 1893; March 22, April 28, June 25, 1894, in the Henry Demarest Lloyd Papers, State Historical Society of Wisconsin, Madison. Unless otherwise indicated, all Lloyd correspondence is from this collection. Lloyd sent Richard T. Ely information about state-owned railways in Australia in October 1893, the same month that the University of Wisconsin debated the public-ownership question; see their letters of September 30, October 1 and 18, 1893. See pages 150–153 of the Bliss *Handbook* and pages 932–938 of the *Encylopedia* for essays on New Zealand reform. Additional information appeared under such entries as arbitration and conciliation in industrial disputes, cooperation, insurance, land, and unemployed. Advance sheets of Bliss's essay on "Arbitration and Conciliation in Labor Disputes" were issued as a pamphlet in the *Publications of the Church Social Union,* Series B, no. 3 (June 15, 1895). For an excellent essay on Frank Parsons,

with a full listing of his articles on New Zealand, see Mann, *Yankee Reformers*, 126–144. For Peebles's reports on antipodean reform, see "If a Little Socialism Is a Good Thing for Labor in New Zealand, Why Not for American Labor?" *Appeal to Reason*, March 19, 1898; "A Conversation with J. M. Peebles on New Zealand—Political, Social, and Religious," *Arena* 29 (April 1903): 397–405. For Wayland's early commentary on New Zealand affairs, see *Appeal to Reason*, February 8, June 13, October 10, 1896; April 17, June 19, September 4, October 30, 1897.

4. See Jencks to Lloyd, October 31, 1900; Lusk to Lloyd, August 13, September 19, October 14, 21, November 9, 23, 1898; March 17, October 18, November 14, December 9, 25, 1899; January 12, February 9, 1900; and Lusk's articles, "Single Tax in Operation," *Arena* 18 (July 1897): 79–89, "Remarkable Success of Woman's Enfranchisement in New Zealand," *Forum* 23 (April 1897): 173–183, "Industrial Emancipation in New Zealand," *Outlook* 62 (May 1899): 167–170, "Old-Age Pensions in New Zealand," *Harper's Weekly* 43 (August 5, 1899): 781.

5. Henry W. Goodrich, E. B. Watson to Lloyd, December 31, October 12, 1898, and an undated handbill announcing a labor rally at Elgin, Illinois, on April 30, 1896, in box 66 of the Lloyd Papers; *Appeal to Reason*, September 4, 1897.

6. Lloyd to William Mather, December 3, 1898. There is a full account of his tour in Chester McArthur Destler, *Henry Demarest Lloyd and the Empire of Reform* (Philadelphia, 1963), chap. 19, which carried the subtitle, "To Altruria," an idea Lloyd included in *Wealth against Commonwealth* and William Dean Howells used in the title of his utopian novel, *A Traveller from Altruria* (1894).

7. Lloyd to Watson, Anna White, October 17, 19, 1898.

8. Undated clipping, *Sheridan Road News-Letter*, in the Lloyd Papers; Lloyd to George Jones, September 14, 1899.

9. This style of reporting characterized his *Country without Strikes: A Visit to the Compulsory Arbitration Court of New Zealand* (New York, 1900) and *Newest England: Notes of a Democratic Traveller in New Zealand, with Some Australian Comparisons* (New York, 1900).

10. Henry Demarest Lloyd, "New Zealand Newest England," *Atlantic Monthly* 84 (December 1899): 789–794, pp. 793–794 for the quotation; Lloyd to Watson, October 19, 1898.

11. Lloyd's magazine articles were "A Visit to the Compulsory Arbitration Court of New Zealand," *Outlook* 63 (December 9, 1899): 877–879; "Some New Zealand Scenes," *Ainslee's Magazine* 4 (January 1900): 752–759; "A Living Wage by Law," *Independent* 52 (September 27, 1900): 2330–2332; "Problems of the Pacific: New Zealand," *National Geographic Magazine* 13 (September 1902): 342–352; "Australasian Cures for Coal Wars," *Atlantic Monthly* 90 (November 1902): 667–674; "Fact and Fancy about New Zealand," *Boyce's Weekly* February 4, 1903; "The Antipodes of Boston," ibid., February 18, 1903; "New 'Song of the Shirt,' " *Sunday School Times* (Philadelphia), March 21, 1903; and "The Abolition of Poverty," *Good Housekeeping* 37 (September 1903): 216–220.

Some of this material reached a wider audience through *Current Literature:* see "Compulsory Arbitration in New Zealand," and "Some New Zealand Experiments," 27 (February 1900): 158, and 29 (November and December 1900): 513–515, 670–674.

See also his essay "Compulsory Arbitration: Arbitration Courts a Logical Necessity," in John F. Peters, editor, *Labor and Capital: A Discussion of the Relations of Employers and Employed* (New York, 1902), 185–199; and for his testimony before the Anthracite Strike Commission, see *Boyce's Weekly,* March 25, 1903, and a collection of his works, *Men, the Workers* (New York, 1909), 201–252.

For newspaper interviews and articles, see *Boston Herald,* June 27, 1899; *Springfield* (Massachusetts) *Republican,* July 21, 1899; "Unique among Peoples—A Country without 'Strikes,' " *New York Herald,* March 25, 1900; *New York Evening Post,* December 29, 1900; *Chicago Record-Herald,* October 22, 1901; *New York Evening Post,* December 7, 1901; "New Zealand Defended," *New York Journal,* January 10, 1902.

On the western lecture tour, see Lloyd to W. E. Ernst, August 1, 1901, to William Pember Reeves, November 5, 1901; *Los Angeles Times,* September 28, 1901; *Portland Evening-Telegram,* October 9, 1901; *Salt Lake Herald,* October 19, 1901; *Denver News,* October 21, 1901; *Omaha Bee,* October 25, 1901.

For examples of editorials and book reviews, see the *Bridgeport* (Connecticut) *Post,* May 12, 1900; *Chicago Tribune,* May 14, 1900; *Boston Globe,* June 21, 1900; *Independent* 52 (November 8, 1900): 2692–2693; Rev. John A. Ryan, "A Country without Strikes," *Catholic World* 72 (November 1900): 147–157; *Indianapolis News,* June 28, 1901.

12. Henry Mortimer Johnson, Gates, Latchford, Watson, and Wilbur F. Atchison to Lloyd, December 19, October 11, 1900; October 25, 1899; August 1, 11, 1902.

13. On academic and forensic influences, see David Lloyd, Charles Zueblin, Jenks, Ely, E. T. Chismore, Thomas J. Towers, E. P. Trueblood, Ernest E. Woods, J. R. Meek, Fred Esch, Trueblood, M. M. Gogg, W. W. Bride, Ely to Lloyd, May 25, October 13, 31, November 8, 1900; November 12, 1902; January 24, February 2, 17, 24, March 2, 14, 27, April 4, August 7, 1903.

For the quotations, see Destler, *Henry Demarest Lloyd,* 413 (*Social Gospel*); *Chicago Tribune,* November 21, 1901; *Outlook* 67 (February 16, 1901): 390–391; *New York Journal,* January 8, 1901. Compare "A Social Reformer," *Arena* 59 (October 1894): 577–589, esp. p. 579, in which Latchford thought that "it may be accounted among the extraordinary and hopeful signs of our time that New Zealand is to-day the most socialistic of all communities and among the most prosperous in the world."

14. Margaret W. Morley in the *Boston Evening Transcript,* November 9, 1901 and March 20, 1901.

15. "Books of the Day," *Arena* 26 (August 1901): 100–105, esp. pp. 100, 101, 105; "In the Mirror of the Present," ibid., 32 (July 1904): 85.

16. *Arena* 25 (January 1901): 90; ibid., 32: 85; "Premier Richard Seddon: Democracy's Lost Leader," ibid., 36 (August 1906): 196–200, p. 196 for the quotation; "Richard Seddon: Democratic Statesman and Master-Builder of a Liberal

Commonwealth," ibid. (November 1906): 449–463, pp. 450, 463 for the quotations.

17. Mann, *Yankee Reformers,* 126–144.

18. "Political Movement of the Nineteenth Century," *Arena* 26 (September 1901): 273.

19. B. O. Flower, *Progressive Men, Women, and Movements of the Past Twenty-Five Years* (Boston, 1914), 115.

20. Frank Parsons, *Politics in New Zealand* (Philadelphia, 1904), edited by C. F. Taylor, i–ii. *The Story of New Zealand* was copyrighted, but Taylor invited editors, journalists, and speakers to make fair use of the material. He declared that *"New Zealand is the most interesting corner of the world today."* See front and back covers of *Politics in New Zealand.*

21. Parsons, *Story of New Zealand,* 691.

22. Ibid., 693, 700, 706, 710. These chapters of contrast (80–81) extend from pages 689 to 755.

23. Ibid., 710–711, 712.

24. Ibid., 713.

25. Mann, *Yankee Reformers,* 140.

26. "Professor Parsons' 'Story of New Zealand,' " *Arena* 31 (April 1904): 424–431, pp. 424, 431 for the quotations.

27. 56 (February 18, 1904): 386; 57 (November 17, 1904): 1141–1142.

28. Parsons, *Politics in New Zealand,* back cover.

29. For Flower's eulogy, see "Professor Frank Parsons, Ph.D.: An Appreciation," *Arena* 40 (November 1908): 497–500, esp. p. 498. Within a month Flower was urging the publication of a memorial edition of Parsons's works and most especially a new edition of *The Story of New Zealand.* It would be "an inspiration and guide to thousands of young men about to enter public life." See ibid., (December 1908): 638–639.

30. Smythe's career can be followed in Edwin R. Bingham, *Charles F. Lummis: Editor of the Southwest* (San Marino, Calif.: 1955), 70, 73, 76, 78, 144–151, 190; Martin E. Carlson, "William E. Smythe: Irrigation Crusader," *Journal of the West* 7 (January 1968): 41–47; Lawrence B. Lee, "Introduction to the 1969 Edition" of William E. Smythe, *The Conquest of Arid America* (Seattle, 1969), xxix–xliii; Lawrence B. Lee, "William Ellsworth Smythe and the Irrigation Movement: A Reconsideration," *Pacific Historical Review* 41 (August 1972): 289–311; Lawrence B. Lee, "William E. Smythe and San Diego, 1901–1908," *Journal of San Diego History* 9 (Winter 1973): 10–24.

31. Lloyd to Smythe, November 29, 1901.

32. Smythe to Lloyd, December 9, 1901; September 21, 1902; *Land of Sunshine* 15 (December 1901): 487–498. Smythe had anticipated some of these themes in two earlier essays, "How to Colonize the Pacific Coast" and "The Perils of Water Monopoly," in ibid., 383–397, in which he cited New Zealand and Australia as places where colonization was a function of government and where traditional English riparian doctrine had been set aside in favor of state control in the public interest.

33. *Land of Sunshine,* ibid., 495.

34. Ibid., 496.

35. See Smythe's columns in *Out West,* "The 20th Century West" and "The California Constructive League," from January 1902 through December 1903.

36. "The Law of Compulsory Arbitration at Work," ibid., 16 (January 1902): 82–88; "The Premier of New Zealand," and "The Government as a Colonizing Agency," ibid., (February 1902): 200–209; "How the People Smashed the Money Ring," ibid., (April 1902): 440–443; "An Important Letter on Compulsory Arbitration, Hitherto Unpublished [Edward Tregear to Harris Weinstock]," ibid. 17 (September 1902): 376–378; ibid. 16: 198; ibid. (March 1902): 319.

37. Smythe to Lloyd, February 5, 1902; "The Procession of Ideas," *Out West* 16 (May 1902): 544–546.

38. See Doubleday, Page & Co. to Smythe, and Smythe to Doubleday, Page & Co., December 19, 1901; January 2, March 20, 1902; Lloyd to Conrad Reno, Smythe, November 29, 1901; Reno to Lloyd, January 23, 1902; Smythe to Lloyd, July 19, August 7, November 21, December 9, 1901; September 21, November 14, 1902; Lloyd's undated commentary on Smythe's ideas, box 26, all in the Lloyd Papers; Lloyd to Caroline M. Severance, n.d., box 25, Caroline Severance Papers in the Huntington Library; Charles F. Lummis, "The Hour and the Man," *Out West* 17 (October 1902): 486–488; Richard F. Pourade, *Gold in the Sun: The History of San Diego* (7 vols., San Diego, 1960–1977) 5: 35–36; *Los Angeles Daily Times,* August 13, 20, 23, 1902.

39. William E. Smythe, "Running for Congress," *Out West* 17 (December 1902): 758–765; Smythe to Severance, September 12, 1906, in the Severance Papers.

40. Smythe to Lloyd, November 14, 1902; Charles F. Lummis, "Their Shadows Before," *Out West* 20 (January 1904): 89; William E. Smythe, "The 20th Century West," ibid., 103–104.

41. New York, 1905.

42. See chap. 7, "The Nation and the Moneyless Man," esp. pp. 414, 417.

43. See pp. 419, 420, 421, 424.

44. See pp. 225–226.

45. Between 1909 and 1916 Smythe promoted a cooperative agricultural settlement near San Diego. See Lawrence B. Lee, "The Little Landers Colony of San Ysidro," *San Diego History* 21 (Winter 1975): 26–51; Robert V. Hine, *California's Utopian Colonies* (San Marino, Calif., 1953), 144–148, 162; Henry S. Anderson, "The Little Landers' Land Colonies; A Unique Agricultural Experiment in California," *Agricultural History* 5 (October 1931): 139–150.

46. Wayland's own account of his career is in his *Leaves of Life: A Story of Twenty Years of Socialist Agitation* (Girard, Kans.: 1912), 7–33. See also, Howard H. Quint, "Wayland Plants Grass Roots Socialism," in *The Forging of American Socialism: Origins of the Modern Movement* (Indianapolis, 1953), 175–209.

47. George Allen England, *The Story of the Appeal* (Girard, Kans., 1914), 11, 70–81, plate facing 159, 270–271, 276, 277; *Appeal to Reason,* April 17, 1897, May 6, 20, September 30, December 9, 1899.

48. George D. Brewer, *"The Fighting Editor" or "Warren and the Appeal"* (2d ed., Girard, Kans., 1910), ix–xvii.

49. *Appeal to Reason*, January 18, February 8, June 13, October 10, 1896. See also, ibid., April 17, June 19, September 4, October 30, 1897; March 19, 1898.

50. Ibid., March 19, 1898.

51. Ibid., April 17, 1897.

52. Ibid., September 4, 1897.

53. Ibid., October 30, 1897.

54. Ibid., March 19, 1898. See also, ibid., June 4, 25, August 13, 1898.

55. Ibid., October 1, 1898.

56. Ibid.; ibid., October 8, 15, November 5, December 17, 24, 31, 1898; January 28, February 4, 25, March 4, 11, April 1, 22, May 20, July 1, 15, August 12, 19, 26, September 16, October 7, 14, November 4, 11, 25, December 9, 1899.

57. Ibid., December 16, 1899; October 15, 1898; December 30, 1899.

58. Wayland to Lloyd, May 5, 1900; *Appeal to Reason*, November 4, 1899.

59. Ibid., February 24, 1900. The special edition may have sold 500,000 copies. For earlier items, see ibid., January 6, 20, 27, February 3, 10, 1900.

60. Ibid., March 3, May 12, 1900. For other comments, see ibid., March 17, 24, 31, April 7, 14, 28, May 5, 1900. They included, for example, Wayland's reaction to a reduction in telegraph rates. "That is the way the poeple degenerate into barbarism under the baleful influence of public ownership!"

61. Ibid., May 20, 1899; October 27, December 29, 1900; August 10, 1901; May 10, 17, 1902.

62. The quotation is from the introduction (p. 4) and may have been written by the compiler, Harvey Howard.

63. Ibid.

64. Ibid.

65. Ibid., 6–7, 22, 27–29, 33–35, 43–45.

66. Ibid., July 21, 1900; January 3, 1903. Orders continued long after the edition had been exhausted. Wayland then offered Parsons's *Politics in New Zealand* as a substitute. See ibid., June 24, 1905.

67. Ibid., August 24, 1901.

68. The campaign may be followed in ibid., February 17, May 12, 19, 26, June 2, 9, 16, 23, 30, July 7, 1900.

69. On circulation, see ibid., December 29, 1900; December 13, 1902; on other matters, see ibid., June 9, 16, 23, July 7, 14, August 11, October 27, December 29, 1900; January 12, 19, 26, February 2, March 16, April 6, 13, 20, May 25, July 6, 20, 27, August 10, 17, 31, September 7, 14, 21, 28, October 19, 26, November 2, 16, December 7, 14, 1901; March 15, April 12, May 10, 17, 31, June 7, 28, July 5, August 16, 23, October 4, November 1, 1902; May 30, July 18, 1903.

70. Ibid., September 12, 1903. Earlier (October 1, 1898), Wayland had described the "semi-socialist character" of New Zealand.

71. Ibid., April 25, 1903. Compare ibid., April 4, 1903.

72. Quint, *The Forging of American Socialism*, 200, 208–209; Charles L. Scott, "Appeal to Reason: A Study of the 'Largest Political Newspaper in the World' " (unpublished master's thesis, University of Kansas, 1957), 19. The shift also reflected the more active role played by Fred D. Warren, the managing editor.

73. See *Appeal to Reason,* June 4, December 17, 1904; June 10, 17, 24, August 19, September 23, 1905; January 6, February 10, July 7, September 29, 1906; August 28, 1909; March 5, 1910; March 25, April 1, 8, August 5, 12, September 30, October 28, November 4, 1911; March 23, June 15, 29, 1912; May 31, July 19, August 16, July 18, 1914.

74. Russell contributed a series of articles to *Everybody's Magazine* under the general title "Soldiers of the Common Good." See 15 (September, November, December 1906): 318–328, 581–593, 784–795.

75. Ibid., 582.

76. Ibid., 795.

77. Russell wrote two articles for *The National Post* 1 (June 17, July 1, 1911): 22–28, 28–32; under the general title "Checking Up New Zealand." The first described "Some Unexpected Results of Its Experiments in Radical Legislation" and the second "The War on Strikes and the Effect." He reported that the masses liked the many innovations that had been tried and that New Zealand was still "the experiment station of progress." He declared compulsory arbitration "an inadequate device," however, and criticized the government for "fooling with half-way measures."

He was much more critical in the seven articles he wrote for *The Coming Nation.* They were "Lessons from the Antipodes. The Labor Party of Australia and How It Fares in Political Policies"; "New Lights on the Common Good: How the 'Low, Common Workingmen' of Australia Conduct the National Machinery"; "More Light on the Common Good: How 'Trust Busting' is Carried On in the Antipodes as in the United States; Practical Workings of State Capitalism in New Zealand; The Collapse of Compulsory Arbitration; and New Zealand Government Housing Schemes for the Working Classes," June 3, 24, July 22, August 5, 12, September 2, 30, 1911. The quotations are from August 5 and 12.

See also, "New Zealand's Present Handicap through Absence of Democratic Machinery," an unsigned editorial, presumably written by B. O. Flower (in *Twentieth Century Magazine* 4 [August 1911]: 459–462), declaring Russell "right. There is no half-way house between democracy . . . and class-rule; between justice and equality of opportunities and rights, and oppression, stagnation and injustice." Only the initiative, referendum, and the right of recall would provide the tools of democracy (see p. 462).

78. G. H. Scholefield, editor, *A Dictionary of New Zealand Biography* (2 vols., Wellington, 1940), 1: 509–510.

79. *New York Times,* April 18, 1898.

80. 42 (May 20, 1899): 167–170; pp. 167, 170 for the quotations.

81. The book was published in New York by Doubleday & McClure Co.

82. See pp. 244, 295.

83. Ibid., 88, 110.

84. For Lusk's articles, see "Old Age Pensions," *Arena* 23 (June 1900): 635–646; "The Successful Prevention of Strikes: Seven Years of Compulsory Arbitration in New Zealand—The Adoption of the Law in Neighboring Colonies," *World's Work* 3 (February 1902): 1781–1783; "Compulsory Arbitration:

The Experience of New Zealand," in Peters, *Labor and Capital,* 221–237; "Government by Laborers," in *Harper's Weekly* 54 (July 16, 1910): 26; "Practical Socialism: A New Study in Political Economy," *Forum* 48 (September 1912): 285–293; "Industrial War," in ibid. (November 1912): 553–564. See also, "Compulsory Arbitration: What It Means in New Zealand; What It Means for America," in *Reports of the Industrial Commission on Labor Organizations, Labor Disputes, and Arbitration, and on Railway Labor,* 17 (Washington, D.C., 1901): 702–706; reprinting Lusk's articles from the *Bricklayer and Mason* for May and June 1901.

85. See p. 287 for the quotation and the *New York Times,* October 6, 1912, for Lusk's full-page summary, "New Zealand's Venture in Social Reform Has Paid."

CHAPTER FOUR. NEW ZEALANDIZING THE UNITED STATES

1. Compare Flower, "Richard Seddon," 458–458, and Russell, "Soldiers of the Common Good: New Zealand—The Advance Guard," *Everybody's Magazine,* 15 (December 1906): 795. See also J. T. Paul, *Humanism in Politics: New Zealand Labour Party Retrospect* (Wellington, 1946); Allen Kelly, "Under the Southern Cross: An Interview with Premier of New Zealand, Mr. Seddon," *Los Angeles Sunday Times* 6 (January 14, 1906): 6. This was the ninth in seventeen columns on Australia and New Zealand appearing in the Sunday editions between December 1905 and March 1906. Kelly's wife, Florence Finch Kelly, also a journalist, accompanied him and wrote a number of articles on New Zealand reforms.

2. Compare Albert Métin, *Le Socialisme sans Doctrines* (Paris, 1910); André Siegfried, *Democracy in New Zealand,* translated by E. V. Burns (London, 1914); Sidney Webb and Beatrice Webb, *Industrial Democracy* (London, 1911); John A. Ryan, "A Programme of Social Reform by Legislation," *Catholic World* 89 (August 1909): 608–614; "Progressive Legislation in New Zealand," *Progressive Review* 1 (December 1896): 225–239.

3. Tregear to Lloyd, April 28, 1894.

4. B. J. Wellman to Chief Postmaster, Christchurch, December 18, 1895, in the Colonial Secretary files, New Zealand National Archives, Wellington; William Dean Howells to Sylvester Baxter, May 11, 1898, HM 41414, William Dean Howells Collection, in the Huntington Library, San Marino, possibly commenting on a lecture by Lusk; *New York Times,* September 30, 1900; and letters from R. B. Thomas, Rev. Walter Howard Moore, John R. Haynes, and Emma Alice Wilkinson, November 18, 1903, March 11, 1908, December 2, 1904, February 2, 1912, in the Colonial Secretary files.

5. On requests for information, see *Appeal to Reason,* April 14, May 19, 1900; J. Mackay, W. G. Eggleston, Sam Bowles to Lloyd, June 8, 1900; May 19, August 6, 1902; C. Mortimer White, Charles McCarthy, Charles W. Hall and friends to the Colonial Secretary, Joseph Schafer to R. J. Seddon, December 12, 1901; October 11, 1904; December 10, 1896; January 27, 1906, in the Colonial Secretary

files; Stanley R. Osborne, Selden Smyser to U.S. Consul, in Miscellaneous Correspondence, Auckland, 3: 137, 10: 103 (November 11, 1902; December 7, 1907), State Department, National Archives, Washington (hereinafter cited as U.S. Consul).

6. For the quotations, see J. V. Rakestraw, Althea Briggs, Elof Anderson, P. R. Sande, November 13, 1904; September 20, 1908; April 29, 1901; October 20, 1906, in the Colonial Secretary files.

7. George B. Harrison, "A New Zealand of Our Own," *Appeal to Reason*, June 2, 1900; *Kansas City Star*, May 29, 1900. See also Edward T. James and others, editors, *Notable American Women, 1607–1950: A Biographical Dictionary* (3 vols, Boston, 1971), 1: 481–482, for Diggs's career.

8. "The New Zealand Innovation," *Spectator* 81 (October 15, 1898): 516–517. See also William Franklin Willoughby, *Workingmen's Insurance* (New York, 1898), for a survey of European programs, both public and private.

9. March 5, April 14, 1899.

10. The quotations are from Lusk's articles, "Old Age Pensions," *Arena* 23 (June 1900): 640, 641, 646, and "Old-Age Pensions in New Zealand," *Harper's Weekly* 43 (August 5, 1899): 781. See also, W. P. Reeves, "The New Zealand Old-Age Pension Act," *National Review* 32 (February 1899): 818–825; and a summary in *Review of Reviews*, 19 (March 1899): 352–353; and Edward Tregear, "Old Age Pensions," *Independent* 51 (March 23, 1899): 799–802.

11. See *Newest England*, pp. 339–363; "The Abolition of Poverty," *Good Housekeeping* 37: 216–217, for the Lloyd quotation; on Parsons, see *Story of New Zealand*, 442–446, 790–798, and the back cover of *Politics in New Zealand* for the quotation; on Reeves, see *State Experiments*, 2: 242–300; on Australia, see Edward Everett Hale, "Old-Age Pensions," *Cosmopolitan* 35 (June 1903): 168–172; "Old Age Pensions in Australasia," *Nation* 82 (February 1, 1906): 96–97; "Old-Age Pensions in Australia," *Independent* 61 (April 10, 1906): 834–835.

12. *Reports of the Industrial Commission*, 16: 240–241; "Old Age Pensions," *Independent* 55 (July 23, 1903): 1761–1762; Lucien C. Warner, "The Socialistic Legislation of New Zealand, as Viewed by an American," *American Monthly Review of Reviews* 28 (October 1903): 467–471. See also, J[ohn] C[ollier], "Old-Age Pensions in Australasia," *Nation* 82 (February 1, 1906): 96–97; "Old-Age Pensions in Australia," *Independent* 61 (April 10, 1906): 834–835; Florence Finch Kelly, "A New Civilization—What New Zealand Has Accomplished in Social and Economic Legislation," *Craftsman* 10 (September 1906): 714–729.

13. Brandeis strongly supported security for the aged but favored voluntary annuities. See his letters to John Edward Pember and Eben Sumner Draper, February 4, June 5, 1908, in Melvin I. Urofsky and David W. Levy, editors, *Letters of Louis D. Brandeis* (5 vols., Albany, 1971–1978), 2 (*1907–1912: People's Attorney*): 73–75, 176–177; Osmond K. Fraenkel, editor, *The Curse of Bigness: Miscellaneous Papers of Louis D. Brandeis* (New York, 1934), 25–29, for "Massachusetts' Substitute for Old-Age Pensions."

14. *Report of* [Massachusetts] *Commission on Old Age Pensions, Annuities*

and Insurance, House Report number 1400 (Boston, January 1910), esp. p. 310 for the quotation; Dr. James T. Buckley, the commission's secretary, to William Pember Reeves, April 25, 1908, in the Colonial Secretary files; Henry Rogers Seager, *Social Insurance: A Program of Social Reform* (New York, 1910), 143–144n; Abraham Epstein, *Facing Old Age: A Study of Old Age Dependency in the United States and Old Age Pensions* (New York, 1922); I. M. Rubinow, *Social Insurance* (New York, 1913); I. M. Rubinow, *The Quest for Security* (New York, 1934); J. Lee Kreader, "Isaac Max Rubinow: Pioneering Specialist in Social Insurance," *Social Service Review* 50 (September 1976): 402–425; Roy Lubove, *The Struggle for Social Security, 1900–1935* (Cambridge, 1968), 34–44.

In 1915 California began considering a comprehensive program. Rubinow served for six months as a consulting actuary. The commissioners concluded that the state could not afford such a program. See *Report of the Social Insurance Commission of the State of California, January 25, 1917* (Sacramento, 1917), esp. pp. 9–10; *Report of the Social Insurance Commission of the State of California, March 1919* (Sacramento, 1919).

15. Compare, Harry Weiss, "Employers' Liability and Workmen's Compensation," in John R. Commons, editor, *History of Labor in the United States, 1896–1932* (4 vols., New York, 1918–1935), 3: 564–610; Malverne Ray Wolfe, "The Evolution of Workmen's Compensation in the United States" (Ph.D. dissertation, University of Pittsburgh, 1950); Robert Asher, "Workmen's Compensation in the United States, 1880–1935" (Ph.D. dissertation, University of Minnesota, 1971); and nine articles by Charles Richmond Henderson on various aspects of industrial insurance, in *American Journal of Sociology* 12 (January–May 1907): 470–486, 717–734, 756–778; 13 (July 1907–May 1908): 34–47, 183–199, 349–379, 489–507, 584–616, 841–854.

16. There is an excellent survey and analysis of these problems in Lawrence M. Friedman and Jack Ladinsky, "Social Change and the Law of Industrial Accidents," *Columbia Law Review* 67 (January 1967): 50–82.

Summarized briefly, workmen's compensation in New Zealand was as follows: in 1882 the General Assembly adopted the new English principle making employers liable where there was a showing of negligence by the employer or his agent; in 1900 the Workers' Compensation Act dispensed with the negligence rule, but apparently provided no benefits if the injury was an inherent consequence of the nature of the work; and in 1908 the employer was made absolutely liable, regardless of inherent risk or finding of fault. Beginning in 1901, employers could choose between private and state insurers of risk; they were not compelled to buy accident coverage.

17. For early developments, see 35 *U.S. Statutes* 65 (1908) applying to interstate railroads; Lindley D. Clark, "Recent Action Relating to Employers' Liability and Workmen's Compensation," *Bulletin of the U.S. Bureau of Labor*, no. 90 (Washington, D.C., September 1910), 675–748; Lindley D. Clark, "Workmen's Compensation and Insurance Bills, 1911," ibid., no. 92 (Washington, D.C., 1911), 97–181; Lindley D. Clark, "Review of Labor Legislation of 1911: Employers' Liability and Workmen's Compensation," ibid., no. 97 (Washington, D.C., November 1911): 904–909; Gilbert Lewis Campbell, *In-*

dustrial Accidents and Their Compensation (Boston, 1911); Thomas I. Parkinson, "Problems and Progress of Workmen's Compensation Legislation," *American Labor Legislation Review* 1 (January 1911): 55–71.

For later developments, see the Workmen's Insurance and Compensation Series, issued as *Bulletins of the U.S. Bureau of Labor Statistics,* which included, beginning in 1917, the "Proceedings of the International Association of Industrial Accident Boards and Commissions"; Ralph H. Blanchard, *Liability and Compensation Insurance: Industrial Accidents and Their Prevention, Employers' Liability, Workmen's Compensation* (New York, 1917); E. H. Downey, *Workmen's Compensation* (New York, 1924).

See also four articles by Robert Asher, "Business and Workers' Welfare in the Progressive Era: Workmen's Compensation Reform in Massachusetts, 1880–1911," *Business History Review* 43 (Winter 1969): 452–475; "The 1911 Wisconsin Workmen's Compensation Law: A Study in Conservative Labor Reform," *Wisconsin Magazine of History* 57 (Winter 1973–1974): 123–140; "The Origins of Workmen's Compensation in Minnesota," *Minnesota History* 44 (Winter 1974): 142–153; "Radicalism and Reform: State Insurance of Workmen's Compensation in Minnesota, 1910–1933," *Labor History* 14 (Winter 1973): 19–41. See also Joseph L. Castrovinci, "Prelude to Welfare Capitalism: The Role of Business in the Enactment of Workmen's Compensation Legislation in Illinois, 1905–12," *Social Service Review* 50 (March 1976): 80–102; Robert F. Wesser, "Conflict and Compromise: The Workmen's Compensation Movement in New York, 1890s–1913," *Labor History* 12 (Summer 1971): 345–372.

18. For example, Minnesota, Illinois, and Wisconsin left the underwriting business to private firms; Ohio, Oregon, Nevada, Washington, West Virginia, and Wyoming gave state insurance offices a monopoly; and California, Colorado, Idaho, Maryland, Michigan, Montana, New York, Pennsylvania, and Utah followed the New Zealand system. Massachusetts underwrote the establishment of an employers' mutual insurance company to compete with private carriers. See also Edward Tregear, "Progress in New Zealand," *Independent* 52 (July 19, 1900): 1716–1719; Edward Tregear, "How New Zealand Is Solving the Problem of Popular Government," *Arena* 32 (December 1904): 574–575.

19. A. J. Pillsbury, "An Adventure in State Insurance," *American Economic Review* 9 (December 1919): 681–692. See also Franklin Hichborn, *Story of the California Legislature of 1911* (San Francisco, 1911), 236–245; *First Report of the Industrial Accident Board of the State of California, from September 1, 1911, to December 31, 1912* (Sacramento, 1913); *Report of the Industrial Accident Commission of the State of California for the Year 1913 and from January 1 to June 30, 1914* (San Francisco, n.d.); *Workmen's Compensation Laws of the State of California* (San Francisco, [1913]), esp. pp. 5–11.

20. Pillsbury, "Adventure in State Insurance," 682–683. See also *San Francisco Call,* January 30, February 20, 21, 22, April 3, 12, 1913; Franklin Hichborn, *Story of the Session of the California Legislature of 1913* (San Francisco, 1913), 345, 347–349; Harris Weinstock, *Why State Insurance?* (San Francisco [?], 1914 [?]); Meyer Lissner to J. O. Hayes, November 6, 1918, box 2, folder 13, Katherine P. Edson Papers, in the University of California Library, Los Angeles; *Report*

of the Industrial Accident Commission of the State of California, from July 1, 1916, to June 30, 1917 (San Francisco, n.d.), p. 23; *Report of the Industrial Accident Commission for the State of California, from July 31, 1917, to June 30, 1918* (San Francisco, 1918), p. 27.

21. Warner, "The Socialistic Legislation of New Zealand," 467–471.

22. John D. Connolly, "Land Taxation and Labor Laws in New Zealand," *U.S. Consular Reports* 53 (January 1897): 38; for the quotation. Ely had briefly described the program in his book *Socialism* (1894), pp. 304–305. See also, "Christian Politics," *New York Times*, April 18, 1898; "Australasia's Condition," ibid., June 11, 1899; Parsons to Lloyd, September 13, 1899; John A. Cockburn, "Sphere of Governmental Action in South Australia," *Annals of the American Academy of Political and Social Science* 14 (November 1899): 388–391; Lloyd, *Newest England*, 104–232; Lusk, *Our Foes at Home*, 63–110; Parsons, *Story of New Zealand*, 140–142, 191–228, 284–288; Smythe's undated statement urging the establishment of a national commission composed of statesmen, economists, irrigationists, and sociologists to promote colonization by either the federal government or a multistate voluntary organization (George Cooper Pardee Papers, Smythe folder, in the Bancroft Library, University of California, Berkeley); William M. Duffus to Sir Joseph Ward, October 23, 1911, in the Colonial Secretary's files; Siegfried, *Democracy in New Zealand*, 195–203.

23. February 1, 1906. For a very different view, see "Pioneering without Pain," *Independent* 71 (August 17, 1911): 382–384.

24. David Lubin, Simon's father, was the half-brother and partner of Harris Weinstock in a dry goods and mail order house in Sacramento. In 1904, convinced that the lack of timely and accurate market information exacerbated worldwide agricultural distress, he went to Rome, where the following year he established the International Institute of Agriculture as an information clearinghouse. It was the predecessor of the United Nations Food and Agriculture Organization.

Simon, born in 1876 and Harvard educated, spent his vacations in social work on New York's Lower East Side, and from 1903 to 1904 he resided at the South End House in Boston. Returning to Sacramento in 1906, he became manager and secretary of the family business, which was an early model, like Edward Filene's department store in Boston, in providing its employees with a voice in management, a credit union program, and retirement benefits.

See Mansel G. Blackford, *The Politics of Business in California, 1890–1920* (Columbus, Ohio, 1977), esp. pp. 28–39; Grace Larsen, "A Progressive in Agriculture: Harris Weinstock," *Agricultural History* 32 (July 1958): 187–193; Grace H. Larsen and Henry E. Erdman, "Aaron Sapiro: Genius of Farm Cooperative Promotion," *Mississippi Valley Historical Review* 49 (September 1962): 242–268; Samuel Edgerton Wood, "The California State Commission of Immigration and Housing: A Study of Administrative Organization and Growth of Function (Ph.D. dissertation, University of California, Berkeley, 1942); Harris Weinstock "Easy Money for the Farmer," *California Outlook*,

November 21, 1914; newspaper accounts of Weinstock's role on the American Commission on Credit and Cooperation in his Scrapbooks beginning in July 1913, in the Bancroft Library, University of California, Berkeley; *Agricultural and Rural Credit in Europe* (63 Congress, 2 session, Senate Document no. 261, pt. 1, serial 6570, Washington, D.C., 1914); *Information and Evidence, May 12 to July 18, 1913* (63 Congress, 1 session, Senate Document no. 214, serial 6519, Washington, D.C., 1913); Earl Sylvester Sparks, *History and Theory of Agricultural Credit in the United States* (New York, 1932), esp. chapter 7; Mead's entry in the *Dictionary of American Biography,* 11 (Supp. 2): 443–444; Weinstock to Rowell, January 22, 1916, urging him to accept an appointment to the Rural Credits Commission, in the Chester H. Rowell Papers, Box 26, Bancroft Library, University of California, Berkeley.

25. *Report of the State [California] Settlement Board, September 30, 1920* (Sacramento, 1921), 49, for the quotation. See also *Report of the Commission on Land Colonization and Rural Credits of the State of California, November 29, 1916* (Sacramento, 1916), esp. pp. 17–19, 63–64, 65–68, 73–76, 82–87, and for a report on Wyoming experience, 116–120; Weinstock to Charles C. Moore, November 20, 1918, urging state colonization to help veterans, in the Rowell Papers, Box 26; *Report of the* [California] *Division of Land Settlement, September 1, 1922* (Sacramento, 1923), 18–19, in which Mead argued that the greatest agricultural progress in the last thirty years had been made in countries with land settlement programs. The experience of Europe, Australia, and New Zealand showed that they "can be made a solvent enterprise." See also "Comparison of Land Settlement Methods in California with Those in Other Countries," mimeograph, pages 25–72 (n.p., n.d., copy in the University of California Library, Berkeley), esp. pp. 25–28, 30–32, 41, 68–69; and in *Helping Men Own Farms: A Practical Discussion of Government Aid in Land Settlement* (New York, 1920), esp. chapters 1, 3, 5–6, 8, 13–14. The mimeograph report, financed by the Commonwealth Club of California, used university students to conduct field studies. It was intended to build public support for a state colonization program. Charles McCarthy urged similar policies in Wisconsin; see the plan he submitted to the Public Affairs Commission in August 1911; his letter to William M. Duffus, March 21, 1912, both in the McCarthy Papers, box 2: 6, box 3: 2, in the State Historical Society of Wisconsin, Madison; and his book, *The Wisconsin Idea* (New York, 1912), 293–294.

26. "Experimenting with Socialism," *New York Times*, June 28, 1896, summarizing a London speech by Reeves; "Laws of New Zealand," ibid., November 21, 1898, summarizing a New York speech by Lusk to the League for Political Education; H. de R. Walker, "Australasian Extensions of Democracy," *Atlantic Monthly* 83 (May 1899): 577–585; Lusk, *Our Foes at Home*, 111–149 passim; Lloyd, *Newest England*, 104–125, 158, 170–171, 181, 370, 375; Parsons, *Story of New Zealand*, 124–125, 191–204, 400–408, 777–785; James Edward Le Rossignol and William Downie Stewart, "Rating on Unimproved Value in New Zealand," *Journal of Political Economy* 16 (January 1908): 13–22; James Edward Le Rossignol and William Downie Stewart, *State Socialism in New*

Zealand (New York, 1910), 117–152; "Tax Evasion Easy," *Morning Oregonian* (Portland), October 28, 1912.

For examples of requests for tax information, see G. M. Palmer to Lloyd, April 14, 1900; L. S. Starr, W. D. Smith, G. G. Curtis, Jr., G. M. Palmer, Lawson Purdy, John Emmeluth, Fred M. Powers, W. N. Johnstone, C. A. Sprague, B. E. Stonebraker, John E. Brindley, and Douglas Sutherland, to U.S. Consul, 98: 249, 99: 103, 00: 145, 01: 122, 1: 64, 121, 3: 178, 5: 132, 14: 64, 16: 57, 17: 163, 18: 94 (July 26, 1898, February 1, 1899; January 11, April 20, 1900; January 30, March 19, 1901; April 29, 1902; February 12, 1904; February 2, 1910; May 22, August 21, 1911; March 8, 1912).

27. T. G. Wilson, *The Grey Government, 1877–9: An Episode in the Rise of Liberalism in New Zealand* (Auckland, 1954), esp. pp. 24–29. Mill had founded a Land Tenure Reform Association in 1870.

28. See, for examples, Lusk's "Single Tax in Operation," *Arena* 18 (July, 1897): 79–89; his chapter, "Profitable Taxation," in *Our Foes at Home;* and Craig Ralston, "Wisconsin Progresses Backwards," *The Public* 18 (April 2, 1915): 329, summarizing a telephone interview with Richard T. Ely, who had recently returned from New Zealand. Ely thought prosperity to be greater and more widely diffused there than elsewhere in the world, but attributed those conditions to population, education, climate, and soil rather than to the taxation of unimproved land values.

29. Single-tax interest in the Antipodes can best be followed in *The Public,* the weekly established in Chicago in 1898 by Louis F. Post and, beginning in 1909, underwritten by the Philadelphia soap magnate, Joseph Fels.

See also, Mervyn J. Stewart, "Present Conditions of the Single Tax Movement in New Zealand," *Single Tax Review* 4 (July 15, 1904): 23–27; P. J. O'Regan, "The Real Truth regarding Land Taxation in New Zealand. What That Country Has Actually Done. Merits and Defects of Its Tax Laws," ibid. 6 (October 15, 1906): 1–10; Arthur Withy and others, "New Zealand," ibid., 12 (September–October 1912): 1–61.

30. Compare *The Public,* March 24, April 7, 14, December 15, 1900; January 12, May 11, August 31, 1901; *New York Times,* March 18, 1900; the testimony of J. H. Ralston in the *Report of the Industrial Commission on Agriculture and Agricultural Labor* (57 Congress, 1 session, House Document no. 179, serial 4340, Washington, D.C., 1901), 10: 1022–1023; The Revenue Commission of Colorado, "The Australasian Tax System," 56 Congress, 2 session, Senate Document no. 209, serial 4340, Washington, 1902); *Laws Passed at the Thirteenth Session of the General Assembly of Colorado* (Denver, 1901), 95–96; David A. Mills, compiler, *Colorado Legislative Manual, 1903* (Denver, 1903), 223–226; Albert H. Jackson to Lloyd, May 15, 1901; *Appeal to Reason,* June 7, 1902.

31. Compare Millicent G. Fawcett, "New Zealand under Female Franchise," *Contemporary Review* 65 (March 1894): 433–437; *Appeal to Reason,* January 18, 1896; *American Fabian* 2 (June 1896): 6; Rev. A. C. Grier, H. G. Ell to Lloyd, October 10, 1899; July 29, 1901; March 13, 1902; P. J. O'Regan, "[Referendum in] New Zealand," and the text of his bill, in 55 Congress, 2 session, Senate Docu-

ment no. 340, serial 3615 (Washington, D.C., 1898), 263–264, 311–312; Lillian Toms, "Referendum in Australia and New Zealand," ibid., 264–266; H. G. Ell, "Direct Legislation in New Zealand," *Arena* 30 (September 1903): 268–272; Parsons, *Story of New Zealand,* xii, 100n, 106, 249–259, 400, 409–417, 511, 693, 743, 766–774; J. Collier, "Democracy in Australasia," *Yale Review* 13 (August 1904): 159–178; "The Prohibition Movement in New Zealand," *Independent* 66 (February 4, 1909): 222; Sir Robert Stout and Sir Joseph Ward, "New Zealand: Its Problems and Policy," *North American Review* 191 (February 1910): 240–250; "The Referendum in Operation," *Quarterly Review* 214 (April 1911): 509–538; "New Zealand Nearly Dry," *Independent* 72 (January 4, 1912): 61–62.

32. John D. Connolly, "Extension of Franchise to Women," December 20, 1893, in U.S. Consular Records, Bay of Islands, 10: 140, State Department, National Archives, Washington; Mary Putnam Jacobi, "Status and Future of the Women Suffrage Movement," *Forum* 18 (December 1894): 406–414; Susan B. Anthony to Clara Colby, December 21, 1895, in the Clara Colby Collection, CC3, in the Huntington Library; Susan B. Anthony, Harriet B. Kells, Anna A. Gordon, Francis E. Willard, Samuel C. Lambert, Clara C. Hoffman, Samuel C. Lambert, Anna A. Gordon, Mary Clement Leavitt, Mary E. Anthony, Carrie Chapman Catt to Kate W. Sheppard, November 7, 1893; March 22, May 24, June 6, September 12, 1894; August 9, 31, September 27, 1895; April 9, 1904; July 18, September 28, December 3, 1906; April 14, 1908, all in the Kate W. Sheppard Papers, in the Canterbury Museum, Christchurch, New Zealand; Edward Reeves, "Why New Zealand Women Get the Franchise," *Westminster Review* 143 (January 1895): 35–47; W. P. Reeves, "Five Years' Political and Social Reform in New Zealand," *National Review* 27 (August 1896): 834–850; Hugh H. Lusk, "Remarkable Success of Woman's Enfranchisement in New Zealand," *Forum* (April 1897): 173–183; "How Women's Franchise Came in New Zealand," *Saturday Review* (London) 87 (March 18, 1899): 328–329; "The Position of Women in New Countries," *Atlantic Monthly* 86 (October 1900): 574–576; "Premier Seddon on Woman Suffrage," *Independent* 54 (August 28, 1902): 2098; Lady Holder [Mrs. Frederick W. Holder], "Women's Suffrage in Australia," *Independent* 56 (June 6, 1904): 1309–1311; Florence Kelley, *Some Ethical Gains through Legislation* (New York, 1905), esp. pp. 196–199; Russell, "New Zealand—The Advance Guard," 786–788; Alice Henry, "Australian Women and the Ballot," *North American Review* 183 (December 21, 1906): 1272–1279; Nellie Alma Martel, "Women's Votes in New Zealand," in Brougham Villiares, editor, *The Case for Women Suffrage* (New York, 1907), 140–143; Jane Addams, "The Working Women and the Ballot," *Woman's Home Companion* 35 (April 1908): 19; "Shall Our Wives and Sisters Be Our Equals or Our Subjects," *Arena* 40 (July 1908): 92–94; Mrs. K. A. Sheppard, *Woman Suffrage in New Zealand* (Pamphlet no. 1, International Woman Suffrage Alliance, n.p., [1908]); Wilhelmina Sherriff Bain to Caroline Severance, September 20, 1908; March 8, 1909; April 29, 1910; July 27, 1911, in the Severance Papers; Sara S. Nolan, "Political Social Reform in the State of New South Wales," in *Report of the International Congress of Women, Held in Toronto, Canada, June 24th–30th, 1909* (Toronto, 1910), 472–474; George Allen England, "The Leaven of Woman Suffrage 'Round

the World," *Lippincott's Monthly Magazine* 85 (January 1910): 123–125. Robert L. Owen, "Introductory Remarks of Presiding Officer," in *Significance of the Woman Suffrage Movement*, Supplement no. 27 to *Annals of the American Academy of Political and Social Science* (Philadelphia, May 1910), 6–9; Hugh H. Lusk, "The Woman's Vote: Some Side-Lights from New Zealand's Experience," *North American Review* 192 (July 1910): 107–116; Paul Kennaday, "Where Women Vote," *Outlook* 95 (May 21, 1910): 117–122; reverse sides of 1910 and 1911 letterheads of The Political Equality League and the Men's Equal Suffrage Campaign League, Los Angeles, for quotations from the Rev. Dr. Francis E. Clark and Cardinal Moran; Rheta Childe Dorr, *What Eight Million Women Want* (Boston, 1910), 287–318; W. Farmer Whyte and Sarah Warder MacConnell, "Where the Women Made Good: In Australia and New Zealand Equal Suffrage Means Equal Responsibility for Public Service," *Delineator* 77 (April 1911): 270, 352; Ida Husted Harper, "The World Movement for Woman Suffrage," *Review of Reviews* 44 (December 1911): 725–729; Carrie Chapman Catt to Premier, January 21, 1913, asking that New Zealand send a delegate to the Budapest Congress, in the Colonial Secretary files; Siegfried, *Democracy in New Zealand*, 280–309; Alice Henry, *The Trade Union Woman* (New York, 1915), 260–262.

33. For examples of the criticism, see J. Grattan Grey in the *New York Times*, March 5, 1899; John Christie, "Women in New Zealand," *North American Review* 168 (April 1899): 509–511; Mark Twain, *Following the Equator: A Journey around the World* (Hartford, 1897), 299–301. For a typical response, see Sheppard, *Woman Suffrage in New Zealand*, 8–9, 14–15, 18, 19, 20, 23, 25–29.

34. Sheppard, *Woman Suffrage in New Zealand*, passim, and p. 13 for the quotation. See also *American Fabian* 5 (May 1899): 8.

35. "The Working Woman and the Ballot," 19.

36. James, editor, *Notable American Women*, 2: 370–372; Jane Addams, *My Friend, Julia Lathrop* (New York, 1935).

37. Josephine Goldmark, *Impatient Crusader: Florence Kelley* (New York, 1953), 102, 106; James Leiby, *A History of Social Welfare and Social Work in the United States* (New York, 1978), 152–155; "Official Mother to Thirty Million Children," *Chicago Inter-Ocean*, May 3, 1914; "New Zealand Society for the Health of Women and Children: An Example of Baby-Saving Work in Small Towns and Rural Districts," Infant Mortality Series, no. 2, Children's Bureau, U.S. Department of Labor (Washington, D.C., 1914).

38. "New Zealand Society for the Health of Women and Children," 5, 6, 7.

39. Ibid., 15–18.

40. Ibid., 3. See also, "How Australia Cares for Her Orphan Children," *Arena* 38 (August 1907): 184–185; "State Subsidies for Large Families," *Harper's Weekly* 43 (September 25, 1909): 32; "How Australia Cares for the Children," *Review of Reviews* 46 (December 1912): 733–744, summarizing an article by Edith Sellers in the *Contemporary Review*; Erik Olssen, "Truby King and the Plunket Society: An Analysis of a Prescriptive Ideology," *New Zealand Journal of History* 15 (April 1981): 3–23.

41. Lloyd, *Newest England*, 104, 106; Sir Joseph A. Ward, quoted in the *New York Times*, July 6, 1906.

42. *New York Times*, July 7, 1906. See also, *Appeal to Reason*, May 11, August 17, October 26, 1901; May 17, 1902; Lloyd, "Australasian Cures for Coal Wars," 668–669; Henry Demarest Lloyd, "Earthly Meaning of Heavenly Words," in the *Saturday Blade* (Chicago), October 3, 1903, for his assertion that New Zealand's policies were designed "to abolish those twin curses of civilization—the millionaire and the pauper"; "Difference between Present Political Conditions in New Zealand and America," *Arena* 32 (July 1904): 85; Parsons, *Story of New Zealand*, 108–112, 420–422, 477–478, 482–487, 571–579, 590–592, 804; Allen Kelly, "Under the Southern Cross: What State Socialists and Totemites Have Done for Australia," *Los Angeles Sunday Times*, March 18, 1906; Guy H. Scholefield, *New Zealand in Evolution: Industrial, Economic and Political* (London, 1909), 318–329.

43. Russell, "New Zealand—The Advance Guard," 795, 792; *New York Times*, June 7, 1911; Russell, "Checking Up New Zealand: Some Unexpected Results of Its Experiments in Radical Legislation," *National Post*, June 17, 1911, pp. 26–28; Russell, "Lessons from the Antipodes: The Labor Party of Australia and How It Fares in Political Policies," *Coming Nation*, June 3, 1911, p. 3; and three articles by Russell under the general title, "More Light on the Common Good: How 'Trust Busting' Is Carried On in the Antipodes as in the United States; Practical Working of State Capitalism in New Zealand; New Zealand Government Housing Schemes for the Working Classes," in ibid., July 22, 1911, p. 3; August 12, 1911, p. 3; September 30, 1911, p. 3.

44. *Appeal to Reason*, September 4, 1897, December 23, 1899; April 14, 1900; Helen Page Bates, "Australian Experiments in Industry," *Annals of the American Academy of Political and Social Science* 12 (September 1898): 193–213; Lloyd, *Newest England*, 55, 181; Howard, "New Zealand in a Nutshell," 18–19; Parsons, *Story of New Zealand*, 88–92, 698; Allen Kelly, "Under the Southern Cross: What the Government of New Zealand Does for the People," *Los Angeles Sunday Times*, February 18, 1906; "Ward on New Zealand's Progress," *Arena* 36 (September 1906): 317–320; William A. Prickett, "New Zealand Government Post-Office Money Depository System," *U.S. Consular and Trade Reports*, no. 327: 238–239 (Washington, D.C., December 1907); F. M. Gill to Secretary of State, January 15, 1909, in the Colonial Secretary files; "Government Savings Banks in Australia," *Independent* 75 (August 14, 1913): 406–407.

45. E. R. L. Gould, *The Housing of the Working People* (Eighth Special Report of the Commissioner of Labor, Washington, D.C., 1895); *American Fabian* 1 (December 1895): 10; James Grattan Grey, "The News of Australasia," *New York Times*, September 3, 1899; "New Zealand," *Independent* 59 (October 5, 1905): 829–830; Kelly, "A New Civilization," 714–715; Edward Tregear, "Recent Humanistic Legislation in New Zealand," *Arena* 37 (April 1907): 366–374; Russell, "New Zealand Government Housing Schemes for the Working Classes," 3–5; *Appeal to Reason*, September 30, 1911; Roy Lubove, *The Progressives and the Slums: Tenement House Reform in New York City, 1890–1917* (Pittsburgh, 1962); Selwyn K. Troen, "The Genesis of a Transatlantic Literature

in Urban Planning: France, England and the United States to the Mid-Nineteenth Century," paper presented at Columbia University, March 1983.

46. *New York Monitor*, 1894, quoted in C. W. Vennell, *Tower of Strength: A Centennial History of the New Zealand Government Life Insurance Office, 1869–1969* (Auckland, 1969), 70, to the effect that the colonists carried more coverage, per capita, than any other people in the world; Fradenburgh, "Social Experiments in New Zealand," 620–621; *Appeal to Reason*, July 15, 1899; February 3, March 17, 1900; September 7, November 2, 1901; Howard, "New Zealand in a Nutshell," 23–24; J. A. Richardson to Lloyd, February 16, 1900; July 12, 1901; Lloyd, "Some New Zealand Experiments," 670–674; Lloyd, *Newest England*, 12–18, 181, 257, 372, 375; John Emmeluth, Norton Chase to U.S. Consul, 1 (January 30, 1901): 64; 14 (January 24, 1910): 187; David J. Lewis to Lloyd, November 11, 1901, reporting his intention to work in the Maryland Senate for a system of state insurance; Warner, "The Socialistic Legislation of New Zealand," 468; W. P. Reeves, "State Insurance in New Zealand," *North American Review* 182 (January 1906): 62–73; Allen Kelly, "What the Government of New Zealand Does for the People," *Los Angeles Sunday Times*, February 18, 1906; Florence Finch Kelly, "Government Insurance in New Zealand," *Independent* 61 (July 12, 1906): 86–88; Kelly, "A New Civilization," 565–566; George Fowlds to Fred A. Binney, March 2, 1907, in the George Fowlds Papers, University of Auckland, New Zealand; A. A. Brown, "New Zealand: A New Democracy," *Arena* 38 (November 1907): 482–487; Le Rossignol and Stewart, *State Socialism in New Zealand*, 153–178; "State Insurance in New Zealand," *Independent* 72 (January 25, 1912): 217; "The Cost of Insurance," ibid., 72 (February 1, 1912): 278; Charles A. Ingram, "The Wisconsin Venture upon State Life Insurance: A 'Life Fund' to Serve the Many Instead of Only the Few," *La Follette's* 4 (May 25, 1912): 7, 15; R. Law to Department of Internal Affairs, June 1, 1913, in Colonial Secretary files; A. G. Fradenburgh, *Elements of Economics* (New York, 1921), 175.

47. Russell, "New Zealand—The Advance Guard," 790. Compare the *Boston Sunday Herald*, December 23, 1900, which editorialized that of all the antipodean reforms, the public trustee system "might stand the best chance of adoption." It functioned "with absolute security, and with freedom from all the dangers and risks attendant upon confidence in individual trustees."

48. "A Conversation with J. M. Peebles," 402; "No Labels," *Independent* 61 (July 12, 1906): 103–104. See also Lloyd to A. B. Stickney, Wm. J. Hill, June 12, 1896; December 13, 1898; Parsons, Samuel Vail, David J. Lewis, W. J. Gordon to Lloyd, April 11, 13, 1900; July 5, November 11, December 6, 1901; June 23, 1902; "Populism in Australasia," *Nation* 63 (September 17, 1896): 206; *Appeal to Reason*, October 30, 1897, August 13, November 5, 1898; May 5, June 2, 9, 23, 1900, January 26, July 20, October 19, 26, 1901; April 12, 1902; Lusk, *Our Foes at Home*, 169–193; H. T. Burgess, "Social Experiments in Australia," *Arena* 23 (January 1900): 132–140; Lloyd, "Some New Zealand Scenes," 752–759; Lloyd, *Newest England*, 31–81 passim; Roland T. Patten to U.S. Consul, 1 (January 11, August 10, 1900): 122, 108; B. O. Flower, "New Zealand in the Van of Progress," *Arena* 27 (April 1902): 429–432; B. O. Flower, "Extension of Public

Ownership of Railways," ibid. 29 (January 1903): 91; Parsons, *Story of New Zealand*, 95–98, 151–162, 379–397; Allen Kelly, "Under the Southern Cross: Government Ownership and Management of Railways in New Zealand," *Los Angeles Sunday Times*," February 11, 1906; Victor S. Clark, *The Labour Movement in Australasia: A Study in Social-Democracy* (New York, 1906), 246–280; Alice Henry, "Industrial Democracy: The Australian Labor Movement," *Outlook* 84 (November 3, 1906): 566–570; Frank Parsons, *The Heart of the Railroad Problem: The History of Railway Discrimination in the United States, the Chief Efforts at Control and the Remedies Proposed, with Hints from Other Countries* (Boston, 1906), esp. pp. 313–332; "New Zealand's Master Concern the Happiness and Prosperity of the People," *Arena* 40 (October 1908): 358–360; unsigned review of Bolton Hall's *A Little Land and a Living* (New York, 1908), ibid., 40 (October 1908): 382–383; J. E. Le Rossignol and W. D. Stewart, "Railways in New Zealand," *Quarterly Journal of Economics* 23 (August 1909): 652–696; Scholefield, *New Zealand in Evolution*, 244–272; J. T. Paul, "New Lines of Progress in New Zealand," *Twentieth Century Magazine* 3 (December 1910): 216–219; Le Rossignol and Stewart, *State Socialism in New Zealand*, 52–67; "Pioneering without Pain," *Independent* 71 (August 17, 1911): 382–384; "Little Editorials from the People: Hon. J. T. Paul Refutes a Slander on New Zealand," *Twentieth Century Magazine* 4 (September 1911): 558–560; Hugh H. Lusk, "Practical Socialism: A New Study in Political Economy," *Forum* 48 (September 1912): 285–293; B. O. Flower, *Progressive Men, Women, and Movements of the Past Twenty-Five Years* (Boston, 1914), 110–115.

49. Lloyd, *Newest England*, 31, for the quotations. See also *Appeal to Reason*, September 4, 1897, November 5, 1898, August 31, 1901; *American Fabian* 4 (April 1898): 3; *Public* 1 (April 9, 1898): 3; Henry Demarest Lloyd, *Sheridan Road Newsletter*, March 25, 1899; "The Railways as Factors in a Popular Educational System," *Arena* 33 (April 1905): 442–443. [Gustav Stickley], "Als Ik Kan," *Craftsman* 10 (August 1906): 665–666, recommending the New Zealand system for municipal utilities in preference to "our fatuous pursuit of *laissez faire*"; unsigned review of *The Works of Charles William Pearson* (Boston, 1908), *Arena* 40 (November 1908): 478, arguing the superiority of public ownership and operation of natural monopolies.

50. Flower, "Extension of Public Ownership of Railways," 91; "The Railways as Factors in a Popular Educational System," 443; Kenneday, "Helping the Small Man," 735. See also Frank Parsons, "National Ownership of Railroads," *American Fabian* 1 (February 1896): 8–10; William E. Smythe, *Constructive Democracy: The Economics of a Square Deal* (New York, 1905), Part II: The Taming of Monopoly, pp. 53–260 passim.

51. "Facts for American Socialists," *American Fabian* 2 (March 1896): 3; "Happy New Zealand," ibid., 2 (May 1896), 2–4, esp. p. 3; "Where Reform Has Sway," *New York Times*, February 21, 1897; *Appeal to Reason*, October 1, 1898; April 14, 1900; "Trade Unionism in Far-Off New Zealand," *New York Times*, April 15, 1900; Lloyd, *Newest England*, 67, 69, 82, 92, 94, 102, 160, 192, 197–232 passim,

245, 366, 372, 373; Fred M. Powers, Wm. M. Leiserson to U.S. Consul, 1 (March 19, 1901): 121; 14 (March 2, 1910): 126; William E. Smythe, "How Tramps Are Turned into Taxpayers," *Out West* 16 (June 1902): 677–682; Tom Mann, "Conditions of Labour in New Zealand," *Nineteenth Century* 52 (September 1902): 393–399; Victor S. Clark, "Labor Conditions in New Zealand," *Bulletin of the U.S. Bureau of Labor*, no. 49 (Washington, D.C., November 1903), 1142–1281, esp. pp. 1157–1159; Parsons, *Story of New Zealand*, 279–283; Victor S. Clark, "Labor Conditions in Australia," *Bulletin of the U.S. Bureau of Labor*, no. 56 (Washington, D.C., January 1905), 9–243, esp. pp. 177–181; Smythe, *Constructive Democracy*, 422–425; W. B. Leffingwell, "New Zealand—A Model Commonwealth: The Institutions of a Country Which Has No Strikes and No Unemployment," *Harper's Weekly* 50 (April 21, 1906), 558–560, 569.

52. *American Fabian* 1 (December 1895): 12; Lloyd to Henry Vivian praising what he called "Labor Copartnership," undated, microfilm reel number 11, frame 56; Jesse Willard Bolte to Lloyd, November 7, 1899; John Christie, "A Letter from New Zealand," *Atlantic Monthly* 86 (October 1900): 520–525; Lloyd, "Some New Zealand Experiments," 515–516; Lloyd, *Newest England*, 82–103, 160, 202, 209–211, 228–229, 371–372; Clark, "Labor Conditions in New Zealand," 1182–1183; Parsons, *Story of New England*, 367–378, including material on producer cooperatives; Kelly, "A New Civilization," 716–717.

53. Reeves, "Five Years' Political and Social Reform in New Zealand," 846–847; W. P. Reeves, "Shops and Shopping Laws in Australia and New Zealand," *Empire Review* 1 (July 1901): 666–675; Lloyd, *Newest England*, 246, 252–255; Reeves, *State Experiments* 2: 181–199; Clark, "Labor Conditions in New Zealand," 1179; Parsons, *Story of New England*, 298–304; Frank Dillingham, "Store and Office Closing Law of New Zealand," *U.S. Consular Reports*, no. 292 (Washington, D.C., January 1905), 100–102; Clark, "Labor Conditions in Australia," 171; E. I. Lewis, "New Zealand Labor Laws and How They Work," *Carpenter* 27 (July 1907): 10–13; "New Zealand Closing Law," *New York Times*, February 20, 1905; Lusk, *Social Welfare in New Zealand*, 95–96.

54. W. P. Reeves quoted in the *New York Times*, June 28, 1896; Reeves, "Five Years' Political and Social Reform in New Zealand," 843–844, 845–846; Reeves, *State Experiments*, 2: 200–215; Parsons, *Story of New Zealand*, 314–315; Russell, "Soldiers of the Common Good: Advent of a Government That Cares Most for the Least Fortunate," 588; Siegfried, *Democracy in New Zealand*, 105–123.

CHAPTER FIVE. MAXIMUM HOURS, MINIMUM WAGES

1. Victor S. Clark made this point in "Labor Conditions in New Zealand," 1166–1167, 1172–1174; "Labor Conditions in Australia," 158–160, 207, 209, 214–215, 220, 229–241 passim; and in *The Labour Movement in Australasia*, 46–47, 233–235, 307–310.

2. That was the general impression given by Lloyd in *Newest England*. Clark disagreed. Working hours were shorter, but living standards were lower, partly because Americans were more productive and had more economic opportunities.

3. For example, Rhode Island, in common with other New England states, attempted to deal with child labor in the 1850s by requiring that young workers receive a minimum number of months of schooling each year. See my earlier study, *The Transformation of Rhode Island, 1790–1860* (Providence, 1963), 75.

4. There is a vast literature on this question, of which the following might be cited: William R. Brock, *Investigation and Responsibility: Public Responsibility in the United States, 1865–1900* (Cambridge, 1984) 149–150, 154, 159, 160, 161, 167, 169, 177; Allen F. Davis, *Spearheads for Reform: The Social Settlements and the Progressive Movement, 1890–1914* (New York, 1967), 123–132, 140, 220, 223, 229; Elizabeth Sands Johnson, "Child Labor Legislation," in John R. Commons, editor, *History of Labor in the United States, 1896–1932* (4 vols., New York, 1918–1935), 3: 403–456; Walter I. Trattner, *From Poor Law to Welfare State: A History of Social Welfare in America* (New York, 1984), 108–134 passim; Robert H. Wiebe, *Businessmen and Reform: A Study of the Progressive Movement* (Cambridge, Mass., 1962), 155, 198–199; Robert H. Wiebe, *The Search for Order, 1877–1920* (New York, 1967), 168, 169, 171, 199, 204, 214, 220, 221, 291. Especially useful is Melvin I. Urofsky, "State Courts and Protective Legislation during the Progressive Era: A Reevalution," *Journal of American History* 72 (June 1985): 63–91, esp. pp.69–71.

5. See, for example, Gerd Korman, *Industrialization, Immigrants and Americanizers: The View from Milwaukee, 1866–1921* (Madison, 1967), 87–135.

6. The case was *Hammer v. Dagenhart* (247 U.S. 251) and involved a congressional prohibition of the interstate shipment of articles produced by child labor.

7. Sutch, *Quest for Security,* 67; Sinclair, *Reeves,* 205.

8. Compare Richard M. Abrams, *Conservatism in a Progressive Era: Massachusetts Politics, 1900–1912* (Cambridge, Mass., 1964), 104–106, 131–132, 232–234, 258–260, 273–276; Elizabeth Brandeis, "Women's Hour Legislation," in Commons, *History of Labor,* 3: 457, 458n, 461–465, 469–471, 472–474; Brock, *Investigation and Responsibility,* 149–155; James Leiby, *Carroll Wright and Labor Reform: The Origin of Labor Statistics* (Cambridge, Mass., 1960); "State Laws Affecting Women: Hours, Minimum Wage, Home Work," *Bulletin of the Women's Bureau,* no. 40 (Washington, D.C., 1924), 1–53 passim; Clara M. Beyer, "History of Labor Legislation for Women in Three States," ibid., no. 66-I (Washington, D.C., 1932), 13–64; Florence P. Smith, "Chronological Development of Labor Legislation for Women in the United States," ibid., no. 66-II (Washington, D.C., 1932), 53–60.

9. Sinclair, *Reeves,* 182–183, 203–205, 213, 216; Brandeis, "Women's Hour Legislation," 469–470.

10. Charles McCarthy to Colonial Secretary, October 11, 1904.

11. On the underlying ideas, see William D. Grampp, *Economic Liberalism* (2 vols, New York, 1965); on the implementation of those ideas, see Lawrence M. Friedman, *A History of American Law* (New York, 1973), 157–158, 203, 300, 314, 385, 397–400.

12. Charles Edward Russell, "More Light on the Common Good: Practical Workings of State Capitalism in New Zealand," *Coming Nation,* August 12,

1911, argued that "Socialism is not a failure in New Zealand because Socialism has never been tried" there and "the State Capitalism of New Zealand is as much of a grewsome failure as the private Capitalism of America" (pp. 3, 7). See also A. M. Simons, "Labor and Socialism," ibid., 12 (August 19, 1911), who declared that labor governments in Australasia had failed to embrace socialism and that their policies had brought "unemployment, strikes, misery, corruption, [and] monopolistic tyranny. . . ." For the conservative perspective and the quotation, see Harold C. Livesay, *Samuel Gompers and Organized Labor in America* (Boston, 1978), 134.

13. See, for example, H. Scott Bennett, "The Truth about New Zealand," *International Socialist Review* 16 (December 1915): 365–366; and Scott Bennett, "Compulsory Arbitration in Australasia," ibid. 17 (February 1917): 458–459.

14. Compare Judith A. Baer, *The Chains of Protection: The Judicial Response to Women's Labor Legislation* (Westport, Conn., 1978); Clyde E. Jacobs, *Law Writers and the Courts: The Influence of Thomas M. Cooley, Christopher G. Tiedeman, and John F. Dillon upon American Constitutional Law* (Berkeley, Calif., 1954); and Benjamin R. Twiss, *Lawyers and the Constitution: How Laissez Faire Came to the Supreme Court* (Princeton, N.J., 1942).

15. *Ritchie v. People,* 155 Illinois 98 (1895); Florence Kelley, *Some Ethical Gains through Legislation* (New York, 1905), 141; Dorothy Rose Blumberg, *Florence Kelley: The Making of a Social Pioneer* (New York, 1966), 145–148; Ray Ginger, *Altgeld's America: the Lincoln Ideal versus Changing Realities* (New York, 1958), 135, 169–170; Josephine Goldmark, *Impatient Crusader: Florence Kelley's Life Story* (Urbana, Ill., 1953), 36–50.

16. Compare Brandeis, "Labor Legislation and the Constitution," in Commons, *History of Labor,* 3: 662–664, 667–673; Ernst Freund, *The Police Power: Public Policy and Constitutional Rights* (Chicago, 1904), 295–303; Friedman, *History of American Law,* 484–494.

17. *Holden v. Hardy,* 169 United States 366 (1898); *In re Morgan,* 26 Colorado 415 (1899). The Colorado decision was not challenged in the U.S. Supreme Court because until 1914 only statutes declared constitutional by a state's supreme court could be tested in the federal courts.

18. 191 United States 207 (1903).

19. See Brandeis, "Labor Legislation," 548–550, 561–562, 673, 678; and, for the cases, *People v. Phyfe,* 136 New York 554 (1893), *Wheeling Bridge & Terminal Co. v. Gilmore,* 8 Ohio Circuit Court 658 (1894), *Re Ten-Hour Law,* 24 Rhode Island 603 (1902), *State v. Cantwell,* 179 Missouri 245 (1904), *Cantwell v. Missouri,* 199 United States 602 (1905), *Baltimore and Ohio Railroad Co. v. Interstate Commerce Commission,* 221 United States 671 (1914).

20. 198 United States 45 (1905).

21. Ibid., 65–74, for Harlan, 74–76, for Holmes.

22. There is substantial literature on the Brandeis brief. The case, *Muller v. Oregon,* is reported at 208 United States 412 (1908). The National Consumers' League reprinted the brief under the title *Women in Industry* (New York, n.d.). It was expanded from barely 100 to more than 500 pages in Josephine Goldmark's *Fatigue and Efficiency* (New York, 1912). See also, "The Con-

sumer's Control of Production: The Work of the National Consumers' League," in supplement no. 24 of the *Annals of the American Academy of Political and Social Science* (Philadelphia, July 1909), 21–22, 41–43; Josephine Goldmark, "The Work of the National Consumers' League during the year ending March 1, 1910," ibid., supplement no. 29 (Philadelphia, September 1910); *The National Consumers' League: The First Quarter Century, 1899–1924* (New York, n.d.), for a list of the briefs prepared and printed by the League; Clement E. Vose, "The National Consumers' League and the Brandeis Brief," *Midwest Journal of Political Science* 1 (November 1957): 267–290; Louis Lee Athey, "The Consumers' Leagues and Social Reform, 1890–1923" (Ph.D. dissertation, University of Delaware, 1965), esp. chap. 8.

Brandeis provided no antipodean evidence in the original brief. However, later versions drew information from the Australian states of New South Wales, Queensland, and Victoria and from New Zealand. See Goldmark, *Fatigue and Efficiency,* 31, 323, 427, 431–432, 461–463, 487; and Felix Frankfurter and Josephine Goldmark, *The Case for the Shorter Work Day, Brief for Defendant in Error, Franklin O. Bunting (Plaintiff in Error) v. The State of Oregon (Defendant in Error). Supreme Court of the United States, October Term, 1915,* which comprised two volumes and 1,121 pages and was published, like the others, by the National Consumers' League (n.p., n.d.). It included in an appendix, pages 961–984, an article by Frankfurter, "Hours of Labor and Realism in Constitutional Law," *Harvard Law Review* 29 (February 1916): 353–373, on which he had been working when Brandeis was nominated to the Supreme Court. On the foreign experience, see 1: 10a–10b; 2: 523–531, 997.

23. Brandeis, "Labor Legislation," 474–489.

24. Ibid., 475–476. See also, Earl C. Crockett, "The History of California Labor Legislation, 1910–1930" (Ph.D. dissertation, University of California, 1931), 5–33; Lucile Eaves, *A History of California Labor Legislation with an Introductory Sketch of the San Francisco Labor Movement* (Berkeley, 1910), 197–228; Spencer C. Olin, Jr., *Prodigal Sons: Hiram Johnson and the Progressives, 1911–1917* (Berkeley, 1968), 47–48; Alexander Saxton, "San Francisco Labor and the Populist and Progressive Insurgencies," *Pacific Historical Review* 34 (November 1965): 421–438.

25. Brandeis, "Labor Legislation," 471–474.

26. The first case was *People v. Williams,* 189 New York 131 (1907), and may have been lost because the state failed to make a persuasive case against night work. In the second case (214 New York 395), Brandeis and Goldmark submitted a 529-page summary of "Facts of Knowledge." The same brief was also submitted in *State of New York, on the Relation of John Krohn v. Warden and Keeper of City Prison, Brooklyn, and John Naumer, City Magistrate,* 168 Appellate Division, Supreme Court of New York 933 (1915), and was reissued in a revised version in 1918 entitled "The Case against Night Work for Women." See also, Brandeis, "Labor Legislation," 479–481, on legislative inertia. However, some states followed the Wisconsin model by empowering an industrial commission to set standards for women. See ibid., 481–483.

27. James Grattan Grey, "Jingoism in Australasia," *New York Times*, November 26, 1899.

28. For early summaries and assessments of the wage-board approach, see Reeves, *State Experiments* 2: 47–68; Clark, "Labor Conditions in Australia," 60–78; and Clark, *The Labour Movement in Australasia*, 138–153.

29. Much of the information available to Americans came through reports on the antipodean system of compulsory arbitration of labor disputes and was more incidental than central to the discussion. The Victorian wage-board model posed the policy question directly; even so, Americans paid it little attention before 1908. For examples not previously cited, see Charles H. Myers, "Compulsory Arbitration," in the *Maryland Bureau of Industrial Statistics* (Baltimore, 1896), 184–202; Arthur Twining Hadley, *Economics: An Account of the Relations between Private Property and Public Welfare* (New York, 1896), 356–363; Frank Parsons, "Compulsory Arbitration," *Arena* 17 (March 1897): 663–676; "Way-Marks of the Labor Movement," *Commons* 51 (October 1900): 7; "Views of a New Zealand Trade Union Official regarding the Industrial Conciliation and Arbitration Act," *Bulletin of the New York Bureau of Labor Statistics* 4 (Albany, March 1902): 55–56; John Bates Clark, "Is Authoritative Arbitration Inevitable?" *Political Science Quarterly* 17 (December 1902): 553–567; Conrad Reno, "Compulsory Arbitration: Industrial Courts to Administer Industrial Justice," in Peters, *Labor and Capital*, 200–220; A. S. Johnson reviewing Reeves's *State Experiments* in *Political Science Quarterly* 18 (December 1903): 710–713; Henry W. Macrosty, "State Arbitration and the Minimum Wage in Australasia," ibid. 18 (March 1903): 112–140; "Fighting It Out," *New York Times*, May 27, 1903: A. D. Weber, "The Report of the Victorian Industrial Commission," *Quarterly Journal of Economics* 17 (August 1903): 614–642; "The Triumph of the Australian Labor Party," *Commons* 9 (April 1904): 151; John A. Ryan, "A Living Wage: Presumptions and Authorities," *Catholic University* Bulletin 11 (April 1905): 126–151; George W. Gough, "The Wages Boards of Victoria," *Economic Journal* 15 (September 1905): 361–372; "A Living Wage," *Massachusetts Labor Bulletin* 10 (December 1906): 438–446; E. I. Lewis, "New Zealand Labor Laws and How They Work," *Carpenter* 27 (July 1907): 10–13.

30. *New Zealand Parliamentary Debates*, 86 (1894): 1113. This statement of the spirit of antipodean reform was quoted with some variations in "Progressive Legislation in New Zealand," *Progressive Review* 1 (December 1896): 225–239.

31. For MacDonald, see 93 (March 1908): 308–325; for Henry, see "Australia's 'New Protection'," 88 (February 8, 1908): 314–317. See also Edward Tregear, "Recent Humanistic Legislation in New Zealand," *Arena* 37 (April 1906): 366–374; H. B. Less Smith, "Economic Theory and Proposals for a Legal Minimum Wage," *Economic Journal* (London) 17 (December 1907): 505–512; "Compulsory Arbitration in New Zealand," *Independent* 65 (September 10, 1908): 579–580; J. Ramsay MacDonald, "Sweating and Wages Boards," in *Nineteenth Century and After* 64 (November 1908): 748–762; William D. P. Bliss and

Rudolph M. Binder, editors, *The New Encyclopedia of Social Reform* (New York, 1908), 769–770; John A. Ryan, "A Programme of Social Reform by Legislation," *Catholic World* 89 (July 1909): 433–444; "Tentative List of References on Wage Boards," in "The Consumer's Control of Production: The Work of the National Consumers' League," in supplement no. 24, *Annals of the American Academy of Political and Social Science* (Philadelphia, July 1909), 33–34; Rheta Childe Dorr, "What Eight Million Women Want: Women's Demand for Humane Treatment of Women Workers in Shop and Factory," *Hampton's Magazine* 23 (December 1909): 794–805, esp. p. 805, and *What Eight Million Women Want* (Boston, 1910), 121–182; Le Rossignol and Stewart, *State Socialism in New Zealand,* 232–235, 238–244, 247–249.

32. Florence Kelley, "Forestalling Shirtwaist Strikes," *Survey* 23 (January 29, 1910): 577–578; Alice Henry, *The Trade Union Woman* (New York, 1915), 169–170; Gladys Boone, *The Women's Trade Union Leagues in Great Britain and the United States of America* (New York, 1942), 74, 114, 141; "Minimum Wage Boards," in "The Work of the National Consumers' League during the Year Ending March 1, 1910," in supplement no. 29, *Annals of the American Academy of Political and Social Science* (Philadelphia, September 1910), 21–22; Arthur N. Holcombe, "Report of the Special Committee on Minimum Wage Boards," in "Work of National Consumers' Leagues," in supplement no. 33, ibid. (Philadelphia, September 1911): 51–52; Athey, "Consumers' Leagues and Social Reform," 171–204; John A. Ryan, "A Minimum Wage and Minimum Wages Boards: With Especial Reference to Immigrant Labor and Woman Labor," in the *Proceedings of the National Conference of Charities and Correction at the Thirty-Seventh Annual Session Held in the City of St. Louis, Mo., May 19 to 26, 1910* (Fort Wayne, n.d.), 457–475, esp. pp. 472–474; John A. Ryan, "Minimum Wages and Minimum Wage Boards," *Survey* 24 (September 3, 1910): 810–820. According to Goldmark, *Impatient Crusader,* 134–135, Florence Kelley learned about Australian and British wage boards at the first International Meeting of the Consumers' Leagues in Geneva.

For other reports, see Paul Kennaday, "The Land without Strikes," *Outlook* 90 (March 5, 1910): 526–530; Paul Kennaday, "Victorian Wages Boards and the New Zealand Conciliation Arbitration Act," *Yale Review* 19 (May 1910): 32–54; Paul Kennaday, "Helping the Small Man," *Outlook* 95 (July 30, 1910): 732–737, esp. p. 737; Paul Kennaday, "Settlement and Prevention of Industrial Disputes in New Zealand," *Annals of the American Academy of Political and Social Science* 36 (Philadelphia, September 1910): 438–444; Annie Marion MacLean, *Wage-Earning Women* (New York, 1910), 178; Frederic Jesup Stimson, *Popular Law-Making: A Study of the Origin, History, and Present Tendencies of Law-Making by Statute* (New York, 1910), 159–160, 210–211, 213, 254–255; Harris Weinstock, *Report on the Labor Laws and Labor Conditions of Foreign Countries in Relation to Strikes and Lockouts* (Sacramento, 1910), 57–144 passim, but especially pp. 57–73.

33. "The Common Welfare: Three States Consider Minimum Wage Boards," in *The Survey* 25 (February 18, 1911): 815; "Women's Wages in Milwaukee," *Milwaukee Bureau of Economy and Efficiency,* bulletin no. 4, (n.p., 1911), 3–18

which was prepared for the Wisconsin Consumers' League and included sections on wage boards in Australia and England, the law proposed for Wisconsin, and an analysis of its constitutionality; "Minimum Wage by Law," *Independent* 70 (April 13, 1911): 806–807; *Report of the* [Massachusetts] *Commission on Minimum Wage Boards* (Boston, January 1912); W. D. Howells, "Elizabeth Gardiner Evans—Appreciation," *La Follette's Magazine* 4 (February 17, 1912): 10–11; Elizabeth Gardiner Evans, "A Legal Minimum Wage: Initial Steps in This Country," ibid. 4 (February 24, 1912): 10; Elizabeth Gardiner Evans, "A Legal Minimum Wage: Some Reasons for Its Adoption," ibid. 4 (March 16, 1912): 10–11; "The Minimum Wage Problem," *Independent* 72 (March 14, 1912): 584–585; Winifred B. Cossitt, "Is a Minimum Wage Not Necessary?" *La Follette's Magazine* 4 (March 16, 1912): 9; Jeanne Robert, "Woman and the Wage Question," *American Review of Reviews* 45 (April 1912): 439–442; "A Leader in the Minimum Wage Movement [Elizabeth Evans]," ibid., 442; "Minimum Wages and the Massachusetts Press," *Survey* 28 (May 18, 1912): 313–314; Elizabeth G. Evans, "The Minimum Wage for Women: The First Effort in America to Follow the Lead of Great Britain in the Most Important Industrial Reform of the Day," *Twentieth Century Magazine* 6 (May 1912): 65–69; "Proposed Minimum Wage Bill [in Wisconsin]," *La Follette's Magazine* 4 (June 8, 1912): 13; Florence Kelley, "Minimum Wage Boards," in the *Proceedings of the National Conference of Charities and Correction*, 39th Annual Session [Cleveland, June 13, 1912] (Fort Wayne, Ind., 1912), 395–403; "Minimum Wage Law for Massachusetts," *Survey* 28 (June 22, 1912): 454–455; "Recognition of the Minimum Wage," *La Follette's Magazine* 4 (July 13, 1912): 3–4; Elizabeth Gardiner Evans, "Massachusetts and the Minimum Wage: An Important First Step toward Establishing a Revolutionary Principle," ibid. 4 (July 13, 1912): 7, 15; Clara E. Laughlin, "Minimum Wages," *Pearson's Magazine* 28 (August 1912): 9–17; Arthur N. Holcombe, "What Is the Minimum Wage?" *Survey* 29 (October 19, 1912): 74–76; Florence Kelley, "Minimum-Wage Boards," *American Journal of Sociology* 17 (November 1911): 303–314; Florence Kelley, "Minimum-Wage Laws," *Journal of Political Economy* 20 (December 1912): 999–1010; Sidney Webb, "The Economic Theory of a Legal Minimum Wage," ibid., (December 1912): 973–998; "The Development of Minimum-Wage Laws in the United States, 1912 to 1927," in *Bulletin* no. 61 of the Women's Bureau (Washington, D.C., 1928), esp. pp. 1–12.

The legislative proposals rested on a growing body of research dealing with wages and living standards in the United States. See, for examples, Louis Marion Bosworth, "The Living Wage of Women Workers: A Study of Incomes and Expenditures of Four Hundred and Fifty Women Workers in the City of Boston," in supplement no. 31, *Annals of the American Academy of Political and Social Science* (Philadelphia, May 1911), 1–90; Scott Nearing, *Wages in the United States, 1908–1910: A Study of State and Federal Wage Statistics* (New York, 1911); Scott Nearing, *Social Adjustment* (New York, 1911), esp. pp. 70–102; Frank Hatch Streightoff, *The Standard of Living among the Industrial People of America* (Boston, 1911), esp. pp. 154–162, 167.

34. "Minimum Wage by Law," *Independent* 70 (April 13, 1911): 806, for the quotation. See also, William Pember Reeves, "Why I Proposed the 'Undesirable Immigrants Exclusion Bill,' " *Review of Reviews,* Australasian Edition, 6 (January 1895): 39–42; Reeves, *State Experiments,* 2: 325–364; Le Rossignol and Stewart, *State Socialism in New Zealand,* 281–283, 305–306; "A Labor Administration in Australia," *Outlook* 95 (July 30, 1910): 708.

35. "An Immigrant Labor Tariff," *Survey* 25 (January 7, 1911): 529–531. See also, Paul U. Kellogg, "Immigration and the Minimum Wage," *Annals of the American Academy of Political and Social Science* 48 (July 1913): 66–77.

36. "Minimum Wage Boards," *Survey* 33 (April 1, 1911): 32–33.

37. "Minimum Wage by Law," *Independent* 70 (April 13, 1911): 806–807.

38. See Brandeis to Evans, August 7, 1887; February, 1893, in Melvin I. Urofsky and David W. Levy, editors, *Letters of Louis D. Brandeis: I. (1870–1907): Urban Reformer* (Albany, 1971), 73, 74: Brandeis to Golden, Rudolph Isaac Coffee, Eugene Noble Foss, Evans, William Howard Taft, Arthur Norman Holcombe, Felix Frankfurter, June 3, 1909; May 25, June 8, December 2, 22, 30, 1911; April 5, 9, 1912, in ibid., *II (*1907–1912): People's Attorney (Albany, 1972), 277, 441, 451, 517–518, 527–528, 531–536, 576, 577–578. Brandeis resisted a proposal for a federal minimum wage law, arguing that it should wait until more states had legislated and a larger body of worldwide evidence had been accumulated. See his letter to Mary E. McDowell, July 8, 1912, in ibid., 639–640. However, he had previously urged President Taft to appoint a national commission to investigate industrial life, including the practicality of minimum wage boards. See ibid., 536.

39. See the commission's report, pages 17, 18, 22, 25, 26; "The Minimum Wage Problem," *Independent* 72 (March 14, 1912): 585.

40. See the commission's report, pages 19–21.

41. Beyer, "Labor Legislation for Women in Three States," 55–61.

42. "A Legal Minimum Wage: Some Reasons for Its Adoption," 10; "The Minimum Wage for Women," 67.

43. Brandeis, "Labor Legislation," 502–503.

44. For the ongoing discussion and compilation of data, see the *Report of the Commission to Investigate the Conditions of Working Women in Kentucky* (n.p., December 1911); "The Minimum Wage," *The City Club Bulletin* (Chicago) (February 14, 1912): 25–32; John A. Ryan, "Guaranteeing a Living Wage by Law," *Life and Labor* 2 (March 1912): 84–85; Evelyn Hubbard, "The Minimum Wage: Past and Present," *Economic Journal* 22 (June 1912): 303–309; R. C. K. Ensor, "The Practical Case for a Legal Minimum Wage," *Nineteenth Century* 72 (August 1912): 264–276; Theodore Roosevelt, "The Minimum Wage," *Outlook* 102 (October 1912): 159–160; Egbert Ray Nichols, editor, *Intercollegiate Debates: A Year Book of College Debating, with Records of Questions and Decisions, Specimen Speeches and Bibliographies* (rev. ed., New York, 1912, 1913), 81–184, for Oklahoma University v. Missouri University, freshman and sophomore debate at Ottawa University, and a bibliography; Edwin V. O'Hara, *Welfare Legislation for Women and Minors* (an address to the Consumers' League of Oregon, Portland, November 19, 1912); "The Minimum Wage," *Life*

and Labor 3 (May 1913): 152–153, for a bibliography; "Waiters and Wage Boards in Australia," ibid., 154–155; William Draper Lewis, "The Proposed Pennsylvania Minimum Wage Act," *Annals of the American Academy of Political and Social Science* 48 (July 1913): 37–40; Scott Nearing, "Wages in the United States," ibid., 41–44; Henry R. Seager, "The Minimum Wage as Part of a Program for Social Reform," ibid, 3–12; "Minimum Wage Laws in Australia," and "Tribunals for the Regulation of Wages in Trades in Australia and New Zealand, 1911," *Life and Labor* 3 (August 1913): 240–241, 256.

45. "Governor Sulzer's Message," and "What Are Minimum Wage Standards?" *Outlook* 103 (January 11, 1913): 51–53. See also, Abram I. Elkus, "Social Investigation and Social Legislation," *Annals of the American Academy of Political and Social Science* 48 (July 1913): 54–65.

46. In addition to the works cited above, see H. LaRue Brown, "A Minimum Wage for Workers," *Bulletin* of the City Club of Philadelphia 6 (January 27, 1913): 202; *Report of the Social Survey Committee of the Consumers' League of Oregon on the Wages, Hours and Conditions of Work and Cost and Standard of Living of Women Wage Earners in Oregon with Special Reference to Portland* (Portland, January 1913), esp. pp. 10–12; "The Success of a Minimum Wage," *American Review of Reviews* 47 (February 1913): 216–217, summarizing Sidney Webb's views from the *Journal of Political Economy;* Jane Addams, "Minimum Wage Boards for Women," *Ladies' Home Journal* 30 (March 1913): 27; Elbert Hubbard, "A Minimum Wage for Women," *Hearst's Magazine* 23 (March 1913): 499–502; James Boyle, "The Legal Minimum Wage," *Forum* 49 (May 1913): 576–584; Samuel McCune Lindsay, "The Minimum Wage as a Legislative Proposal in the United States," *Annals of the American Academy of Political and Social Science* 48 (July 1913): 45–53; "Labor Legislation in the Australian Elections," *American Review of Reviews* 48 (August 1913): 223–224, summarizing J. H. Harley in the *Contemporary Review;* Joseph Lee, "What the Minimum Wage Means to Workers–A Criticism," *Survey* 31 (November 8, 1913): 156–157; Raymond V. Phelan, "Minnesota Minimum Wage Law, 1913," *American Economic Review* 3 (December 1913): 989–990; American Federation of Labor, *Proceedings,* 1913 (Washington, D.C., 1913), 59–64; H. LaRue Brown, "Massachusetts and the Minimum Wage," *Annals of the American Academy of Political and Social Science* 48 (1913): 13–21; The Board of Public Welfare Bureau of Labor Statistics, "Report on the Wage-Earning Women of Kansas City (Kansas City, 1913); Clara E. Laughlin, *The Work-a-Day Girl: A Study of Some Present-Day Conditions* (Chicago, 1913), esp. pp. 173–176; John Mitchell, *The Wage Earner and His Problems* (Washington, D.C., 1913), esp. pp. 100–102; Scott Nearing, *Financing the Wage Earners' Family* (New York, 1913); Thomas H. Russell, *The Girl's Fight for a Living: How to Protect Working Women from Dangers Due to Low Wages* (Chicago, 1913), esp. pp. 22–23, 27, 178–180, including a summary of Alice Henry's speech to the Cook County (Chicago) Real Estate Board on March 18, 1913; C. C. Williamson, *The Minimum Wage: A Preliminary List of References* (New York, 1913); John A. Ryan, "Minimum Wage Legislation," in Jeremiah S. Young, editor, *Papers and Proceedings of the Minnesota Academy of Sciences,* 6 (1913):

110–122; Ambrose Tighe, "The Police Power and Economic Welfare," in ibid., 21–33.

47. Glendower Evans, "A Minimum Wage for Workers," *Bulletin* of the City Club of Philadelphia, 6 (January 27, 1913): 204; Henry Rogers Seager, "The Theory of the Minimum Wage," *American Labor Legislation Review* 3 (February 1913): 81–91, and the comments of John R. Commons, George W. Anderson, Edward F. McSweeney, Paul U. Kellogg, Henry Abrahams, George G. Groat, M. B. Hammond, G. W. Noyes, and Emily Greene Balch at pp. 92–115; Matthew B. Hammond, "The Minimum Wage in Great Britain and Australia," *Annals of the American Academy of Political and Social Science* 48 (1913): 22–36.

48. Webb, "The Economic Theory of a Legal Minimum Wage," 973–998.

49. Hammond, "The Minimum Wage in Great Britain and Australia," 22–36.

50. "The Minimum Wage," *Atlantic Monthly* 112 (September 1913): 289–297.

51. Summarized in "The 'Minimum Wage' from a New Angle," *Literary Digest* 46 (April 5, 1913): 744–745.

52. Boyle, "The Legal Minimum Wage," 576–584, esp. p. 576 for the quotation.

53. Ibid., 579.

54. Ibid., 584.

55. Charles Wells Reeder, "Bibliography on the Minimum Wage," Report no. 1 of the Department of Investigation and Statistics, Industrial Commission of Ohio (n.p., March 6, 1914), 23–33. See also C. C. Williamson, "Select Bibliography," in the *Third Report of the* [New York] *Factory Investigating Commission, 1914* (Albany, 1914), 489–513; H. A. Millis, "Some Aspects of the Minimum Wage," *Journal of Political Economy* 22 (February 1914): 132–159.

For other discussions, see Elizabeth G. Evans, "A Case for Minimum Wage Boards: Experience vs. Prophecy," *Survey* 31 (January 10, 1914): 440–441; Edwin V. O'Hara, "The Minimum Wage: Legislative Aspects," *Catholic University Bulletin* 20 (March 1914): 200–210, "Wage Boards in Australia," *Life and Labor* 4 (June 1914): 179–180; Mary Chamberlain, "Settling Labor Disputes in Australia," *Survey* 32 (August 1, 1914): 455–458, summarizing an interview with Justice Henry Bournes Higgins, president of the Arbitration Court; Irene Osgood Andrews, "Minimum Wage Legislation," in the *Third Report of the* [New York] *Factory Investigating Commission*, 173–382; *The Minimum Wage: A Debate. The Constructive and Rebuttal Speeches of the Representatives of the University of Chicago in the Sixteenth Annual Contests of the Central Debating League against Michigan and Northwestern, January 17, 1914* (Chicago, 1914).

56. John A. Ryan, "Minimum Wage Laws to Date," *Catholic World* 100 (January 1915): 433–443; John A. Ryan, *A Living Wage* (New York, 1915); Florence Kelley, "Status of Legislation in the United States," *Survey* 33 (February 6, 1915): 487–489; Louis D. Brandeis, "The Constitution and the Minimum Wage: Defense of the Oregon Minimum Wage Law before the United States Supreme Court," in ibid., 490–494, 521–524; M. B. Hammond, "Where Life Is More than Meat: The Australian Experience with Wage Boards," in ibid., 495–502; John A. Hobson, "The State and the Minimum Wage in England,"

in ibid., 503–504; Howard B. Woolston, "Wages in New York," in ibid., 505–511; N. I. Stone, "Is the Minimum Wage a Menace to Industry?" in ibid., 512–514. See also, Esther Packard, "Just Getting Along," in ibid., 514–515, for an analysis of wage rates in department stores and factories in New York. Florence Kelley edited the series under the title, "The Case for the Minimum Wage," *Minimum Wage Series Number 11* (National Consumers' League, n.p., n.d.). See also, Chas. H. Verrill, "Minimum-Wage Legislation in the United States and Foreign Countries," in *Bulletin Number 167, Miscellaneous Series No. 8, U.S. Bureau of Labor Statistics* (Washington, D.C., April 1915), esp. pp. 104–173, 210–294, 313–316 for the Australasian data, and 321–328 for a bibliography. Another bibliography appeared in P. M. Pearson, editor, *Intercollegiate Debates* (New York, [1913]), 3: 181–184.

57. The case was *Stettler v. O'Hara*, 69 Oregon 519 (1914). The National Consumers' League published the 207-page brief. See Louis D. Brandeis and Josephine Goldmark, *Stettler v. (State of Oregon) Industrial Welfare Commission. Supreme Court of Oregon, October term, 1913.*

58. Brandeis and Goldmark again prepared the brief (398 pages) for the October term, 1914, and for the associated case, *Simpson v. (State of Oregon) Industrial Welfare Commission.* See esp. pp. 7–15, 101, 120, 253, 266, 272, 278–280, 298, 300–302, 305–323, 331–353, 357–359, 361–381, 386, 392.

59. Reeves was not cited in the much longer (843-page) 1916 brief, which included many additional references to Australasian experience. See *Oregon Minimum Wage Cases. Stettler v. O'Hara; Simpson v. O'Hara. Supreme Court of the United States, October Term, 1916. Brief for Defendants in Error upon Re-Argument* (New York, n.d.), 1–4, 108–109, 167–168, 225–226, 337–338, 351–352, 452–454, 498–501, 517–529, 534–536, 546–551, 563, 567–570, 586–590, 594–596, 608–615, 622–623, 630–632, 643–650, 653–660, 675–679, 686–693, 695–700, 703–704, 708, 710–718, 723–725, 727–732, 735–740, 742–743, 758, and esp. p. 722 for the statement that "the experience of those states and countries which have longest had minimum rates of pay fixed by law has proved successful. In Victoria the officials of the Employers' Association and the Chamber of Manufacturers, which originally led the opposition to the wage-board system, no longer opposes it."

60. See the 1914 brief, pages 3-6.

61. Brandeis, "Labor Legislation," 503; *Laws of Utah*, Chap. 63, March 18, 1913. It is ironic that New York, the state that produced the most extensive investigation and that had the greatest influence on the reform movement, itself failed to enact a law until 1933. The state supreme court struck that measure down in 1936 but reversed itself the following year. See the *Fourth Report of the* [New York] *Factory Investigation Commission, 1915* (5 vols., Albany, 1915), esp. 1: 1–50, 291–298, 389–887; 2: 1–635; 4: 1846–2280; 5: 2671–2905. The Australasian minimum-wage experience figured prominently in these volumes in replies to questionnaires, a symposium, oral testimony, and in an extended essay by Paul S. Collier, "Minimum Wage Legislation in Australasia," 4: 1851–1955. Many prominent reformers testified, including LaRue Brown, Clark, Commons, Goldmark, Hammond, Kelley, Kellogg, Ryan, Seager,

Seligman, and Weber. See also Thomas J. Kerr IV, "The New York Factory Investigation Commission and the Minimum-Wage Movement," in *Labor History* 12 (Summer 1971): 373–391, for an analysis of the reform effort and its opponents.

62. See Constance D. Leupp, "A Substitute for Charity," *Pearson's Magazine* 33 (January 1915): 103–113; reprinted by the National Consumers' League as no. 9 in its *Minimum Wage Series* (n.p., n.d.); Edwin V. O'Hara, "Wage Legislation for Women," *Catholic World* 100 (January 1915): 443–450; Walter Lippmann, "The Campaign against Sweating," *New Republic* 2 (March 27, 1915): 3–29, which also appeared in pamphlet form; Henry Bournes Higgins, "A New Province for Law and Order: Industrial Peace through Minimum Wage and Arbitration," *Harvard Law Review* 29 (November 1915): 13–39, reprinted by the National Consumers' League as no. 14 in its *Minimum Wage Series* (n.p., n.d.), and in the *Monthly Labor Review* 2 (February 1916): 1–22; Paul Leland Haworth, *America in Ferment* (Indianapolis, 1915), esp. pp. 173, 190, 198; Arthur E. Suffern, *Conciliation and Arbitration in the Coal Industry of America* (Boston, 1915), esp. chaps. 8–9.

The volume of publications remained modest over the following years. For examples, see W. J. Ghent, "How the Minimum Wage Works," *Independent* 89 (February 5, 1917): 219–220; M. B. Hammond, "The Regulation of Wages in New Zealand," *Quarterly Journal of Economics* 31 (May 1917): 404–446; Dorothy W. Douglas, "American Minimum Wage Laws at Work," *American Economic Review* 9 (December 1919): 701–738; "Development of the Labor Situation in Australia," *Monthly Labor Review* 11 (July 1920): 59–66, summarizing the view of A. W. Ferrin, the U.S. Trade Commissioner in Melbourne; "Minimum Wage Laws for Women," a map of the United States supplied by the Women's Bureau of the U.S. Department of Labor, *Life and Labor* 11 (February 1921): 49; Mary W. Dewson, "Outlines for Study Courses: Minimum Wage Commission Legislation," *Woman Citizen*, May 7, 1921, esp. Lesson II for Australasian models and experience; Alice Henry, *Women and the Labor Movement*, 137, 143–165.

63. Brandeis, "Labor Legislation," 507, 512–522; Rome G. Brown, *"Brief and Argument for Plaintiffs in Error," Cases Nos. 507 and 508 before the Supreme Court of the United States; Stettler v. O'Hara; Simpson v. O'Hara; October Term, 1914* (Minneapolis, n.d.); Rome G. Brown, *The Minimum Wage, with Particular Reference to the Legislative Minimum Wage under the Minnesota Statute of 1913* (Minneapolis, n.d.); Helen Marot, "Trade Unions and Minimum Wage Boards," *American Federationist* 22 (November 1915): 966–969; Marie L. Obenauer, "The Status of the Minimum Wage Controversy," typescript, 8 pp., pointing to the difficulty of extrapolating from the Australasian experience, in the Katherine P. Edson Papers, University of California Library, Los Angeles, box 7, folder 5; Norris C. Hundley, Jr., "Katherine Philips Edson and the California Minimum Wage, 1912–1923," *Pacific Historical Review* 29 (August 1960): 271–285, esp. pp. 274–276; Kerr, "The New York Factory Investigating Commission," 379–385; and the testimony of businessmen and labor spokesmen

in the *Fourth Report of the Factory Investigating Commission,* 1: 769–826, and indexed in 5: 2275–2277.

64. Brandeis, "Labor Legislation," 519–522; Hoyt Landon Warner, *Progressivism in Ohio, 1897–1917* (Columbus, 1964), 335–343, 402.

65. Hundley, "Katherine Edson," 271–278; Harris Weinstock, Florence Kelley, Walter G. Mathewson to Edson, November 14, 22, December 3, 1914, Katherine Philips Edson, "Industrial Problems as I See Them," typescript, ca. 1913, "Minimum Wage Constitutional Amendment," a pamphlet prepared by Edson, Mrs. Charles Farwell Edson, "Industrial and Social Conditions, " ca. 1913, Edson's three-page memorandum on the history of the minimum-wage movement in California, typescript, ca. 1923, and an unsigned memorandum summarizing the history of the California Industrial Welfare Commission, three typescript pages, ca. 1933, all in the Edson Papers, box 2, folders 2, 6, box 7, folders 5, 4; Earl C. Crockett, "The History of California Labor Legislation, 1910–1930" (Ph.D. dissertation, University of California, 1931), 335–343 passim, 402; George E. Mowry, *The California Progressives,* (Berkeley, 1951), 153; Olin, *California's Prodigal Sons,* 72–74; William Bradley Wait, "A Historical and Comparative Study of the Development of Minimum Wage Legislation in California and New York" (Ph.D. dissertation, Cornell University, 1952), 162–235; *San Francisco Bulletin,* March 17, 1913, for Weinstock's support, citing Australasian experience as justification.

66. See Florence Kelley, John A. Ryan to Edson, January 16, February 21, 20, 1916, in the Edson Papers, box 2, folders 11, 10.

67. *Stettler v. O'Hara,* 243 United States 629 (1917). Simpson worked for Stettler and argued that she could live adequately on a lower wage and that she would lose her job if her employer had to pay the minimum, $8.64 a week. See also Edwin V. O'Hara, *A Living Wage by Legislation: The Oregon Experience* (Salem, Ore., 1917), esp. pp. vi–ix, xii–xv, 45–56; Mary D. Hopkins, "Do Wages Buy Health? The Oregon Minimum Wage Case Re-Argued," *Survey* 37 (February 3, 1917): 517–519, reprinted by the National Consumers' League as no. 15 in its *Minimum Wage Series* (n.p., n.d.).

For several years, however, state courts sustained the constitutionality of minimum-wage laws. See *State v. Crowe,* 130 Arkansas 272 (1917); *Williams v. Evans,* 139 Minnesota 32 (1917); *Holcombe v. Creamer,* 231 Massachusetts 99 (1918); *Larsen v. Rice,* 100 Washington 642 (1918); *Miller v. Minimum Wage Commission,* 145 Minnesota 262 (1920); *Spokane v. Younger,* 113 Washington 359 (1920); and *Poye v. Texas,* 230 South West 116 (Texas Court of Criminal Appeals, 1921).

68. Brandeis, "Labor Legislation," 503–504; *First Biennial Report of the Industrial Welfare Commission of the State of California, 1913–1914* (n.p., 1914), esp. pp. 11–22; *Second Biennial Report of the Industrial Welfare Commission of the State of California, 1915–1916* (Sacramento, 1917), esp. pp. 13–18; *Third Biennial Report of the Industrial Welfare Commission of the State of California, 1917–1918* (Sacramento, 1919), esp. p. 8.

69. "Minimum Wage for Women and Children," *Hearings before the Subcommittee of the Committee on the District of Columbia, House of Repre-*

sentatives, 65 Congress, 2 session, April 16, 1918 (Washington, D.C., 1918).

70. The case was *Adkins and Others v. Children's Hospital,* 261 United States 525 (1923).

71. Felix Frankfurter and Mary W. Dewson prepared the 520-page brief for the initial case, *District of Columbia Minimum Wage Cases—Children's Hospital of the District of Columbia v. Minimum Wage Board of the District of Columbia; Lyons v. Same. Court of Appeals of the District of Columbia, October Term, 1920.*

72. *Adkins v. Children's Hospital,* 567–568.

73. Ibid.

74. Brandeis, "Labor Legislation," 505, 513, 515, 519–522, 539, 690–691. The cases were *Commonwealth v. Boston Transcript Company,* 249 Massachusetts 477 (1924); *Folding Furniture Company v. Wisconsin Industrial Commission,* 300 Federal Reports 991 (1924); *People v. Laurnaga & Co.,* 32 Puerto Rico 766 (1924); *Murphy and O'Connor v. Sardell,* 269 United States 530 (1925); *Stevenson v. St. Clair,* 161 Minnesota 444 (1925); *Topeka Laundry Company v. Court of Industrial Relations,* 119 *Kansas* 12 (1925); and *Donham v. West Nelson Manufacturing Company,* 273 United States 657 (1927). Frankfurter and Dewson prepared a brief for *Helen Gainer v. A. B. C. Dohrman et al., members of the Industrial Welfare Commission of California* for submission to the California Supreme Court, but the case was dropped before it came on for argument. The National Consumers' League published the 179-page brief in June, 1924. The California Industrial Welfare Commission filed a friend-of-the-court brief in the Arizona case, *Murphy and O'Connor v. Sardell.* It included a summary of American and foreign minimum-wage laws, pp. 4–13, and a bibliography, pp. 39–42.

For reactions to the *Atkins* decision, see *The Supreme Court and Minimum Wage Legislation: Comment by the Legal Profession on the District of Columbia Case* (New York, 1925); John A. Ryan, *The Supreme Court and the Minimum Wage* (New York, [1923]), which drew heavily on his earlier writings; and E. M. Burns, *Wages and the State: A Comparative Study of the Problems of State Wage Regulation* (London, 1926), esp. chapters 4–6.

75. Brandeis, "Labor Legislation," 513, 538–539.

76. See, for example, the *Gainer* brief. It was supported by the California Federation of Women's Clubs, the California League of Women Voters, the Los Angeles United Garment Workers, the Los Angeles Waitresses and Cafeteria Workers, and both the Northern and Southern branches of the Women's Christian Temperance Union. See also, a five-page statement on the status of minimum-wage legislation prepared for the Women's Organizations of California, April 22, 1922, in the Edson Papers, box 7, folder 5.

77. Delaying tactics stalled enactment in Ohio until the *Atkins* decision ended all hope of reform. See Brandeis, "Labor Legislation," 519–522; "In the Ohio Senate on Feb. 21, 1923," *Ohio Council on Women in Industry* (March 1923): 1–4; "Minimum Wage," ibid., (May 1923): 1.

CHAPTER SIX. THE COMPULSORY ARBITRATION OF LABOR DISPUTES

1. The full title of the statute was "An Act to Encourage the Formation of Industrial Unions and Associations, and to Facilitate the Settlement of Industrial Disputes by Conciliation and Arbitration." See *New Zealand Statutes, 1894* (Wellington, 1894), 22–44.

2. Interested Americans first learned about the system from several sources: W. P. Reeves, "Labor Troubles: Hints of New Remedies from the Antipodes," *Review of Reviews* 10 (August 1894): 178–184; *Introduction to the Labour Laws of New Zealand* (Wellington, 1895), 2–3; W. D. P. Bliss, *Arbitration and Conciliation in Industrial Disputes* (Boston, 1895), a fifteen-page pamphlet reprinted from the advance sheets of his *Encyclopedia of Social Reform* (New York, 1897); E. R. Gould, "Industrial Conciliation and Arbitration in Europe and Australasia," *Yale Review* 3 (February 1895): 376–407; J. G. Ward, "Suggestions from New Zealand," *Review of Reviews* 12 (August 1895): 203–204; "New Zealand's Legislators Seem to Rank People above Property," *New York Times*, June 28, 1896, summarizing a lecture Reeves gave in London; Reeves, "Five Years' Political and Social Reform in New Zealand," 847; "Progressive Legislation in New Zealand," 233.

3. See Carroll D. Wright, *Eighth Annual Report*, Massachusetts Bureau of Labor Statistics (Boston, 1877); Carroll D. Wright, *Industrial Conciliation and Arbitration* (Boston, 1881); Horace E. Denning to Lloyd, September 20, 1893; Carroll D. Wright, *The Industrial Evolution of the United States* (Meadville, Pa., 1895), 290–291; Myers, "Compulsory Arbitration," 184–201, reporting a debate in 1892 between Wright, who supported voluntarism throughout his career, and the Reverend H. L. Wayland, former president of the American Association of Social Science. Wayland argued that "if the State is to come in at the finish with the bayonet, it may well come in at the start with" compulsory arbitration. Such a system, "beneficent" and "just," was sure to come.

In fact, Reeves was not even the pioneer in the Antipodes. C. C. Kingston, the premier of South Australia, had introduced a similar bill in 1890, and in New Zealand Willam Downie Stewart introduced a private bill that same year. See C. C. Kingston, *Notes on the Industrial Conciliation Bill of the South Australian Parliament* (Adelaide, 1894); C. C. Kingston, "Industrial Agreements and Conciliation," *Review of Reviews* 10 (December 1894): 647–650; Holt, "Political Origins of Compulsory Arbitration in New Zealand," 100; Holt, "Compulsory Arbitration in New Zealand," 180; Sinclair, *Reeves*, 105–112, 116, 120, 138, 151–153, 182, 203, 209–210; [William Pember Reeves], *State Arbitration and the Living Wage. With an Account of the New Zealand Law and Its Results* (Fabian Tract no. 83, London, 1898).

Some American groups, notably the iron molders and the construction trades, already provided for arbitration in their labor contracts, and some states, notably Massachusetts and New York, had established conciliation and arbitration agencies, though with little success, which explains why Reeves turned to the compulsory concept. See Josephine Shaw Lowell, compiler, *Industrial Arbitration and Conciliation: Some Chapters from the Industrial History of the Past Thirty Years* (New York, 1893), 64–109; C. R. Lowell, "The Rights of Capital and Labor," *Publications of the Church Social Union*, no. 38 (Boston, June 15, 1897), for data on the construction trades in Boston, Chicago, and New York City; George Milton Janes, *The Control of Strikes in American Trade Unions* (Baltimore, 1916), esp. pp. 29–37; and Ting Tsz Ko, *Governmental Methods of Adjusting Labor Disputes in North America and Australasia* (Studies in History, Economics and Public Law, vol. 123, no. 2, Columbia University, New York, 1926).

4. Lloyd told Edward Everett Hale, "People constantly misunderstand my purpose. They seem to think I want the U.S. to imitate New Zealand; on the contrary, I want our country to give New Zealand something to imitate." Nevertheless, he judged the colony's labor program "the best . . . in the world," thought the arbitration law "the most important piece of social legislation . . . enacted in recent years," and described Reeves as "one of the constitutional geniuses of our time." Edward Tregear, the New Zealand Secretary of Labor, thanked Lloyd "for the interest you take in our work." See Lloyd to Hale, Samuel Gompers, Charles Sprague Smith, and Sylvester Baxter, September 12, 1901; June 22, 1894; October 3, 12, 1899; and Tregear to Lloyd, April 28, 1894.

5. For a typical conference, see *Industrial Conciliation: Report of the Proceedings of the Conference Held under the Auspices of the National Civic Federation* (New York, 1902). Lusk gave a paper, "The Experience of New Zealand." He left the conference critical of both capital and labor for rejecting the compulsory concept. See *Chicago Tribune*, December 18, 20, 1900, and Lusk to Lloyd, December 23, 1900.

On the legislative efforts, see James T. Smith, Thomas P. Rixey, E. W. Harris, W. P. Potter, F. C. Chalfant, and Henry W. Goodrich to Lloyd, June 22, August 6, November 17, December 17, 22, 1900; May 31, September 12, 1902; *Buffalo Express, New York World, Oakland Enquirer, Syracuse Post Standard, Newport Herald, San Francisco Bulletin*, and *Boston Evening Transcript*, March 20, May 30, December 11, 13, 14, 1900; May 21, 1901; March 5, 1902; "Arbitration Voluntary and Compulsory," in the *Biennial Report of the Colorado Bureau of Labor, 1899–1900* (Denver, 1900), 206–215; "Gov. Lind on Compulsory Arbitration," in the *Seventh Biennial Report of the* [Minnesota] *Bureau of Labor, 1899–1900* (St. Paul, 1900), 323–324; "The Strike," *Independent* 54 (September 18, 1902): 2214; and William A. Stone, "Compulsory Arbitration," ibid., 2219–2220.

6. Lloyd, *A Country without Strikes*, 178–180. Reeves wrote a foreword. "I have pitched it in rather a mild key," he told Lloyd, thinking "it best to leave you to do the fighting." Reeves to Lloyd, March 4, 1900.

7. Clark, "Labor Conditions in New Zealand," 1184–1211; Weinstock, *Report on Foreign Laws*, 143; Kelly, "A New Civilization," 721–722. Kelly's assessments were more favorable than she recalled in her autobiography, where she complained of difficulties in placing her articles. Nevertheless, her work attracted

attention and brought many appreciative letters. See *Flowering Stream* (New York, 1939), 350–357.

For her husband's report, "Under the Southern Cross: How New Zealand Tamed Trade Unions and Abolished Strikes," see the *Los Angeles Times*, January 7, 1906. He confirmed that the colony was governed by neither cranks nor fanatics and that it was not rushing toward "social disaster and industrial ruin." On the contrary, he noted a "conspicuous common sense and humanity" in government and an amazing prosperity "for so young and sparsely-settled a country." Later he told his readers, ibid., January 21, 1906, that "The colony is not the industrial Garden of Eden described by some enthusiasts, but neither is it a boycotters' hell like San Francisco, nor a grafting walking delegate's happy hunting ground like New York."

8. Of the dozens of reports and assessments appearing between 1901 and 1910, several might be cited as illustrative: "Compulsory Arbitration in New Zealand," a condensation of the Backhouse Report to the New South Wales Royal Commission of Enquiry, in *Massachusetts Labor Bulletin*, 20 (Boston, November 1901): 128–137; "Compulsory Arbitration in New South Wales," in ibid., 21 (Boston, February 1902): 26–31; Hugh H. Lusk, "The Successful Prevention of Strikes. Seven Years of Compulsory Arbitration in New Zealand. The Adoption of the Law in Neighboring Colonies," in *World's Work* 3 (February 1902): 1781–1783; New York Board of Mediation and Arbitration, "Report of Royal Commission of Inquiry, New South Wales, Australia, into the Working of the New Zealand Compulsory Conciliation and Arbitration Law," Part 4, *Fifteenth Annual Report for the Year 1901*, Assembly Documents, vol. 23, no. 61, pt. 3, 381–424 (Albany, New York, 1902); "Working of Compulsory Conciliation and Arbitration Laws in New Zealand and Victoria," in *Bulletin* of the U.S. Department of Labor, 7 (40): 552–560 for the report and 561–574 for the text of the New South Wales law (Washington, D.C., May 1902); Kennaday, "Victorian Wages Boards and the New Zealand Conciliation-Arbitration Act," 32–54. The *Outlook* predicted that "the New Zealand law is sure of transplantation upon this side of the globe" and reported that Ontario already had the system under consideration for its railroads. See 71 (January 1902): 902–903.

9. Lloyd's running headings in *A Country without Strikes* made his case: "The Better Way," "Debate instead of War," and "Compulsion Means Peace." He asked, "Is not this a civilized way for civilized people to settle their differences?" (p. 55). Both he and Lusk pressed these ideas on the *Industrial Commission on Labor Organizations, Labor Disputes, and Arbitration, and on Railway Labor*, House Document 186, 57 Congress, 1 session, serial 4347 (Washington, D.C., 1901), esp. pp. cx–cxii, cxxiv, 519–545, 701–706. The commission also reprinted Lusk's two-part article, "Compulsory Arbitration: What It Means in New Zealand" and "What It Means for America," from the *Bricklayer and Mason*, May–June 1901. See also, Lusk to Lloyd, August 30, September 9, 1900, saying that the commissioners wanted to know if compulsory arbitration could be introduced into the United States.

10. Lloyd, "Australasian Cures for Coal Wars," 667, 674. A presidential com-

mission settled the strike but rejected compulsory arbitration. See Carroll D. Wright, *Report to the President on the Anthracite Coal Strike* (Washington, D.C., 1902); and *Report of the Anthracite Commission* (Washington, D.C., 1903). Lloyd told a New Zealand official, however, that the president had intervened because of "the inspiration derived from the laws of your country," and Allen Kelly confirmed that Roosevelt had "watched its legislation very closely. . . . The Older World," the president declared, "has a great deal to learn from New Zealand." See Lloyd to Joseph Ward, March 31, 1903; Kelly, "Under the Southern Cross: Results of the Empiric Policy of Trying Things On—The Arbitration Act in New Zealand," *Los Angeles Sunday Times*, January 21, 1906.

11. "The Abolition of Strikes and Lockouts," *Arena* 31 (January 1904): 1–11; "The Political Revolution in New Zealand Which Laid the Foundation for the Establishment of Industrial Arbitration on Demand," ibid. (May 1904): 464–471.

12. Smythe, "A Program for California," *Land of Sunshine* 15 (December 1901): 487–498; Smythe, "The California Constructive League: Arbitration and the Workers," *Out West* 16 (March 1902): 333–334; and Smythe, "The Law of Compulsory Arbitration at Work," 82–88. Compare *Chicago American*, June 28, July 27, 1901, and Edward Tregear, "Industrial Arbitration in New Zealand," *Independent* 55 (August 13, 1903): 1908–1910, for similar views.

13. The words quoted are from the title of his pamphlet and pages 13–14 and 23, published in New York, probably in 1900. In a letter to Lloyd dated September 14, 1901, Francis reported that he had been apprenticed to the printing trade in Dunedin, New Zealand, in the 1860s and had published *The Otago Punch*, beginning in 1866. He had also gained "experience as a Union Man and Proprietor . . . in London, and the U.S. West and East." Two printing unions, he said, pressmen and typographers, supported arbitration and he hoped that "the day is not far distant when the horizon will be cleared of the strike question."

14. "Necessity of Industrial Arbitration," *Annals of the American Academy of Political and Social Science* 36 (Philadelphia, July–December 1910): 311–320. This was one of nine essays on arbitration in that issue.

15. "Compulsory Arbitration under Storm-Sails," *Arena* 40 (August–September 1908): 137–141.

16. See *A Country without Strikes*, especially chap. 2, "The Shoemaker Sticks to the Last," chap. 3, "Better Committees than Mobs," and pp. 114–116, 120, 122–123, 154, and 166–168.

17. "A Country without Strikes," *Catholic World* 72 (November 1900): 147–157.

18. "A Program for California," 496.

19. "Industrial Peace through Arbitration," *Arena* 32: 303. Flower declared that the American people should "act for their own protection, as well as for the maintenance of law, order, and the principles of free government. New Zealand has shown the way."

20. *Strikes Are War! War Is Hell!* 23.

21. "Compulsory Arbitration: The Experience of New Zealand," in Peters, *Labor and Capital*, 221–237. This was one of fifty papers, mostly reprinted from the Hearst newspapers as part of the publisher's effort to stimulate debate

on labor questions. See also, Tregear to Parsons, quoted by Benjamin O. Flower, "In the Mirror of the Present," *Arena* 32 (July 1904): 85–86, saying that no employer dared disobey the arbitration court for fear of being branded as exploitative and unjust.

22. Dorr, "What Eight Million Women Want," 805. Compare Paul Kennaday, "The Land without Strikes," *Outlook* 90 (March 5, 1910): 526–530, saying that New Zealand "would rather sacrifice the industry than the worker."

23. Quoted from an interview he gave Mary Chamberlain in "Settling Labor Disputes in Australia," *Survey* 32 (August 1, 1914): 455–458.

24. Lloyd, *Newest England*, 275.

25. Smythe, "The Law of Compulsory Arbitration at Work," 87; Conrad Reno, "Compulsory Arbitration: Industrial Courts to Administer Industrial Justice," in Peters, *Labor and Capital*, 200–220.

26. Edward Tregear, "How New Zealand Is Solving the Problem of Popular Government," *Arena* 32 (December 1904): 569–577; Lloyd, "Problems of the Pacific," 352; A. S. Johnson in the *Political Science Quarterly* 18 (December 1903): 710–713; Weinstock, *Report on Foreign Laws*, 142; Lusk, *Social Welfare in New Zealand*, 287.

27. Lusk, "The Successful Prevention of Strikes," 1783. Compulsory arbitration, he argued later, would bring Americans "justice and fair-play, . . . brotherhood and kindness, . . . especially to those who have been . . . deprived of these things for the supposed benefit of others." See Lusk, "Practical Socialism," 293.

28. Reno, "Industrial Courts," 219–20; Clark's words are quoted from pages 5 and 6 in Frank L. M'Vey, "Minneapolis Conference of Employers and Employes," *Commons* 7 (November 1902): 1–12.

29. "Compulsory Arbitration. A Half-Way House to Socialism?" *North American Review* 175 (November 1902): 597–606.

30. Fieldhouse's article for the Hearst syndicate, "Need of a National Court of Arbitration," also appeared in Peters, editor, *Labor and Capital*, 179–184.

31. See his *Methods of Industrial Peace* (Boston, 1904), esp. "Legal Regulation of Labor Disputes in New Zealand" and "The Case for Legal Regulation," pp. 364–408.

32. In addition to the sources cited at note 5 above, see, for example, Stanley Bowmar, "Progressive New Zealand," *Public* 15 (July 5, 1912) 628–630; Richard T. Ely, *Studies in the Evolution of Industrial Society* (New York, 1903), 351–353, 382–384; Richard T. Ely, "How to Avert Strikes," *Boston Evening Transcript*, August 3, 1901; Richard T. Ely and George Ray Wicker, *Elementary Principles of Economics* (New York, 1912), 285–287; Gilman to Lloyd, June 25, 1900.

33. On Costigan and Allen, see the text below at notes 52–53.

34. Quoted from the *Louisville Courier* in Smythe to Lloyd, August 29, 1901.

35. Thomas J. Hogan, "Voluntary Arbitration: Experience of Stove Manufacturers, in Peters, editor, *Labor and Capital*, 280–286. In Wisconsin, for example, the sponsor of an arbitration bill argued that without it, the state would have "to keep an army to maintain the peace between capital and labor," but

the governor opposed a compulsory system, questioning both its constitutionality and the willingness of capital and labor to "surrender . . . rights which men hold to be very sacred. . . ." Compare the *Milwaukee Journal*, February 22, 1895, and *Wisconsin Public Documents* 1 (Madison, 1895): 14.

36. Compare Martin Fox, "Voluntary Arbitration: Experience of Iron Moulders," in Peters, editor, *Labor and Capital*, 287–298; Spahr to Lloyd, October 2, 1899; Myers, "Compulsory Arbitration," 201; Samuel Gompers, "Labor Unions: Labor Unions and Strikes," in Peters, editor, *Labor and Capital*, 62–74; Samuel Gompers, "From the Address [to] the Arbitration Conference, . . . December 17, 1900," in ibid., 448–457. After extensive reading on the subject of compulsory arbitration, Gompers declared himself "unconverted." Though the system might work in good times, he predicted failure when hard times struck, and the punitive provisions of the New South Wales law appalled him. And so he rejected the counsel of Lloyd in Chicago and Ben Tillet, the London dock union leader, responding instead to the urgings of the National Civic Federation to lead labor's opposition to the New Zealand principle. See Lloyd to Gompers, June 22, 1894, and the letters to and from Tillet and Ralph Easley in the American Federation of Labor Papers, January 4, May 21, November 11, 26, 1902, Series 11, File A, box 1, in the State Historical Society of Wisconsin, Madison.

37. See, for examples, Gompers in *Labor and Capital*, 72, 448, 456; N. F. Thompson, secretary of the Southern Industrial Convention, as reported in the New York *Evening Post*, June 13, 1900; and Kennaday, "The Land without Strikes," 528–529.

38. E. E. Clark of the Railway Conductors, "Arbitration of Labor Disputes," *Annals of the American Academy of Political and Social Science* 24 (July 1904): 285–295.

J. Ramsay MacDonald, a founder of the British Labour Party, agreed. Compulsory arbitration had "steadied . . . the industrial machine" by putting "obstacles in the way of war," but it had not dealt with "the maldistribution of wealth" or with the "mechanism of industrial relationships." "In the end," he declared, "practically nothing has happened except that a generation's effort has been wasted." Reeves admitted as much, agreeing that the New Zealand program did not "go to the root of the relations of labour with capital, of currency with wealth, or of exchange with production." See MacDonald, "Arbitration Courts and Wages Boards in Australasia," 312, 316, 325; Reeves, "Five Years' Political and Social Reform in New Zealand," 850.

39. See, for example, Fox, "Experience of Iron Moulders," in Peters, editor, *Labor and Capital*, 295, 297.

40. See pages 364–375 for his criticism. Compare an unsigned review in the *Nation* 72 (October 3, 1901): 259–260; and John Collier, "The Crisis of Industrial Arbitration," ibid. 81 (July 20, 1905): 50–52.

41. For examples, see "Compulsory Arbitration," *Independent* 53 (July 25, 1901): 2372; *Louisville Courier*, quoted in Smythe to Lloyd, August 29, 1901; *New York Times*, May 8, 1905, commenting on a proposal for compulsory

arbitration in public service industries; B. K. Miller, a Milwaukee attorney, quoted from the *Los Angeles Times* in Bomar, "Progressive New Zealand," 628; and "Compulsory Arbitration in Australia Fails," *New York Times,* November 12, 1915.

42. See Wayland's column, "The Economic Struggle," *Appeal to Reason,* April 25, 1903; and an unsigned review of Lloyd's *Newest England* in the *Nation* 72 (April 18, 1901): 322. For examples of Wayland's earlier views, see *Appeal to Reason,* December 31, 1898; August 31, September 7, November 2, December 7, 1901; April 12, August 16, 1902.

43. Compare Charles Edward Russell, *Bare Hands and Stone Walls: Some Recollections of a Side-Line Reformer* (New York, 1933), 171 and 178 for the quotation, and 179–182 for his puzzled reflections on why he had initially praised the New Zealand system; Charles Edward Russell, "The War on Strikes and the Effect," *National Post* 1 (June 14, July 1, 1911): 22–28, 28–32; "More Light on the Common Good: The Collapse of Compulsory Arbitration," *Coming Nation,* September 2, 1911.

44. Charles Edward Russell, "Lessons from the Antipodes: The Labor Party of Australia and How It Fares in Political Policies," *Coming Nation,* June 3, 1911.

45. For an analytical summary of industrial disputes in New Zealand, 1895–1912, see *The Official New Zealand Year Book, 1912* (Wellington, 1912), 684–700; and for confirmation of labor's restlessness with the system, see Harry R. Burrill, "New Zealand Labor Questions," in *U.S. Monthly Consular and Trade Reports,* no. 322 (Washington, D.C., July 1907): 241–243.

See also "A General Strike against Compulsory Arbitration," *New Review: A Critical Review of International Socialism* 2 (May 1914): 314–316; W. H. Triggs, "Syndicalism in New Zealand," *Quarterly Review* 221 (July 1914): 200–215; Bennett, "The Truth about New Zealand," 365–366; Bennett, "Compulsory Arbitration in Australasia;" 458–459; Charles Edward Russell, "How Compulsory Arbitration Worked," *Carpenter* 37 (June 1917): 16–17; "Direct Action in Australia," *Independent* 92 (October 20, 1917): 120; Hugh H. Lusk, "The Australian Strike for National Control," *Bellman* 24 (June 22, 1918): 658–689.

46. P. Airey, "The 'Australia Remedy,' " *National Review* (London) 59 (August 1912): 1030–1035. See also "Doubtful Efficacy of the 'Australian Remedy' for Strikes," *American Review of Reviews* 46 (September 1912): 367–368, for a summary.

For typical criticism, see the *New York Evening Post,* December 18, 1900, September 26, October 3, 1901. For Lloyd's rejoinders, see ibid., December 29, 1900; August 20, 23, 30, December 7, 1901; *Chicago-Record Herald,* October 22, 1901; *New York Journal,* January 10, 1902; "Abolition of Poverty," *Good Housekeeping* 1 (September 1903): 216–220; "Fact and Fancy about New Zealand," *Boyce's Weekly,* February 4, 1903; "New 'Song of the Shirt,' " *Sunday School Times,* March 21, 1903. For Lloyd's correspondence on this problem, see the letters to or from Samuel Bowles, Henry Mortimer Johnson, Edward Tregear, Richard Holton James, William Pember Reeves, Joseph Ward, Hugh Lusk, Richard John Seddon, and Horace White, August 20, September

15, October 15, 18, November 5, 11, 12, 18, 27, December 3, 1901. See also H. Parker Willis to White, October 22, 1901, copy in the Lloyd Papers.

47. Edward Tregear, "Compulsory Arbitration," *Locomotive Firemen's Magazine* 30 (April 1901): 468–474; Edward Tregear, "The Labor Situation in New Zealand," *Independent* 53 (November 21, 1901): 2742–2743; Edward Tregear, "Compulsory Arbitration under Storm-Sails," *Arena* 40 (August–September 1908): 137–141; "Has Compulsory Arbitration Failed?" *Independent* 72 (April 25, 1912): 885–887.

48. That was the position taken by Victor S. Clark in his report to the U.S. Bureau of Labor Statistics in 1903 and in his dissertation, published as *The Labour Movement in Australasia.*

49. That assessment was reflected by Cornelius J. Doyle, chairman of the Illinois Arbitration Board, "Compulsory Arbitration in the United States," *Annals of the American Academy of Political and Social Science* 36 (September 1910): 302–310.

50. Compare Ely, *Studies in the Evolution of Industrial Society,* 351–353, 382–384; and Hadley, *Economics,* 356–362.

51. Weinstock, *Report on Foreign Laws,* 152–157; *Final Report and Testimony* [of] *the Commission on Industrial Relations* (62 Congress, 1 session, Senate Document no. 415, serial 6929, Washington, D.C., 1916), 120–124.

52. Edward P. Costigan, "The Compulsory Investigation of Labor Disputes," in Colin B. Goodykoontz, editor, *Papers of Edward P. Costigan Relating to the Progressive Movement in Colorado, 1902–1917* (Boulder, Colo., 1941), 357; Edward P. Costigan, "Statement [to the Joint Industrial Relations Committee of the Colorado General Assembly, February 19, 1917] on Industrial Relations," in ibid., 359–360.

53. Compare, Dominico Gagliardo, *The Kansas Industrial Court: An Experiment in Compulsory Arbitration* (Lawrence, Kans., 1941); Henry J. Allen, *The Party of the Third Part* (New York, 1921), esp. 221–240; Julia E. Johnsen, compiler, *Kansas Court of Industrial Relations* (New York, 1922), a debating manual; and Edith M. Phelphs, editor, "Kansas Court of Industrial Relations," in the *University Debaters' Annual, 1921–1922* (New York, 1922), 151. The case quoted was *Wolff Packing Co. v. Court of Industrial Relations,* 262 United States Reports 522 (1923) and 45 United States Supreme Court Reports 441 (1924).

54. For the breakdown of the antipodean system, see W. B. Sutch, *The Quest for Security in New Zealand, 1840–1966* (Wellington, 1966), 99–122.

55. John Collier, "The Crisis of Industrial Arbitration," 52.

CHAPTER SEVEN. AMERICAN PROGRESSIVISM AND THE WORLD OF REFORM

1. Laissez faire was more an ideology than a guide to policy, especially after the Civil War. Since the beginning of the Republic, states, as well as the federal government, had intervened in a variety of ways to promote economic growth, regulate business activity, and provide some social welfare. Pragmatic ex-

pediency spurred most of these efforts, whether in the form of subsidizing railroad construction, regulating exports, or requiring banks to support homes for the blind, and it was businessmen who most commonly sought government favors.

Although expediency and pragmatism continued to shape public policy in the Progressive years, particularly on specific measures, the demand for state intervention became increasingly based on new concepts of the proper role of government as a manager of economic and social affairs.

2. Smythe to Caro Lloyd Withington, February 2, 1905, in the Lloyd Papers.

3. See his letters of March 3 and January 25, 1915, in the Ely Papers, State Historical Society of Wisconsin, Madison.

4. New Zealand attracted far more attention than Australia, probably because of two factors: first, the reform movement came earlier in New Zealand and developed both comprehensively and swiftly, providing foreign observers with a broad range of programs to evaluate; second, visitors and commentators found it much more difficult to deal with the six separate colonies on the other side of the Tasman Sea and after 1901 with the Commonwealth as a seventh entity. Some states joined the reform movement sooner than others and there were important programmatic differences among them.

5. Compare Walter H. Page, F. N. Doubleday, and Doubleday, Page & Co. to Lloyd, August 17, 1900; October 3, November 6, 1902; August 1, 1904, and Reeves to William Downie Stewart, June 30, 1908, in the William Downie Stewart Papers, Hocken Library, Dunedin, New Zealand.

6. For examples, see E. T. Chismore, Thomas J. Towers, E. P. Trueblood, Ernest E. Woods, Fred Esch, M. M. Fogg, and W. W. Bride to Lloyd, November 12, 1902; January 24, February 2, 17 March 2, 14, 27, and April 25, 1903; and Edward M. Hulme, H. Leslie Wildey to U.S. Consul, A: 33, A(4): 32, February 4, 1900; January 24, 1903.

7. *The Handbook Series, Intercollegiate Debates,* and the *University Debaters' Annual* were the most important. It was later claimed by one of the editors that an account of a debate on minimum wages for women had been instrumental in the introduction and passage of the California law. Compare Egbert Ray Nichols, editor, *Inter-Collegiate Debates* (22 vols., New York, 1909–1941), 3: 81–184; Egbert Ray Nichols and Joseph H. Baccus, editors, *Selected Articles on Minimum Wages and Maximum Hours* (New York, 1936), 15.

8. Farmers worldwide had considerable difficulty reconciling the older ideology of individualism and self-reliance with the newer demand for state assistance. It is not without point, therefore, that interventionism everywhere initially took the form of improving rural welfare by lowering production, credit, and transaction costs and by increasing efficiency, market access, and commercial information. It was only later, primarily after the First World War, that policy makers sought to raise farm income through the control of output and by restricting the flow of agricultural commodities across national boundaries.

9. See J. D. N. McDonald, "New Zealand Land Legislation," *Historical*

Studies, Australia and New Zealand 5 (November 1952): 195–211.

10. Compare Eric E. Lampard, *The Rise of the Dairy Industry in Wisconsin: A Study in Agricultural Change, 1820–1920* (Madison, 1963), and Roy V. Scott, *The Reluctant Farmer: The Rise of Agricultural Extension to 1914* (Urbana, Ill.: 1970).

11. See, for example, *Agricultural Cooperation and Rural Credit in Europe* (63rd Congress, 1 session, Senate Document no. 214, serial 6519, Washington, D.C., 1913). For the Federal Farm Loan Act (July 17, 1916) and the Federal Warehouse Act (August 11, 1916), see 30 *United States Statutes* 360, 486.

12. On the broad impact of the Expansion of Europe, see Walter Prescott Webb, *The Great Frontier* (Boston, 1952), esp. chapters 10–12; on the impact of Old World thought, see Forrest McDonald, *Novus Ordo Seclorum: The Intellectual Origins of the Constitution* (Lawrence, Kans., 1985); on later linkages with European ideas, see David F. Bowers, editor, *Foreign Influences in American Life: Essays and Critical Bibliographies* (Princeton, N.J., 1944), 207–219; Robert Kelley, *The Transatlantic Persuasion: The Liberal-Democratic Mind in the Age of Gladstone* (New York, 1969), passim.

13. Clark's career is summarized in the *Dictionary of American Biography,* 11 (Supp. 2): 105–108. On Scudder, see her autobiography, *On Journey* (New York, 1937); her entry in the *Dictionary of American Biography,* Supp. 5: 616–617; and Barbara Sicherman and others, editors, *Notable American Women. The Modern Period: A Biographical Dictionary* (Cambridge, Mass., 1980), 636–638.

14. The Chautauqua movement falls into this pattern. Though many of the programs had little to do with reform, they did present tens of thousands of Americans with new political ideas, often from the mouths of prominent politicians, suffrage leaders, socialists, and other activists. See Arthur Eugene Bestor, Jr., *Chautauqua Publications: An Historical and Bibliographical Guide* (Chautauqua, N.Y., 1934); and Theodore Morrison, *Chautauqua: A Center for Education, Religion, and the Arts in America* (Chicago, 1974), esp. chaps. 5 and 10; and the files of the *Chautauquan.*

15. On Wright's career and influence, see Leiby, *Carroll Wright and Labor Reform.*

16. See, for example, the 16th and 19th annual reports of the U.S. Bureau of Labor, 1901 and 1904, dealing with "Strikes and Lockouts," and "Wages and Hours of Labor"; and John Graham Brooks, compiler, "Compulsory Insurance in Germany," 1893.

17. Compare, for example, Clark, "Labor Conditions in New Zealand"; and Weinstock, *Report on Foreign Laws.*

18. Commons trained at the Johns Hopkins with Richard T. Ely and held various teaching and research posts before being appointed to the faculty at the University of Wisconsin in 1904. Clark, by contrast, was trained as a classicist in Europe and at Columbia. His first important appointment was to the administration in Puerto Rico. See Commons' autobiography, *Myself* (Madison, Wis., 1963), and his entry in the *Dictionary of American Biography,* 11 (Supp. 3): 176–180; and Clark's obituary notice in the *American Historical Review* 51 (July 1946): 797–798.

19. Kelley eventually found an outlet for her activism when she served as director of the National Consumers' League, where she campaigned vigorously for women's legislation. See Goldmark, *Impatient Crusader; Dictionary of American Biography,* 11 (Supp. 1): 462–463; James, editor, *Notable American Women,* 2: 316–319.

On Lathrop, see her entry in ibid. 2: 370–372; and Jane Addams, *My Friend, Julia Lathrop* (New York, 1935).

20. Beginning in 1917 the association's proceedings appeared as annual bulletins of the U.S. Bureau of Labor Statistics.

21. See James Penick, Jr., *Progressive Politics and Conservation: The Ballinger-Pinchot Affair* (Chicago, 1968).

22. Leiby, *A History of Social Welfare,* 152–155; Goldmark, *Impatient Crusader,* 102, 106; "Official Mother to Thirty Million Children," *Chicago Inter-Ocean,* May 3, 1914. One of the bureau's earliest publications dealt with the activities of the Plunket Society: "New Zealand Society for the Health of Women and Children: An Example of Baby-Saving Work in Small Towns and Rural Districts," Infant Mortality Series, no. 2, *Children's Bureau, U.S. Department of Labor* (Washington, D.C., 1914).

23. "Workmen's Insurance and Compensation Systems in Europe," *Twenty-Fourth Annual Report of the U.S. Commissioner of Labor* (2 vols., Washington, D.C., 1911). See, also, Rubinow's *Social Insurance,* and *The Quest for Security.*

24. Kreader, "Isaac Max Rubinow," 402–425; Lubove, *The Struggle for Social Security,* 34–44.

25. The commission's report was previously cited at note 11. See, also, Harris Weinstock, "Easy Money for the Farmer," in *The California Outlook,* November 21, 1914; and Larsen, "Harris Weinstock," 187–193.

26. There is a brief summary of Hammond's career in *Who Was Who in America. Vol. 1, 1897–1942* (Chicago, 1943), 513–514.

27. See McCarthy's *Wisconsin Idea* for his own account.

28. Compare Division of Bibliography, Library of Congress, *Select List of Books (with References to Periodicals) on Labor, Particularly Relating to Strikes* (Washington, D.C., 1903); and Charles Wells Reeder, "Bibliography on the Minimum Wage," in Report no. 1, *Industrial Commission of Ohio, Department of Investigation and Statistics* (Columbus, Ohio, 1914).

29. There is a brief account in Edward H. Beardsley, *Harry L. Russell and Agricultural Science in Wisconsin* (Madison, 1969), 25–34. See also, Lampard, *The Rise of the Dairy Industry in Wisconsin,* 145–195; R.M. Burdon, *New Zealand Notables* (series two, Christchurch, 1945), 104–105; and Harold G. Philpott, *A History of the New Zealand Dairy Industry* (Wellington, 1937), passim.

A NOTE ON SOURCES

This book is based on several categories of sources: unpublished archival records, manuscripts, published documents, newspapers, periodicals, and books.

The Miscellaneous Correspondence of the U.S. Consul, Bay of Islands and Auckland, New Zealand, Record Group 84 of the State Department, in the National Archives, Washington, D.C., provided useful insights into the kinds of questions Americans asked about antipodean reform. So too did the files of the Colonial Secretary in the National Archives, Wellington, New Zealand, though the volume of correspondence proved much smaller than contemporary accounts indicated. That was probably because a fire some years ago destroyed the records of the Department of Labour, the agency reportedly inundated by requests for information.

The Henry Demarest Lloyd Papers in the State Historical Society of Wisconsin, Madison, yielded a great deal of information. Lloyd corresponded widely, especially in connection with his books and with the various causes he espoused. The papers include a rich collection of newspaper clippings, mainly but not exclusively bringing together the reviews of his books. Most of the other likely collections at the Historical Society—the John R. Commons Papers, the Richard T. Ely Papers, the Samuel Gompers Papers, the Morris Hilquit Papers, the Robert M. La Follette Papers, the Charles McCarthy Papers, the Raymond Robins Papers, the Algie Simons Papers, and the William English Walling Papers—yielded little. There were better though still modest returns in collections in the Bancroft Library at the University of California, Berkeley—the George Cooper Pardee Papers, the Chester H. Rowell Papers, and the Harris Weinstock Scrapbooks—and in the University of California Library, Los Angeles—the Katherine Philips Edson Papers.

Several collections in New Zealand repositories proved especially useful: at the University of Auckland the Sir George Fowlds Papers showed his links to American single taxers and at the Canterbury Museum in Christchurch the Kate W. Shephard Papers showed links to American feminists. Two collections in the Alexander Turnbull Library, Wellington—the John Ballance Papers and the Sir Robert Stout Papers—provided insights into the Lib-Lab movement in New Zealand.

Published documents, both public and private, have been a rich source. The reports of various federal agencies and commissions, especially in the labor field, have proved invaluable, as have the reports of state and municipal agencies, also in the labor field but also on such questions as rural credits, old age pensions, and village settlements. The publications of private agencies have also been helpful, especially those of the National Consumers' League, the National Civic Federation, and the American Academy of Political and Social Science.

Newspaper files provided much commentary and information. However, only Wayland's *Appeal to Reason,* the *Los Angeles Times,* and the *New York Times* were scanned over a run of years. Other newspaper data came either from clippings in such collections as the Lloyd and Stout papers or from specific issues cited in other sources.

As the footnotes show, the periodical literature, both academic and popular, has been mined for antipodean linkages. For example, a good deal of scholarly analysis appeared in such journals as the *American Labor Legislation Review,* the *Journal of Political Economy,* and *Yale Review.* On the popular side a formal listing of all the articles, editorials, and reviews would cover hundreds of items, though they would be heavily concentrated in such periodicals as *Arena, Everybody's, Independent, Outlook,* and *Public.* As readers will appreciate, extracting these items over several decades may have given antipodean influences a larger significance than they actually had.

The study also rests on many books published during the Progressive years, some such as Lloyd's *Newest England* or Clark's *Labour Movement in Australasia,* written by American visitors. Many of the others, such as Parson's *Story of New Zealand* or Walling's *Socialism as It Is,* were derivative but nevertheless influential works, as were the many books published in support of the intercollegiate debating system.

Wherever possible, the study also draws on the secondary literature. Since scholars have had very little to say about the linkages between Australasia and the United States, the work has drawn instead upon the many articles and books dealing with the Progressive movement in general and with specific reforms—such as social insurance or minimum wages—in particular.

INDEX

Addams, Jane, 92, 160, 178
Ahl, Frances N., 162
Allen, Henry J., 141
Alpers, O. T. J., 16, 160
American Academy of Political and Social Science, 160, 189
American Association for Labor Legislation, 117, 128, 160, 180, 184, 189
American Commission on Credit and Cooperation, 87, 185
American Economic Association, 180
American Fabian Society, 180
American Federation of Labor, 105
American Medical Association, 184
American Socialist Party, 71
Anderson, George W., 114
Andrews, E. B., 56
Anti-Saloon League, 180
Antitrust movement, 9, 93–94, 174
Appeal to Reason, 62–63, 188
Association of Western Manufacturers, 141
Atkins v. Children's Hospital (1923), 125–127
Atkin v. Kansas (1903), 106
Arizona, 125, 127
Arkansas, 123, 127
Australasia: child care in, 93; labor laws in, 100; labor movement in, 50; land reforms in, 88; old-age pensions in, 83; as reform model, 6, 52, 75, 82, 99, 129, 164–165, tax reform in, 88–90; wage regulation in, 109, 119, 126. *See also* Australia, New Zealand
Australia: adopts New Zealand reforms, 76, 83, 86, 135; hour regulation in, 108; labor conditions in, 181; labor reforms in, 98; land reform in, 88; public ownership in, 65; old-age pensions in, 82, 83; state interventionism in, 12; village settlements in, 86; wage regulation in, 98, 115, 117, 118, 119, 120, 121, 122, 127
Australian ballot, 112
Aves, Edward, 119

Ballance, John, 21, 25, 28, 29, 94
Ballinger-Pinchot controversy, 183
Bates, Helen P., 157
Baxter, Sylvester, 78
Bellamy, Edward: influence in New Zealand, 25, 31, 45, 77, 78–79; influence in United States, 77, 178
Bliss, William D. P., 47
Boston, 189, 205(n24)
Bowmar, Stanley, 141
Boyle, James, 119–120
Brandeis, Louis D.: on hour regulation, 107–108, 109, 190; on old-age pensions, 82, 202(n13); on wage regulation, 114, 121, 122, 123, 125, 126, 190
Brewster, Eugene J., 78–79
Brotherhood of the Kingdom, 48
Bucklin, James W., 159
Butler, Pierce, 126

California: agricultural reforms in, 87–88, 169, 187–188; compulsory arbitration of labor disputes in, 134, 136, 148, 159, 182; hour regulation in, 108, 124, 125, 126, 127; wage regulation in, 115; workmen's compensation in, 83–86, 159, 204(n18)
California Bureau of Labor Statistics, 124
California Colonization and Rural Credits Commission, 87
California Constructive League, 57, 59, 60
California Federation of Labor, 108, 120
California Federation of Women's Clubs, 124
California Industrial Accident Board, 159
California Land Settlement Board, 87–88
Canada, 12, 148, 173, 182
Capitalism, 165–167, 171, 173
Carpenter, Frank G., 69
Casualty Actuarial and Statistical Society of America, 184
Chartism, 7, 17, 26
Chautauqua movement, 189, 236(n14)
Chicago, 189
Child, Richard W., 82
Child labor: abolition of, 98, 100–101, 156, 159, 171; women's suffrage and, 91–92

Christian socialism: in Great Britain, 5, 77; in United States, 141, 155, 179, 189
Christie, John, 160
Church Social Union, 188
Civil service reform, 10
Clark, John B., 118, 140, 141, 157, 179
Clark, Victor S.: on compulsory arbitration of labor disputes, 135; on foreign labor conditions, 100, 110–111, 159, 162, 181, 213(n1), 234(n48); and labor reform, 182; on wage regulation, 120
Clyden, Arthur, 47
Colorado: compulsory arbitration of labor disputes in, 134, 141, 148; hour regulation in, 106; labor disputes in, 113, 138; tax reform in, 89–90; workmen's compensation in, 204(n18)
Coming Nation, 62
Commons, John R., 100, 157, 182
Commonwealth Club of California, 206(n25)
Conference of Charities and Correction, 110–111, 189
Connecticut, 104, 115
Connolly, J. D., 16
Conservation movement, 10, 163, 174, 183, 191(n8)
Consumer legislation, 173
Conwell, Russell H., 56, 141
Cooperative movement, 194n
Cooperatives: in California, 58, 59, 60, 188; in Europe, 58; in New Zealand, 50, 60, 65, 97
Cooper Union, 48, 74
Costigan, Edward P., 141
Cuba, labor conditions in, 181

Denmark, agricultural reform in, 187, 188
Dependency, concept of, 174–175
Diggs, Annie L., 80
Direct democracy: in New Zealand, 7, 64, 88, 90, 200(n77); Progressivism and, 7, 14, 53, 88, 90, 163
District of Columbia, 125
Duffus, R. D. L., 25

Edson, Katharine P., 124
Eight-hour movement, 49, 64, 66, 99
Electrical Workers Union, 141
Ell, H. G., 160
Ely, Richard T.: on compulsory arbitration of labor disputes, 141; on land reform, 87; on New Zealand, 157, 207(n28); on railroad reform, 47; on wage regulation, 111
Evans, Elizabeth G., 114, 115, 117

Fabian socialism, 5, 31, 77, 141
Federal Farm Loan Act (1916), 185
Federal Farm Loan Board, 87
Federal Trade Commission, 182
Federation of Women's Clubs, 128
Fels, Joseph, 207(n29)
Fieldhouse, Walter, 141
Filene, Edward, 205(n24)
Fitzgerald, James E., 20
Flower, Benjamin O.: on Australasian reforms, 52; on compulsory arbitration of labor disputes, 138, 141; on Henry D. Lloyd, 52–53; on New Zealand, 52–53, 64, 73, 75, 76, 156; as Progressive, 77
Fox, Martin, 143
Fradenburgh, A. G., 47
Francis, Charles, 136, 138, 141
Frankfurter, Felix, 125, 126
Franklin, E. C., 157
Funk, I. S. E., 56

Gates, George H., 51
George, Henry: influence of in New Zealand, 24, 31, 89; and Progressivism, 45, 77, 169, 178
Germany: Bismarkian socialism in, 5, 167; old-age pensions in, 80, 82, 83; social insurance in, 188; state interventionism in, 12
Gilman, Nicholas P., 141, 157
Gilman, Theodore, 141
Girard, Kans., 62–63
Golden, John, 114
Goldmark, Josephine, 107–108, 122, 123
Gompers, Samuel, 64, 105, 120, 143
Goodwin, Etta R., 92
Great Britain: child care in, 93; labor conditions in, 181; old-age pensions in, 82, 83; socialism in, 5; town planning in, 5; wage regulation in, 109, 110, 117, 120–121, 127; workmen's compensation in, 84
Greeley, Horace, 3
Grey, Sir George, 20
Grey, J. Grattan, 81, 144, 162

Hale, Edward E., 82, 228(n4)
Hammond, Matthew B., 116, 117–118, 121, 157, 186
Hard, Anne, 82
Harland, John M., 107
Harrison, George B., 79–80
Henry, Alice, 111, 116, 189

Higgins, Henry B., 139, 160
Hobson, J. A., 121, 140, 141
Hoeneck, Ernest, 67
Holcombe, Arthur N., 112–113
Holmes, Oliver W., 106, 107, 113, 125–127
Hoover, Herbert, 128, 178
Howells, William D., 78
Hull House, 92, 182
Hunter, Robert, 60

Idaho, 204(n18)
Illinois: compulsory arbitration of labor disputes in, 134; hour regulation in, 49, 105, 108; probation law in, 92; wage regulation in, 115
Illinois Board of Charities, 92, 183
Immigration restriction, 112
Indiana, 115
Industrial Commission of Ohio, 120, 124
Infant care reform, 92–93, 158, 164
International Association of Accident Boards and Commissions, 182
International Institute of Agriculture, 187, 205(n24)
Interstate Commerce Commission, 182
Ireland, land reform in, 163
Iron, Steel, and Tin Plate Workers Union, 141
Irrigation movement, 57, 59, 60, 65
Italy, state interventionism in, 12

Java, labor conditions in, 181
Jenks, Jeremiah W., 48
Johnson, A. S., 139–140, 141
Johnson, F. N., 141
Johnson, Hiram, 87, 124, 185
John Stuart Kennedy Foundation, 82
Juvenile courts, 91, 92

Kansas, 123, 126, 127, 141, 149
Kelley, Florence: as factory inspector, 105, 182; on hour regulation, 105–106, 107; on New Zealand reforms, 160; on wage regulation, 111, 121
Kellogg, Paul U., 112, 190
Kelly, Allen, 161, 201(n1), 229(n7)
Kelly, Florence F., 135, 161, 201(n1), 228–229(n7)
Kennaday, Paul, 141
King, Truby, 93
Kingston, C. C., 227(n3)
Klamouth, Louis, 63
Knights of Labour, in New Zealand, 25, 45
Krauskopf, Joseph, 137, 141

Laissez faire, 105, 106, 134, 155, 178
Latchford, Henry, 51, 196(n13)
Lathrop, Julia C., 92–93, 182, 183
Lawrence, Mass., 115
League of Industrial Courts, 139
Lefavour, Henry, 114
Le Rossignol, James E., 157, 162
Lewis, David I., 211(n46)
Lewis, Frank W., 82
Lind, John, 141
"Living-wage" concept, 110, 112, 114, 127, 128, 137, 138, 158, 162
Lloyd, Henry D.: on compulsory arbitration of labor disputes, 133–136, 142, 145, 147–148, 149, 150–151, 232(n36); and Julius A. Wayland, 61, 66–67, 69; on land reform, 87; and Hugh H. Lusk, 48, 73; on New Zealand reform, 47, 49–52, 64, 75, 76, 82, 88, 110, 133–136, 156, 161, 162, 163; on old-age pensions, 81–82; as Progressive, 72, 75, 77, 141, 156, 157–158, 159, 164; on tax reform, 88; on wage regulation, 110; and William E. Smythe, 57, 59, 156
Lochner v. New York (1905), 107, 108, 109
Los Angeles United Garment Workers, 226(n76)
Los Angeles Waitresses and Cafeteria Workers, 226(n76)
Lubin, David, 185, 187, 205(n24)
Lubin, Simon, 87, 187–188
Lumis, Charles F., 57
Lusk, Hugh H.: on Australasian reforms, 48, 49; on compulsory arbitration of labor disputes, 138, 140, 141; and Henry D. Lloyd, 48, 73; on land reform, 87; on New Zealand reforms, 69, 72–75, 76, 157, 162; on old-age pensions, 81; and Progressivism, 48, 49, 73–75; on wage regulation, 110

McCarthy, Charles, 103, 141, 186–187, 206(n25)
McCrosty, H. W., 157
MacDonald, J. Ramsay, 111, 232(n38)
McKenna, Joseph, 125–127
McKenzie, John, 30–31, 40, 187
McReynolds, James C., 126–127
Maine, 104
Manchester school of economics, 177
Maryland, 141, 204n, 211(n46)
Massachusetts: compulsory arbitration of labor disputes in, 134; hour

regulation in, 102, 104, 108; mediation of labor disputes in, 131, 227(n3); old-age pensions in, 82, 83, 159; wage regulation in, 109, 112, 114–115, 123, 125, 127
Massachusetts Bureau of Labor Statistics, 102, 104, 181
Massachusetts Federation of Labor, 112
Maternal care reform, 92–93, 164
Mead, Elwood, 46–47, 87–88
Melville, Herman, 3
Mexican Revolution, 169
Mexico, labor conditions in, 181
Michigan, 115, 204(n18)
Mill, J. S.: influence in New Zealand, 31, 73–74, 89; influence in United States, 31, 77; and unearned increment, 24, 169; and women's suffrage, 192(n3)
Millis, H. A., 120–121, 157
Minnesota: compulsory arbitration of labor disputes in, 134, 141; wage regulation in, 112, 115, 125, 127; workmen's compensation in, 204(n18)
Missouri, 134, 141
Montana, 204(n18)
Muller, Mary A., 19–20
Muller v. Oregon (1908), 108, 109, 122, 125–126
Municipal reform movement, 9–10, 14, 88–89
Myers, Charles H., 141

National Association of Stove Manufacturers, 142
National Civic Federation, 160, 232(n36)
National Consumers' League: Felix Frankfurter and, 126; and hour regulation, 107, 190; and Progressivism, 160, 180, 237(n19); and wage regulation, 111, 112, 121, 128, 190
National Convention of Chiefs and Commissioners of Bureaus of Labor Statistics, 181
Nebraska, 115
Nevada, 204(n18)
New England, 104
New Hampshire, 104
New South Wales, 82, 99, 150, 216(n22), 232(n36)
New York: compulsory arbitration of labor disputes in, 134; factory commission in, 159; hour regulation in, 107, 108, 109; labor mediation in, 131, 227(n3); wage regulation in, 115, 116, 126, 223(n61); workmen's compensation in, 84, 204(n18)
New York City, 93, 184, 229(n7)
New Zealand: American criticism of, 50, 71, 72, 83, 87, 94, 105, 119–120, 127, 142–146; antitrust movement in, 9, 93–94; compulsory arbitration of labor disputes in, 34–35, 50, 53, 55, 61, 69, 70, 109, 118, 130–132, 156, 157, 158, 173, 194(n3); concentration of wealth in, 71; corruption in, 71; direct democracy in, 7, 90; education in, 40, 50, 91; electoral reform in, 7–8, 27–28; European criticism of, 40–41; functions of government in, 10, 38, 65, 66, 70, 72, 76, 85, 94, 95–96, 142, 158, 174, 194(n3); hour regulation in, 33, 102–103, 108, 109, 216n; housing conditions in, 9, 72; ideology in, 26, 37, 76, 78; immigration restriction in, 112; industrialization in, 98–99, 119; labor movement in, 67; labor reform in, 32–35, 50, 54, 64, 65–66, 76, 91, 97, 98, 157; labor relations in, 34, 55, 76; land monopoly in, 24, 29, 30, 86–87, 94; land reform in, 25, 29–31, 48, 50, 54, 57, 59, 60, 64, 66, 74, 76, 86–87, 157, 169; liberalism in, 6, 7, 8, 9, 10, 25–41, 77; old-age pensions in, 39, 50, 54, 68, 70, 76, 80–83, 91, 157, 158, 159, 164; political structure in, 8, 26–27; poverty in, 71; productivity in, 118; prosperity in, 70, 73, 89, 96, 139; rural credit in, 30, 50, 55, 60, 67–68, 70, 76, 86, 149, 158, 162, 170; shopping laws in, 64, 97, 103, 173; socialism in, 70–71; tax reform in, 30, 31, 72, 86, 88–90, 169; temperance movement in, 90; trusts in, 71, 94; unemployment in, 21, 22–23, 36–37, 50, 53, 54, 60–61, 68, 71, 86, 97; village settlements in, 86, 88; wage regulation in, 109–110, 117, 118, 120, 121, 122, 129, 149; welfare state in, 155–165; women's rights in, 39–40, 91; women's suffrage in, 7–8, 19–20, 28–29, 65, 76, 90–92; workmen's compensation in, 32, 38, 91, 203(n16)
Nineteenth Century Club, 48
North Dakota, 125

Ohio, 115, 124, 186, 204(n18)
Ohio Coal Mining Commission, 186
Ohio Health and Old Age Insurance Commission, 186
Ohio Industrial Commission, 186
Olney, Richard, 114

Ontario, 229(n8)
Oregon: hour regulation in, 108, 159; wage regulation in, 115, 123, 124, 125, 126; workmen's compensation in, 204(n18)
Oregon Consumers' League, 116

Peace movement, 163
Parsons, Frank: on compulsory arbitration of labor disputes, 48, 136; and Hugh H. Lusk, 73; on New Zealand reform, 41, 53–56, 72, 75, 76, 82, 88, 100, 156, 157, 160, 162; on old-age pensions, 82; as Progressive, 57, 64, 75, 77, 141, 156, 164; on tax reform, 88; on village settlements, 87; on wage regulation, 111
Peebles, J. M., 48, 64–65, 95–96
Pennsylvania: compulsory arbitration in, 134, 141; strikes in, 69, 74, 136; wage regulation in, 115; workmen's compensation in, 204(n18)
People v. Charles Schweinler Press (1915), 109
Pettigrew, R. F., 56
Pillsbury, A. J., 85–86, 159
Pinchot, Gifford, 183
Plunket Society, 93
Pomeroy, Elmweed, 64
Populism, 45, 63
Post, Louis F., 207(n29)
Progressivism: and agriculture, 166–167, 170, 186, 187; and the banking industry, 74; and businessmen, 166, 173–174; characteristics of, 4–11, 155, 177–190; and concentration of wealth, 74, 168; and corruption, 8–9, 53, 54; historiography of, 11–15; and hour regulation, 14, 92, 101–109, 156, 158, 159, 171, 190; and housing reform, 168, 188; and industrial regulation, 156, 159, 172; and industrial relations, 53, 58, 59, 61, 109, 130, 132–142, 156, 157, 158, 159, 162, 172–173; and insurance industry, 65, 66, 70, 95, 158, 174, 194(n3); and land monopoly, 5, 48, 50, 54, 57, 58, 59, 60, 64, 66, 74, 86–87, 94, 168, 169; and mining industry, 68, 159; and old-age pensions, 50, 54, 68, 70, 76, 80–83, 91, 157, 158, 159, 162–163, 164; and public housing, 174, 188; and public ownership, 9, 10, 19, 20, 37–38, 48, 53, 54–55, 65, 70, 95, 162, 173, 174, 194(n3); and railroad exploitation, 96; and rural credit, 5, 50, 55, 60, 67–68, 70, 149, 158, 159, 162, 164, 170–171, 185; and shopping laws, 173; and social insurance, 5, 80–86, 156, 163, 175, 184–185, 188; and tax reform, 54, 55, 65, 74, 163; and trust movement, 9, 74, 79; and unemployment, 60–61, 68, 86, 97, 168, 188, 194(n3); and village settlements, 86–88, 158, 164, 187; and wage regulation, 14, 92, 109–129, 149, 156, 158, 159, 164, 172, 190, 219(n33); and women's suffrage, 7–8, 14–15, 65, 76, 90–92, 157, 162; workmen's compensation, 83–86, 91, 95, 149, 156, 158, 159, 163, 164, 172, 182, 184; and zoning laws, 174
Prostitution, 119
Puerto Rico, 125, 127

Queensland, 110, 216(n22)

Ramsay, David, 3
Ranstead, William, 67
Rauschenbusch, Walter, 48, 178
Rees, W. L., 20
Reeves, William P.: book reviewed, 139–140; book sales, 162; and compulsory arbitration of labor disputes, 34–35, 131–132, 133, 150, 232(n38); Henry D. Lloyd on, 228(n4); and New Zealand labor reforms, 31–37, 40, 100; and old-age pensions, 81, 82; and wage regulation, 110, 111, 114, 122–123, 128
Reno, Conrad, 139, 140, 141
Rhode Island, 104, 214(n3)
Ritchie v. People (1895), 105–106, 107
Rixey, Thomas P., 141
Rome, Italy, 187
Roosevelt, Franklin D., 178
Roosevelt, Theodore, 230(n10)
Rowell, Chester, 87, 94–95
Rubinow, Isaac M., 83, 184–185
Ruskin, John, 62, 179
Ruskin College of Social Science, 53
Russell, Charles E., 71–72, 76, 145, 161
Russell, Harry L., 187
Russell Sage Foundation, 108, 160, 189–190
Russian Revolution, 169
Ryan, John A.: and compulsory arbitration of labor disputes, 137–138, 141; and old-age pensions, 82; as Progressive, 158; and wage regulation, 111, 112, 116–117, 121, 128, 157

St. Ledger, Anthony J., 162
Sanford, Edward T., 126–127

San Francisco, 124, 136, 229(n7)
Scholfield, Guy H., 162
Scudder, Vida, 178, 179
Seager, Henry R., 82, 83, 117, 157
Seddon, Richard J.: Benjamin O. Flower on, 53; Julius A. Wayland on, 71; and old-age pensions, 39; as politician, 35–36, 39, 40–41, 76; as prime minister, 26; William E. Smythe on, 58; and unemployment, 35, 37; and women's suffrage, 28–29
Sheppard, Katherine W., 91–92
Sheppard-Towner Act (1921), 93
Siegfried, André, 40–41, 162
Simons, A. M., 215(n12)
Single tax, 24–25, 29, 89
Smith, Adam, 105, 165, 176
Smith, James T., 141
Smythe, William E.: and compulsory arbitration of labor disputes, 58, 59, 136, 138, 139, 141; and Hugh H. Lusk, 73; New Zealand influences on, 57–61, 64, 75, 156, 157; as political candidate, 59–60, 80, 87; as Progressive, 72, 75; and rural credit, 158; and village settlements, 57, 58, 87, 158, 205(n22)
Social sciences, 5, 78, 168
Socialism, 50, 63, 64, 65. *See also* State socialism
Society of Christian Socialists, 47
South Australia, 110
South Dakota, 125
South End House, 205(n24)
Spahr, Charles B., 143
Spencer, Herbert, 31, 106, 113
Starr, Ellen G., 178
State interventionism, 12, 164, 166–167, 178, 189
State Rivers and Water Supply Commission (Victoria), 87–88
State socialism: criticism of, 105; in New Zealand, 74–75, 76, 129, 161; and Progressivism, 177. *See also* Socialism
Stern, Carl, 112
Stettler v. O'Hara (1916), 122, 124–125, 126
Stewart, William D., 160–161, 162, 227(n3)
Stickley, Gustav, 212(n49)
Stone, N. I., 121
Stone, William A., 141
Stout, Sir Robert A., 21, 160–161
Strong, Josiah, 56, 141
Sultzer, William, 116
Sutherland, George, 126–127
Taft, William H., 126–127, 220(n38)
Tasmania, 110
Taylor, C. F., 54, 56
Taylor, Clementia, 192(n3)
Temperance movement, 28–29, 90
Texas, 125, 134
Tillet, Ben, 232(n36)
Town planning, 5
Tregear, Edward: on compulsory arbitration of labor disputes, 137, 139, 146; on New Zealand reforms, 160–161; on old-age pensions, 81; reports interest in New Zealand reforms, 99, 228(n4); as secretary of labour, 33, 35, 100
Trollope, Anthony, 40

United Nations Food and Agriculture Organization, 187, 205(n24)
U.S. Anthracite Coal Commission, 186
U.S. Bureau of Labor, 82, 99–100, 159, 181, 182
U.S. Children's Bureau, 92–93, 160, 182, 183
U.S. Food Administration, 186
U.S. Forest Service, 183
U.S. Industrial Commission, 148
U.S. War Labor Policies Board, 186
Universal Postal Union, 179
Utah, 106, 109, 123, 204(n18)

VanDevanter, Willis, 126
Vermont, 104
Victoria: compulsory arbitration of labor disputes in, 82; hour regulation in, 216(n22); irrigation in, 87–88; as reform model, 99; wage boards in, 110, 117–118, 120–121, 223(n59)

Waddell, Rutherford, 23
Wagner Act (1935), 133, 151
Waihi, New Zealand, 149
Wakefield, Edward G., 17–18
Walker, H. de R., 162
Wallace, Alfred R., 24, 31, 77, 169
Ward, Sir Joseph G., 26, 160–161
Warner, Lucien C., 82
Warren, Fred, 62
Washington, 126, 204(n18)
Watson, Tom, 51–52
Wayland, H. L., 141, 227(n3)
Wayland, Julius A.: and *Appeal to Reason*, 62–63, 69–70; criticizes Richard J. Seddon, 71; criticizes New Zealand, 72, 145; early career of, 61–62; and Hugh H. Lusk, 73; on

New Zealand as reform model, 48, 64–71, 75, 76, 141; and "New Zealand in a Nutshell," 68–69; as socialist, 63, 71
Webb, Sidney B., 116, 117
Weinstock, Harris: and agricultural reform, 187–188; and compulsory arbitration of labor disputes, 100, 135, 140, 141, 148, 159, 181–182; and rural credit, 87, 185, 187–188
Welfare state: characteristics of, 155, 169–177; New Zealand origins of, 155–165; and Progressivism, 155, 177–190; world trend toward, 165–169
West Virginia, 204(n18)
Wilkinson, Emma A., 79, 80
Williams, W. J., 23
Wilson, Woodrow, 120, 185
Wisconsin: compulsory arbitration of labor disputes in, 141, 231–232(n35); hour regulation in, 108; New Zealand as reform model for, 103; regulation of dairy industry in, 187; tax reform in, 88; wage regulation in, 112, 113, 115, 125, 126, 127, 218–219(n33); workmen's compensation in, 204(n18)
Wisconsin Livestock Sanitary Board, 187
Wisconsin Consumers' League, 112
Woolston, Howard B., 121
Women's Christian Temperance Union, 28, 226(n76)
Women's Trade Union League, 111, 128, 180, 189
World Peace Foundation, 180
Wright, Carroll D., 181, 182, 227(n3)
Wyoming, 204(n18)

Young Women's Christian Association, 128